REGRET
Developmental, Cultural, and Clinical Realms

Edited by

Salman Akhtar and Shahrzad Siassi

KARNAC

First published in 2017 by
Karnac Books Ltd
118 Finchley Road
London NW3 5HT

British Library Cataloguing in Publication Data

A C.I.P. for this book is available from the British Library

ISBN-13: 978-1-78220-589-0

Typeset by Medlar Publishing Solutions Pvt Ltd, India

www.karnacbooks.com

To

Our children,

Kabir and Nishat
                    —SA

Guilan and Dara
                    —SS

with ordinary parental regrets but with much more pride and love

CONTENTS

ACKNOWLEDGMENTS

We are deeply grateful to the distinguished colleagues who contributed to this volume. We appreciate their effort, their sacrifice of time, and their patience with our requirements, reminders, and requests for revisions. We are also thankful to Jan Wright for her skillful help in preparing the manuscript of this book. Oliver Rathbone and Kate Pearce of Karnac Books gave unerring support to this project and shepherded it through various phases of publication. To both of them, our sincere thanks.

Salman Akhtar and Shahrzad Siassi

ABOUT THE EDITORS AND CONTRIBUTORS

Salman Akhtar, MD, is professor of psychiatry at Jefferson Medical College and a training and supervising analyst at the Psychoanalytic Center of Philadelphia. He has served on the editorial boards of the *International Journal of Psychoanalysis*, the *Journal of the American Psychoanalytic Association*, and the *Psychoanalytic Quarterly*. His more than 300 publications include eighty-two books, of which the following eighteen are solo-authored: *Broken Structures* (1992), *Quest for Answers* (1995), *Inner Torment* (1999), *Immigration and Identity* (1999), *New Clinical Realms* (2003), *Objects of Our Desire* (2005), *Regarding Others* (2007), *Turning Points in Dynamic Psychotherapy* (2009), *The Damaged Core* (2009), *Comprehensive Dictionary of Psychoanalysis* (2009), *Immigration and Acculturation* (2011), *Matters of Life and Death* (2011), *The Book of Emotions* (2012), *Psychoanalytic Listening* (2013), *Good Stuff* (2013), *Sources of Suffering* (2014), *No Holds Barred* (2016), and *A Web of Sorrow* (2017). Dr. Akhtar has delivered many prestigious invited lectures including a plenary address at the 2nd International Congress of the International Society for the Study of Personality Disorders in Oslo, Norway (1991), an invited plenary paper at the 2nd International Margaret S. Mahler Symposium in Cologne, Germany (1993), an invited plenary paper at the Rencontre Franco-Americaine de Psychanalyse meeting in Paris, France (1994), a keynote address at the 43rd IPA Congress in Rio de Janeiro, Brazil (2005), the plenary address at the 150th Freud Birthday Celebration sponsored by the Dutch Psychoanalytic Society and the Embassy of Austria in Leiden, Holland (2006), and the inaugural address at the first IPA-Asia Congress in Beijing, China (2010). Dr. Akhtar is the recipient of numerous awards including the American Psychoanalytic Association's Edith Sabshin Award (2000), Columbia University's Robert Liebert Award for Distinguished Contributions to Applied Psychoanalysis (2004), and the American Psychiatric Association's Kun Po Soo Award (2004) and Irma Bland Award for being the Outstanding Teacher of Psychiatric Residents in the country (2005). He received the highly prestigious Sigourney Award (2012) for distinguished contributions to psychoanalysis. In 2013, he gave the commencement address at graduation ceremonies of the Smith College School of Social Work in Northampton, MA. Dr. Akhtar's books have been translated in many languages, including German, Italian, Korean, Romanian, Serbian, Spanish, and Turkish. A true Renaissance man, Dr. Akhtar has served as the film review editor for the *International Journal of Psychoanalysis*, and is currently serving as the book review editor for the *International Journal of Applied Psychoanalytic Studies*. He has published nine collections of poetry and serves as a scholar-in-residence at the Inter-Act Theatre Company in Philadelphia.

Susan L. Donner, MD, is a child, adolescent, and adult psychiatrist and psychoanalyst in private practice in Woodland Hills, CA. She graduated from the adult and child psychoanalytic programs and is now a senior teaching faculty member, training and supervising analyst, child and adolescent supervising analyst, and the chair of the Child Psychoanalytic Program at the New Center for Psychoanalysis in Los Angeles. A graduate of Harvard University and UCSF School of Medicine, she is an assistant clinical professor in psychiatry at UCLA where she teaches and supervises child psychiatry fellows and residents. She was a contributor to Lenore Terr's 2007 book, *Magical Moments of Change*, as well as the author of two JAPA book reviews. Dr. Donner has presented at IPA, APA, and AACAP Western Regional conferences and other meetings on development, diagnostics, attachment disorders, psychoanalytic perspectives on the use of medications, and case presentations of child, adolescent, and adult psychoanalytic treatment.

Theodore Fallon, MD, is a faculty member of the Psychoanalytic Center of Philadelphia. He has been a physician for over thirty-five years, trained in understanding and working with families, children, adolescents and adults. Dr. Fallon obtained his medical degree from the Pennsylvania State School of Medicine and did his psychiatric training at the University of Pittsburgh Medical College and at the University of Rochester Medical Center. He completed his adult and child psychoanalytic training at the Western New England Psychoanalytic Institute, affiliated with Yale University. He has extensive academic, clinical, and community-based experience. His training in many different modes and modalities of therapy allows him to select what will be most helpful for any particular person and situation. Dr. Fallon has published many significant papers on mourning, child development, psychoanalytic listening, and, more recently, a co-authored book, *Disordered Thought and Development: Chaos to Organization in the Moment* (Rowman & Littlefield, 2013). He maintains a private practice of adult and child psychotherapy and psychoanalysis in suburban Philadelphia.

Ingrid M. Geerken, PhD, received her doctorate in English literature and language from Harvard University in 2003. She taught at Kenyon and Oberlin colleges before training as a psychoanalyst in Cleveland. She has served on the faculties of the Cleveland Psychoanalytic Center and the Case Western Reserve medical school, and on the editorial boards of JAPA and the IJP. She writes in the fields of literature, narrative theory, and psychoanalysis. Currently, she maintains a full-time clinical practice in Cleveland Heights and Oberlin, Ohio.

Nilofer Kaul, PhD, is a Delhi-based training analyst. She is also an associate professor of English at Hansraj College in Delhi University. Her doctorate work was on "Masks and mirrors: configurations of narcissism in women's short stories" (2012). She has since then written on bisexuality—presented at IPSO, Istanbul, 2013; child sexuality—"Afterwords" in *Dark Room* (ed. Pankaj Butalia); on "Separation" (at the Second International Psychoanalytic Conference in Fortis, Delhi); "Myth, Misogyny, Matricide" (ed. Anup Dhar et al., in press); on homosexuality—"Morphology of the closet: some secrets of Indian life" in the *Psychoanalytic Review*, 102: 827–842 (2015); on "The Rehearsed Language of Unconscious" (a paper presented at the International Conference on Psychoanalysis in Mumbai, 2016), and has written "On Strangeness" (forthcoming in *Division 39/Review*). She is also a part of a supervision group of the Delhi Chapter (Indian Psychoanalytic Society) and Psychoanalysis India.

Susan Kavaler-Adler, PhD, ABPP, NPsyA, DLitt, is a psychologist and psychoanalyst in private practice, working with individuals and groups. She is the founder of the Object Relations Institute for Psychotherapy and Psychoanalysis in New York City, where she has served as executive director, training analyst, senior supervisor, and faculty member. She is also a prolific author who has published five books and over sixty articles, and has eleven awards for her writing. Her books are: *The Compulsion to Create: Women Writers and Their Demon Lovers* (Routledge, 1993, Other Press, 2000); *The Creative Mystique: From Red Shoes Frenzy to Love and Creativity* (Routledge, 1996); *Mourning, Spirituality and Psychic Change: A New Object Relations View of Psychoanalysis* (Routledge, 2003, winner of the National Gradiva Award from NAAP); *The Anatomy of Regret: From Death Instinct to Reparation and Symbolization in Vivid Case Studies* (Karnac, 2013); and *Klein-Winnicott Dialectic: New Transformative Metapsychology and Interactive Clinical Theory* (Karnac, 2014). Dr. Kavaler-Adler integrates psychoanalytic work on creativity, spiritual self-evolution, and erotic transference with mourning as a developmental process, and addresses the addictions to bad/traumatic eroticized objects that forestall mourning.

Joan Lachkar, PhD, is a licensed marriage and family therapist in private practice in Sherman Oaks, California, an affiliate member for the New Center for Psychoanalysis, an internationally renowned therapist, and author of numerous publications including, *The Many Faces of Abuse: Treating the Emotional Abuse of High-Functioning Women (1998)*; *The Narcissistic/Borderline Couple: Psychoanalytic Perspective on Marital Treatment (2003)*; *The V-Spot (2007)*; *How to Talk to a Narcissist* and *How to Talk to a Borderline*; *The Disappearing Male; New Approach to Marital Therapy (2010)*; *Common Complaints in Couples Therapy* (2014). Dr. Lachkar is also a psychohistorian, has published numerous publications on marital and political conflict in the *Journal of Psychohistory*, *Frontpage*, and *Family Security Matters*, including her paper, "The Psychopathology of Terrorism" presented at the Rand Corporation.

Apurva Shah, MD, is a child and adolescent psychiatrist, currently working at Kaiser Permanente in Lancaster, California. After finishing his medical school in Ahmedabad, India, he moved to New York City where he did his residency and fellowship training at the Albert Einstein

College of Medicine. He became a candidate at the New York Psychoanalytic Institute, but left it to move back to India. In Ahmedabad, he started a not-for-profit company, Antarnad Foundation, for teaching psychoanalysis and training psychoanalytic psychotherapists. Under his patronage, Antarnad has thrived and he teaches and supervises there on his annual visits and via Skype. In southern California, he is a professional affiliate member and the co-coordinator of the Film and Mind Series at the New Center for Psychoanalysis. In his presentations and publications, he focuses on the intersection of psychoanalysis and culture, often through the analysis of movies.

Shahrzad Siassi, PhD, is a psychologist/psychoanalyst with a PhD from University of Pittsburgh and a PhD in psychoanalysis from the Southern California Psychoanalytic Institute (now the New Center for Psychoanalysis). A senior faculty member at the New Center for Psychoanalysis and a supervising and training analyst at the Newport Psychoanalytic Institute, she is the recipient of the 2003 Karl A. Menninger Memorial Award of the American Psychoanalytic Association. Her areas of research and interest include healthy aspects of human relatedness, with a special focus on the role of culture and religion in psychodynamic psychotherapy as well as shifting significance of transference in male patients and female analysts. Dr. Siassi is the author of *Forgiveness in Intimate Relationships: Psychoanalytic Perspectives* (Karnac, 2013). She maintains a private practice of psychotherapy and psychoanalysis in Los Angeles, CA.

Richard Tuch, MD, is a training analyst at the New Center for Psychoanalysis, Los Angeles and at the Psychoanalytic Center of California. He is clinical professor of psychiatry at the David Geffen School of Medicine, University of California at Los Angeles. He was presented with the Karl A. Menninger Memorial Award for Psychoanalytic Writing in 1995, and was presented with the Edith Sabshin Teaching Award in 2008. He has published a number of articles in all three of the major psychoanalytic journals and is a frequent presenter at meetings of the American Psychoanalytic Association. Dr. Tuch is the author of *The Single Woman-Married Man Syndrome* (Rowman & Littlefield, 2002), a book about marital infidelity. He maintains a private practice of psychotherapy and psychoanalysis in Los Angeles, CA.

INTRODUCTION

While ubiquitous in human experience, the emotion of regret has received little attention from psychiatry and psychoanalysis. This is in sharp contrast to its phenomenological twin, remorse. The latter, though occasionally conflated with guilt, has been at the center of many psychoanalytic conceptualizations, especially those of Melanie Klein. Regret, which differs from remorse in being less object-related and more narcissistically oriented, has been ignored. The meagre literature that does exist is scattered, heuristically "thin," and insufficiently related to clinical praxis.

Our book aims to fill this gap in psychoanalytic literature. It is comprised of essays by nine distinguished psychoanalysts who address the state of regret from diverse theoretical, developmental, cultural, and clinical perspectives. The first section of the book is devoted to the developmental substrate of regret and of its vicissitudes over the life span. The second section of the book deals with fiction, poetry, and movies pertaining to regret. The final section of the book addresses the clinical issues pertinent to this realm. This section elucidates the psychopathological dimension of ego restriction associated with regret. Utilizing illustrative clinical vignettes, the contributors discuss masochism, wishful fantasies of reversing the flow of time, nostalgia, and temporal fracture of life in poignant and instructive details. The result is a harmonious gestalt of enhanced understanding of an nonoptimally investigated emotion of profound existential significance.

PART I

DEVELOPMENTAL REALMS

CHAPTER ONE

The capacity for regret in children and adolescents

Susan L. Donner

Regret can be summarized as the sorrowful affect experienced from the realization that one's past action or inaction has caused harm to the self (Akhtar, 2009). Most adults can recognize regret as the terrible feeling accompanying the awareness that they made an error leading to a painful or negative outcome that cannot be easily undone. This contribution offers an opportunity to examine the capacity for the manifestation of regret in children and adolescents. Do children and adolescents experience regret in the same way as adults? If not, what does regret look like at different ages and stages of development? A literature review of child and adolescent psychiatric, psychological, and psychoanalytic literature reveals almost no citations relevant to this topic and, when the topic is addressed, divergent definitions are used.[1] In the absence of guidance from the psychoanalytic and other clinical literature, how might an analyst address the presence or absence of regret in child and adolescent cases? Is regret a by-product of psycho-analytic treatment as affects are differentiated and verbalized? Is it a symptom that needs to be resolved in the course of treatment? Would there be a construct that might serve as a tool for beginning to explore regret in these younger age groups?

The Passover Seder in the Jewish tradition offers a parable called "The Four Children"[2] that presages by a few millennia an interest in children's minds. This story focuses the attention of the parents and Seder leaders on the necessity to utilize different approaches to reach children of varying ages, developmental stages, and capacities as the Passover story is told again and again. "The Four Children" are traditionally described as the wise one, the wicked one, the simple one, and the one who does not know how to ask. A child psychoanalytic reframing of these four archetypal children might be described as the following:

1) The *wise one* is the curious and verbal child who demonstrates his (or her) intellect by asking questions and engaging the adults with answers and discussion;
2) The *wicked one* is the rebellious child who refuses to take part and separates himself from the community at the table;
3) The *simple child* is the limited one who can process only fragments of the information given constitutional and/or developmental conditions; and
4) The *one who does not know how to ask* is the child who is not able to formulate questions and needs the adults to reach out to and find him.[3]

These representational categories might be used to organize our understanding not only of the development and clinical manifestations of regret in children and adolescents, but also of the technical approaches in the child psychoanalyst's toolbox needed to work effectively with children, given differences in ages, capacities, and states of mind. The "wise" child may not need much of a shift from classical psychoanalytic technique and thus might be considered "wise" since she can work well with transference manifestations and interpretations. In this chapter, this child will be represented by Lori, an adolescent girl who suffered from depression but who, through her analytic work, was able to achieve a reasonably stable depressive position. She came to endure the weight of her decisions, recognize and take responsibility for her "errors" which caused "damage to herself," and consider new possibilities in the wake of disappointment, sadness, and regret.

The "rebellious" child connects with his objects via hostility and other uncomfortable affects. James, a most difficult and inconsolable child, chronically organized his disorganized family with his intolerable affects and behaviors. Unable to bear any negative affect, let alone regret and remorse, he projected massively into his objects. In treatment, the exploration of the meaning of his connections required a different approach that circumvented his feeling of "being analyzed like a rat in a laboratory," as he referred to himself. Coming from a more paranoid and persecuted stance, he necessitated an approach that encouraged self-reflection and mentalization without further increasing his defensive stance. He needed assistance over time to tolerate the intolerable and to reintegrate the projected parts of himself, including the pain of regret and remorse.

The "simple" child is, in reality, anything but. Serena was the young, developmentally delayed child who was considered unreachable and unteachable by her preschool and unmanageable by her overwhelmed parents. The focus of her psychoanalytic treatment was to build the structures of her mind to allow for connections and self-regulation through very active play where various self-states could be experienced and reorganized (Solnit, 1987). Assisting Serena to experience regret in a way she could make meaning of could indeed be viewed as a feat.

Representing the "child who cannot ask" is Adam, an adopted child, now an older teenager, who constructed a protective bubble for himself. From therein, he would not have to commit to any identity or direction and thus never seemed to develop agency or motivation beyond maintaining his closed-state equilibrium. Reaching Adam, a calm and polite young man, was more difficult than reaching James. He had constructed a narcissistically sealed world for himself where there existed no past, present, or future and only a few basic and muted emotional states. Missing among other affects, such as desire, anger, anxiety, and discomfort, was regret. The child and adolescent analyst's work in this case was different still. Words would simply wash over Adam. Yet he came to treatment uncoerced, and we began by tolerating the presence of the other. Experiencing painful affects like regret seemed to be eons away.

Beginning with the "wise" (and the most easily accessible) child, Lori was a sixteen-year-old adolescent girl, the oldest of two children of professional parents, who came to treatment after the breakup of her first romantic and sexual relationship that had lasted over a year. Initially she presented with depressive symptoms, including difficulty sleeping, feelings of worthlessness, self-reproach, anhedonia, and social withdrawal. She had been a good student but was having difficulties concentrating, and her grades had dipped. She could not stop thinking about her ex-boyfriend, her sense of being betrayed by him, her loss of her identity as a member of a couple, and her self-criticism and terrible regret about no longer being a virgin.

Lori was very distressed by her depressed and miserable state but simultaneously was very curious about the functioning of her mind. After a three-month consultation period, she and her parents agreed to a psychoanalytic treatment four days a week with regular parent sessions. What emerged within her history and within the transference was a close, even enmeshed, relationship with her mother. They shared similar temperaments and social and artistic interests that had allowed them to spend much time together over many years. They were each other's closest confidantes and emotional supports. The mother knew intimate details about Lori's relationships, and, in turn, Lori knew a great deal about mother's complex family, relationship history, and marital issues. In contrast, Lori's brother was impulsive and opposi-tional and related better to their father, who was less available given his work schedule and hobbies. I speculated to myself that perhaps this first romantic relationship was Lori's attempt at object removal (Katan, 1951) with several potential goals: to separate and individuate herself from her mother, to renounce oedipal designs on her father, and to con-solidate her own sexual identity. Perhaps the simultaneous failure on so many fronts resulted in her significant clinical collapse.

Lori engaged immediately with me and demonstrated that she was able to develop an observing ego and examine her thoughts, feelings, and actions. She brought in her dreams and readily associated to them. Her symptoms rapidly remitted, and her academic successes returned. Although delightful to work with given her enthusiasm and return-ing energy, Lori seemed to be trying almost too hard to please me and become my most special patient.

After several months, I realized that she was never, ever late and would start a new topic with two minutes to go at the end of the session that required considerable effort on my part to end on time. I discerned a certain clinginess that made me wonder if the former boyfriend had been similarly overwhelmed by the same feeling of possessiveness. When I brought the end of the session pattern to Lori's attention by wondering aloud if she could verbalize what she was feeling, she said she worried she was disappointing me. She associated to a dream that had been lovely but was rudely interrupted by her morning alarm.

She recounted feeling so angry that she had to get up and go to school. At the end of the session, I mused aloud if she was disappointed in having her session come to an end. She looked so surprised, perhaps as much by the announcement of the end of the session as by her affective state. Then she looked angry and muttered, "Maybe." Endings, especially surprising ones, of relationships, dreams, and now sessions were evidence of Lori's inadequate omnipotent control and her emerging irritation and anger.

In and out of sessions, the overly sweet, adorable persona gave way to an aggressively critical voice towards her friends, family, and her analyst. Her mother commented that Lori was critical and angry, and no one in the house could do anything right. In my office, Lori complained that the pillows in the chair had been changed or rearranged and were uncomfortable. She went on to disparage the artwork and express her distaste for the furniture design. I commented that we were all so imperfect in her eyes and disappointed her so dreadfully. She paused and started to cry. She realized that it wasn't everyone else who was so imperfect but her. She felt small, incompetent, tarnished. She regretted so many things: rushing into the relationship with the former boyfriend, having sex, getting some bad grades, picking wrong friends, again having sex, and no longer being a virgin. She ruminated about that former state of "purity" that was now gone forever. She berated herself for not having been omniscient and not foreseeing what could happen that she might regret in the future.

She then began thinking about her parents and their complex relationship and the ties that now seemed too close with her mother. She realized that her mother had a boyfriend in her early teenage years, and the patient now felt the mother encouraged Lori too much to get involved sexually with the boyfriend. I commented that it seemed that she felt she was being obedient for being involved with the boy and now she was criticizing herself. I said that it almost sounded like she wanted it to be her mother's fault, so she could escape the confusion. She said sadly that she wished she could stay little and have her parents and me have to take the responsibility for her bad feelings and mistakes. I interpreted that she was in a paradoxical position. On one hand, she wanted her independence of action and of thought but, on the other hand, she wanted protection from painful feelings, like blame and regret, and wanted to stay under the large, seemingly omnipotent wings of the "adults."

In parallel to Lori's treatment, her parents were also actively involved in their own parent work with me (Novick & Novick, 2005). There were very clear limits about confidentiality around Lori's work, and her parents were very interested in the evolving process of parenting. The sessions allowed the two of them to focus together on their children and quickly resulted in a renewed sense of teamwork and collaboration as well as a different perspective on parenting where they could step "out of the trenches," so to speak. They developed new perspectives on both of their children and their own shifting roles and responsibilities as they appreciated differences in their children's needs, sensitivities, and developmental stages. Specifically with regard to Lori, her mother, with the crucial support of her father, was more conscious of hierarchical boundaries and the emotional space necessary for Lori to develop more separately, especially with regard to emotional regulation and identity. Over the period of the treatment, they also used the opportunity to discuss their own expectations, disappointments, errors and, of course, remorse and regret as they looked more objectively at their actions and inactions with regard to their children and themselves. Their overall parental ability to tolerate unpleasant affects, thoughts, and fantasies provided an implicit and explicit support for Lori's affect tolerance and second separation-individuation process (Blos, 1967).

Thus, as Lori grappled with the disintegration of her omnipotent defenses, there evolved a new space in our analytic world and in her mind for her reality testing to develop so that she could accept responsibility for her actions, both past and present. Her sense of being irreversibly changed through the course of the failed relationship was a tremendous source of regret, but her eventual recognition of the brutal harshness of her own superego allowed for her to begin to relinquish her omnipotent and omniscient powers (Gray, 1987). It was her harsh judgment of herself that had eroded her willingness to separate and use her emerging agency to take independent action.

From a technical point of view, Lori had a capacity to shift back and forth in her treatment between the real and transference levels, that is, an ability to achieve symbolic functioning as part of depressive position functioning (Segal, 1957). Lori felt that I sat back in my chair and judged her from an imperious throne. She took my silences to indicate my boredom and lack of connectedness with her. Any separation seemed to be a betrayal. She brought in a dream in which her mother was driving, and she was in the passenger seat listening to music that she chose.

Her mother changed to a news station on the radio, and the patient became enraged. Then her mother changed direction, and the patient started screaming at her. The mother then picked up her brother and his friend, and the patient sat in a furious silence. The dream ended when the car crashed into another, and she woke up in a panic.

Lori focused on her anger with her mother and her competitive feelings with her brother but then became angry with me as I signaled the end of the session. "I was not finished. I will forget by tomorrow. Why can't I go on for a minute till your light goes on?" I noted her upset with me too, not just her mom, and her resistance at any separation that was not her choice. She left in a bit of a huff but returned the next day apologetic. She said she recognized how angry she was at not being able to control everyone, even sometimes her own anger. She was embarrassed and regretted the intensity of her emotions in the dream but also in my office. I asked her what she meant by regret. She said she wished she could have a "do-over" and take it back. She laughed and said she knew that that must sound silly, but she really wished it, like they all did when they were little. Then she was very serious. She talked about how intense her feelings had been in the moment and how they changed even in a few hours. Maybe she didn't have to feel held captive and mortified by her emotions.

Through her dream work and transference feelings, Lori was able to acknowledge her destructive, hateful wishes towards herself, her mother, her sibling, and me, and the accompanying "disgraceful" affects of greed, envy, and jealousy. She recognized wanting her father to herself. Given his relative inaccessibility and her mother's availability, reality worked with her own wishes to mask some of her competitive strivings. Lori's courage to look at herself with greater clarity and less shame allowed her to occupy a more secure depressive position where she could feel more resilient and not as tortured by competitive thoughts and actions which stimulated remorse towards her objects and regret towards her idealized self.

With Lori, regret began as a persecutory affect, an emotional imprint of failure, rejection, and imperfection. The collapse of her omnipotent defenses left her depressed and frightened. Her analytic work allowed her to move gradually to a firmer depressive position where she could observe her conscious and unconscious desires and attacks with a shift in regret and remorse. Her experience of damaging her internal objects was also understood as being less powerful and less real and contrasted

with her parents' evolution into more effective, thoughtful, and separate figures. Thus her survival of her own imaginary attacks, including
the weapon of regret and her once unrealistically cruel superego, created a new sense of resilience and sturdiness.

The affect of regret was thus transformed from a symptom into a
signal to activate her new capacity for reflective thinking. Within the
new potential space, Lori could then turn to other possibilities, like new
goals, new relationships, and a new college environment, none of which
were experienced as particularly threatening, and, as a result, did not
demand the return of former compromising defenses such as merger
identifications. Like the wise child in the Passover parable, she was able
to make great use of the analytic setting and expanded her capacities to
manage her affects with greater patience and flexibility.

James, in stark contrast, represents the wicked or rebellious child from
the Passover liturgy. He was the first child of privileged parents, both
of whom had histories of trauma and great difficulties consoling and
containing themselves even before James was born. They described him
as an irritable infant who alternately clung to and rejected his objects.
He was referred to me during early adolescence for cutting and mood
instability with a provisional diagnosis of borderline personality traits.
James had no investment in school, sports, hobbies, or close friends and
ran with a pack of fungible middle school peers. He paid little attention to his well-being, never complained about his cuts or scars, and
engaged in impulsive and risky behaviors. There was neither remorse
nor regret for harm he caused to others or himself. If derailed from the
blur of constant activity, he would feel persecuted and would join frantically with any available object.

Within a week of beginning analysis four times a week, the cutting stopped. I silently hypothesized that James was responding to the
containment in a predictable setting and/or a trial merger with a new
developmental object, one who might be available to help him tolerate
separation and his unsteady movements as he began to take steps on
his own. What also became clear within the first weeks was his splitting
between a loved, depressed symbiotic maternal object and a hated,
vital, and independent paternal one. He seemed to use the analysis as a
safe zone between his internal claustrophobic and agoraphobic cycling
and the chaos of his external world.

During the first year of treatment, James recounted tales of "The
Wild," stories of the wolf pack with whom he ran. It was an opportunity
for me to practice analytic restraint as I heard stories of unsupervised

early adolescents pushing every boundary possible, often late at night in public spaces. With great relish, James would tell stories of other girls and boys, but we both knew that many of the tales were autobiographical. As in the play of a young child, we spoke about various characters in displacement and used the setup to discuss possible thoughts, feelings, and motivations in the "others" to try to understand some of their "incomprehensible" decisions and behaviors. James was clearly identifying with my armchair position to observe himself and others and to identify sequences and affects in the frenzied situations.

Similarly to Lori's parents, I worked with James's parents weekly with the hope of providing an experience of affect tolerance and reflective thinking that might reverberate through the household. Neither was fundamentally engaged in the development of their roles as parents or willing to engage with each other as teammates. In retrospect, each session felt like starting again from the beginning as we managed whatever weekly crisis James created to attempt to keep them attentive and parental. I also tried to address the manifestation of their superego lacunae that allowed James to continue to act out in obvious ways with no or ineffective parental response (Johnson & Szurek, 1952).

In spite of environmental concerns, James surprised me with the diligence with which he worked in the analysis as he discovered his separate mind in his dreams, where the productions were his alone, even the terrifying aggressive ones. Ever so slowly, he began to differentiate between fantasy and reality, lies and truths. He used the privacy and confidentiality of treatment to share secrets that he had been burdened with over the years by friends and family. I thought of these confidences as *quid pro quo* gifts for my keeping his own confidential world separate. Many sessions felt like moments to refuel in a quiet space and reorganize his internal world. James questioned others' motivations and even began to think about his own. He tried on others' perspectives and exhibited real empathy for the new "real" friends emerging from the pack.

James, however, continued to have great difficulty pursuing sustained independent pursuits outside the analysis, like school or extracurricular activities or work. At other times that would only be revealed long after the fact, he would hint provocatively at his drug and alcohol use and sadomasochistic bisexual relationships. It was as if he could only tolerate the tension of separation and individuation for a limited period of time and then would have to regress into a complex and shameful fusion.

Two and one-half years into analysis, during a vacation break, James "confessed" to his father that he had kept the mother's prescription pill addiction quiet for ten years. What was not even a poorly kept secret was treated as duplicitous treachery. There was an emergency family session, and it turned out to be the last time I saw the patient. I wondered aloud about the patient's potential motivations behind the revelation and articulated his worry and care for his mother. James screamed that he did it out of hatred, not love. In that moment, I realized that James's internal world, under stresses that he could or would not describe in this setting, seemed to collapse back into "psychic equivalence" (Fonagy & Target, 1996, p. 225). The space that we had created in his mind, his actual analytic work and play within the consultation room, his fragile status of separation-individuation, and any achievement of ambivalent feelings appeared to have evaporated.

As he exclaimed that he would never return to treatment, I received the simultaneous nonverbal message that his accomplishments were secrets that were too dangerous to reveal, and the analyst's mandate was to hold them in absolute confidence. I recognized that, to preserve the relationship with his mother, he would need to sacrifice publicly his gains, continue to cast himself as the crazy, unmanageable child who could never be an object of envy, and to keep the lines between self and other blurred. His successful pathological accommodation in order to preserve familial equilibrium would trump his individual progressive movement, at least at that particular crossroads (Brandchaft, 2007). In his dramatic termination, James needed to demonstrate to his family that the fusion was still intact and he was still "ruthless," in spite of the analytic treatment (Winnicott, 1945). James had to convince his primary objects that he had not changed and was clearly the same aggressive child who could show no concern (or "ruth," in Winnicott's language) towards himself or his objects. There was to be no evidence of any loyalty conflict between his mother and his analyst.

In spite of his protestations at that last session, James had made some progress beyond the state of ruthlessness. Although I agree with James that aggression, hate, and hard-fought separation from and triumph over his damaged mother were components of the revelation of her addiction, there was also real concern for his object and, more important, for himself that had started to emerge during the previous and subsequent weeks as his actions demonstrated his separation and differentiation from various merger states, including the analytic one.

With his need to obfuscate so much of his true emerging self and possible budding feelings of guilt towards his objects, it is difficult to assess from James's words his ability to achieve the state of "ruth" or "the capacity for concern" (Winnicott, 1965, pp. 73–79), let alone any hints of the depressive position (Klein, 1940). One of the advantages of fantasied mergers is that self and object do not have to be clearly separated and affects can be fluidly projected. James could thus try to limit his vulnerability to internal and external persecutory attacks but at a price of emotional and ego integrity.

Winnicott wrote about the importance of being able to use an object beyond a "bundle of projections," where the object is a separate entity that exists outside the mind of the subject, "the ability to place the object outside the area of subjective phenomenon" (Winnicott, 1971, p. 86). James's ability to place his objects outside of his subjective experience was still in a nascent stage and deteriorated under threat to the relationship with his primary object. His ability to "play with reality" (Fonagy & Target, 1996, p. 217) collapsed back into a world of psychic equivalence where the concrete is real and the symbolic is not. Perhaps one has to be able to see both oneself and the object as separate to be able to experience regret or remorse, respectively. James was not yet in a position to consider his remorse towards exposing his mother or his regret about the termination of his own analytic treatment.

The work of the analyst with James during this two and a half year period was different than with Lori. Although relative anonymity and neutrality allowed for the transference and collection of projections to be assembled, Lori could tolerate the return of those projections and their transformation in the form of interpretations. James was much too terrified and persecuted to allow for the return of but a few of his projections during the years of our work together and always with careful reformulation. Perhaps over time, he could have continued to develop greater ego strengths, including affect tolerance and superego modifications, to tolerate that level of work but, at the time of termination, that was not possible. The analyst was left holding the bag, so to speak.

The feelings of sadness, loss, and failure as well as the positive ones, including love, respect, and fulfillment from collaborative productivity, had to be safely and definitively projected into the analyst with no opportunity for return. The sorrow from the abrupt termination of treatment could not be expressed publicly or even in a private termination session. Thus, the harm James had done to his true self and the damage he inflicted on his emerging healthier parts could not be recognized outside of the analyst's mind (Winnicott, 1956). Furthermore, the progress that had been made had to be denied and negated, externally and potentially internally. That exquisitely painful realization and understanding of the cost of the destruction, including the associated regret, had to be experienced solely by the analyst.

Ultimately, I felt sad and wished I could have changed the outcome. Still, like a young child with a parent, James expected me to hold on to the painful affects so that he could maintain his relationships that he depended on in the concrete world. Being forced to bear the feelings of helplessness, shame, rejection, and regret about his different clinical course than the one we had begun to imagine together was a bitter pill to swallow. I realized in retrospect that James had trust in me not to return the projections, not to retaliate, and not to destroy confidentiality.

The third child in the parable is the "simple" one with extraordinary medical and psychiatric complexity. Serena's parents came to me for a consultation about their three-and-a-half-year-old daughter who had been given a provisional diagnosis of autism in order to provide speech and language, physical, and occupational therapies and behavioral interventions for her developmental delays. She was a beautiful preschooler whose difficulties in motor skills and coordination, articulated speech and language, enuresis and self-regulation kept her in a much younger symbiotic state with her mother than her age would suggest. What became clear within a few weeks of the beginning of her psychoanalytic treatment and monthly parent sessions was the huge contribution of anxiety and panic to Serena's hyperactivity.

Except for some environmental sensitivities, Serena exhibited no symptoms of autism with her engaging personality and her reciprocal and imaginary play with peers and adults. Her anxieties were notable in various symptoms, including phobias, nightmares, inability to be alone, and terror of using a toilet, among others. In sessions, her issues with separation framed the playtime with a recurring, prolonged separation process from her mother or father in the waiting room and long-lasting screams or screeches at the end of her sessions.

Serena's mother, it was learned slowly, suffered from fragile and complicated health conditions that may have impacted Serena prenatally and clearly affected her postnatally. Her mother's energy and ability to attend were often unpredictably low, and her search for effective medical management and time-consuming treatments also diminished her availability and responsiveness. The mother was reasonably attuned to Serena emotionally, but felt she could not keep up with her intense energy, demands, and constant need for limits. Serena's father also was overwhelmed with his job and financial responsibilities and would often bring Serena to her many appointments but then would have to work late to compensate. Grandparents and other family supports were either ill themselves or lived too far away to be regularly helpful.

Serena's experiences of object loss were not minimal and, in fact, were traumatic for her. Her mother's medical illnesses and their delayed diagnoses and prolonged treatments created physical and emotional absences that could not be explained or contained well enough for Serena. Serena's ability to internalize a consistently available good internal object eluded her and, in fact, the maternal object she internalized was damaged, whether from her real experiences or her fantasied attacks. Thus, her continuous anxieties were communicated with panic, controlling behaviors, and aggression.

Normally, the dance of a toddler is fueled with positive affects towards actions of separation and individuation and negative affects that often bring regressive behaviors, which allow for proximal reconnection with primary objects. Although she made some forward movement like separation at school, she frequently collapsed into symbiotic states and used her distress and aggression to engage her objects regressively. She forced her objects to console her or contain her, often physically since her receptive and expressive use of language was not stable enough to be used alone. Her use of her objects in this manner limited her opportunities to feel separate and to experience her actions as her own (Winnicott, 1958). Thus, the recognition of harm to oneself or another and of cause and effect relationships, both necessary to experience regret and remorse, were still not regularly apparent to this child. Serena experienced the world as the root of her pain and distress, since she had no consistent sense that she could be an agent of predictable action and therefore be responsible for the way in which she interacted with herself, others, and things in the external world.

Serena began treatment with her mother in the room. I needed her mother to translate her poorly articulated speech that I could not decipher, and the mother needed to begin to trust me and internalize my very different psychoanalytic approach from the regional center's and school professionals' behavioral interventions. I used affectively attuned narration of her affects and play, as well as simple but containing interpretations that allowed Serena to develop and sustain her play with her mother and then increasingly me. Within two months, the distortions of Serena's speech and her disruptive anxiety and hyper-activity markedly improved, and the mother-child dyad could separate for the sessions (Sherkow, 2001). Still, the waiting room was the stage for variable separation delays at the beginnings of sessions and screeches at the ends.

About four months later, Serena forced her mother and me to endure a twenty-minute blood-curdling tantrum in the waiting room. While she wailed, she effectively blocked out our words, clung to her mother, and demanded to be held like a baby. Both of us were effectively paralyzed while we waited for each screaming cycle to end and for her to re-equilibrate, only to be surprised when she resumed screaming. When she was finally ready, she decided that she would come with me to my office kitchen and calm down with a cup of water. After a sip, she put down the cup and then ordered me to sit on the rug so we could play "Duck, Duck, Goose." I explained that it was not safe to play that game in the office and repeated that several times to make sure she might hear and understand. She agreed as I was ordered to sit on the rug and I complied. Then, she defiantly ran in a circle and cried, "Duck, Duck … Goose" and, in an instant, turned and crashed into the wooden playhouse and dropped to the floor.

Shocked from the impact and pain, Selena froze for several moments and then began to cry. I stayed where I was sitting to indicate my calm and our separateness and suggested empathically that she rub her leg to help her pain. She cried, "I hurt, I hurt my leg," but did listen and followed directions in between sobs. When she was calmer, I linked her running to her getting hurt. She stayed quiet. Perhaps physical pain provided a rare opportunity for self-awareness at this developmental stage like no other stimulus. I repeated that the game was not safe in the space of the playroom since it was much smaller than the yard at school. I commented that she made a choice that resulted in her, and only her, getting hurt. She repeated the rule that we don't run in the office and then requested another sip of water in the kitchen. Then she drank and repeated the rule about not touching the hot water tap. I was hopeful that we were at a turning point in the session, but, to my dismay, she began to climb on chairs and nonverbally requested that she needed more reassurance by my physical and verbal containment.

In this particular sequence, Serena and I experienced a moment where her sensorium, emotions, and cognition coalesced into an integrated and separate state of "self" that contrasted strikingly with the apparent lack of separation-individuation evidenced by the twenty minutes in her mother's arms screaming at the beginning of the session. Linked to that experience was the observation that the analyst translated into words of cause and effect that she alone caused and experienced the effect of that action. Time and action seemed to slow in this moment of relative separateness, autonomy, and self-awareness. My role as witness, narrator, and separate object allowed her an emotional and mental space where she could physically and then symbolically link her pain. Was there a brief moment in which she could bear the responsibility of her painful state and therefore experience regret? I believe there was, for she then returned to a state of impulsive, "naughty" actions that necessitated my return to a role as the "boss," rather than her acceptance of that self-regulating responsibility.

Serena ravenously engaged in her treatment and demanded much from her analyst. I played many roles, often simultaneously. What could not be kept in her mind, I had to keep in my mind. I needed to keep both of us safe, and I often referenced that limit when necessary. In that moment, I was a paternal transference object, responsible for rules but also a new developmental object with a level of consistency that Serena tested religiously (Faimberg, 2014; Settlage, 1989). I was also a comforter in my role as maternal transference object but also a dissimilar developmental object since I did not take my patient into a cuddle when she was hurt or upset and instead would use my words, slowly, repetitively, and calmly. I was a playmate who would join in every scenario Serena would imagine as an actor in a panoply of roles that became more differentiated over time: organizer, janitor, monster, leader, follower, boss, source of disappointment and pain, time keeper, doctor, patient, teacher, pupil, and her favorite role for me, "bad girl."

Within a few months, Serena became an expert at playing with reality and would often inform me, if I became confused, when play was pretend. Her symbolic functioning was developing faster than her language, but she worked hard at making herself understood and took pride in her new words that described emotions and bodily feelings, events, time, characters, and friends. She frequently referenced that time when she was not safe and crashed into the little house. Her linking of time, cause and effect, and intentionality had coalesced into an important memory that hopefully will allow her reasonable regulatory control of her body and emotions so that she can experience feelings of regret and remorse within longer and longer moments of the depressive position.

Work with Serena's parents continued to evolve with their ability to recognize earlier when Serena needed more immediate containment. Her lively dad also was able to take a more active role with her physical play where there was both intensity and safety needs being addressed. As Serena became more verbally expressive and less anxious about her mother's slowly improving condition, her mother was able to sit with her and play or read with longer and longer circles of communication (Greenspan, 2007). As the parental anxieties diminished, the focus in the parent sessions shifted to addressing their communication, teamwork, and our collaboration towards helping Serena to realize her developmental goals that were not always aligned with school expectations. Exploring their disappointments and self-blame allowed for them to comfort and reassure the other. That kinder and gentler ambiance then contributed to a home with more room for affects but also with mechanisms to reflect upon them. Serena, like James, desperately and repetitively behaved in ways to demand parental containment, which would allow her to restabilize after emotional upsets. Serena, however, was able to shift along with her parents to a different, healthier state of equilibrium where they could tolerate more of a depressive position as a family unit. Over time, perhaps, continued work around negative emotions in the parents and child will allow for greater affect tolerance, including constructive and durable experiences of regret and remorse.

Finally there is Adam, an example of a child who truly "does not know how to ask." Adam came to analytic treatment as a fifteen-year-old adopted young man in a family of a couple who later had their own biological daughter, now eight years old. Adam's biological parents were teenagers who, when the mother got pregnant, realized they could not raise a child alone or together. His adoptive parents were present at the time of delivery and were thrilled to bring their healthy baby home. He was a particularly easy baby who demanded very little and went along with his parents' routines. His milestones were within normal range, but the parents had concerns when he started preschool. He was friendly but did not seem to seek out friendships. When his sibling was born, he was happy but not particularly engaged with her either. He seemed bright, sweet, and communicative but just in his own world. He floated through school and did the bare minimum to get by with little interest and energy. Although seen by a number of mental health practitioners, he didn't seem to improve, no matter what the intervention. Feeling helpless and confused, his parents came to me for a consultation.

Adam was a nice looking and pleasant boy who would only talk if I asked him questions. Otherwise he was content just to sit with me and watch me. His answers were short, typically one to six words. He was remarkably concrete but did not have psychotic or autistic symptoms. I learned about the few things that interested him and would try to establish contact. During the first few months, he would dutifully arrive on time but occasionally nodded off to sleep for fifteen or twenty minutes. There were no other symptoms of narcolepsy or other sleep disorders and, after unsuccessful attempts to awaken him, I relaxed and allowed myself to enter into a kind of "maternal reverie." I was curious about his need to be watched while he slept, but then the slumbering phase ended. I felt helpless and confused, much like his parents.

Adam attended regularly, but it was unclear if he was attached to me or to the routine. Curiously, he never missed a session unless I had to cancel for illness or vacation, but then he would miss multiple sessions in a row with no acknowledgment or emotional response. He could not understand my attempts to link my cancelled sessions to his missed ones. My attempts to engage his curiosity or powers of observation failed. I silently mused that his experience of powerlessness when required to separate from me disrupted his carefully constructed narcissistic equilibrium (Rosenfeld, 1964). He would just sit in the chair opposite me for an interminable amount of time and verbalize nothing unless I initiated. He prided himself on needing and wanting very little. He spoke about his mind as "his empty box," but he made no attempts to fill it. His main focus was video games, which he played after school and into the night and told me that he could imagine playing during school and even in session. I experienced him as a self-sufficient, sedentary, complacent young man who could achieve his basic needs with parental support and thus maintain his omnipotent womb-like fantasy of self-containment (Ferenczi, 1916).

I believed that parent work would be an important component of Adam's treatment since I surmised to myself that the excavation of histories and meanings and complex communications would only help open up his insulated system. Unfortunately, it became clear that unspeakable parental traumas and complex dynamics prevented them from joining with me in parent work. I was filled with curiosity, sadness, frustration, and anger, likely intolerable affects that the family needed to split off and project into me. Adam and I were left to our own devices to make our own way, much as I imagined he had felt growing up. At this point in treatment, the analytic work was to respect his cocoon structure and look for opportunities to stretch it with experiences within the consultation room (Bromberg, 1983).

When his parents expressed anxiety that he might not graduate high school given his poor work habits and inconsistent grades, he compliantly did enough of the work necessary to not embarrass them. He wasn't interested in college and, when given a job opportunity, he proved to be a hard worker. He dutifully followed directions without much emotion, although he enjoyed the camaraderie of the other workers. A couple of friends would contact him during their breaks from college, and he would hear stories of the larger world. Perhaps, I hoped, the job or peers' experiences would awaken a larger sense of desire, ambition, excitement, or even feelings of boredom, loneliness, pain, or possibly regret, but there seemed to be no traces of these positive or negative emotions.

One session, Adam came in and plopped into the chair in his routine way. This day, however, he was quiet and seemed to have more tension in his body. We sat in silence. He told me that his bird was ill and might die soon. I asked him to tell me more, but he remained silent and still. All of a sudden, he sobbed, head down. About ten minutes later when he started to settle, I said he seemed upset. He talked about the bird and taking care of her and his love for her. At the beginning of the next session, he told me that she had passed away by the time he had returned home that day. He was no longer emotional but talked about his organization of her memorial service and burial in the garden. I realized later that he had chosen to come to his session and leave his dying bird. In retrospect, I realized he was choosing life, even with its painful separations.

Over the next several months, little by little, I began to hear more about various losses. A good friend cut off contact over the summer after graduation. He began to describe loneliness when his friends from high school no longer wanted to play video games online as they became more involved with their lives at college. Then, for the first time, he showed curiosity about me, and he asked me where I went when I had to cancel two sessions. I was astonished at his interest in me and told Adam that I had been at a conference. He exhaled sharply, looked relieved, and then smiled. I imagined that, in his mind, I had been lost and now I had been found. I had become an object that could help him to discover and recognize himself as potentially interesting, maybe even worthwhile (Alvarez, 2012).

As he continued to discover me, little by little, as a separate person, I realized that he was beginning, ever so subtly, to venture out of the narcissistic bubble he had created. He would ask me questions. I recognized that this birth of curiosity was a dramatic step. He still could not link the internal experience and his questions with my words, but I noted that he was beginning to talk more about the past and occasionally the future. Time and space seemed to begin to differentiate. Almost imperceptibly, he was beginning to take the initiative. If I were able to tolerate the remoteness and wait for him to show himself, he would begin to talk, just a short sentence at a time.

One day, there was a major shift. Adam did not move within the office but within his own mind. He said to me that he decided that he did not want to live forever with his parents. He added that he knew that they could never ask him to leave. These two sentences revealed so much of the development that had taken place over the last several years. Adam was able to picture himself years from now in the same position living at home, isolated and unchanged. And the preservation of the bubble was no longer a purely comforting thought! My persistent curiosity about his states of mind, his motivations, his thoughts and fantasies allowed him to imagine that they might exist somewhere in his "empty box." Fantasies of himself as a separate person still felt like too aggressive and isolating an act, but our work had created a frame of comings and goings that helped make separateness and separations both more real and somewhat more tolerable.

Although Adam is still a long way away from achieving his purported goals, the fact that he can begin to imagine a life beyond his bubble is a first step. His vision of living at home forever was ego-dystonic in a new way and the fear of his perpetual paralysis was a powerful motivating force. That seed of regret, that is, the feeling that he might be disappointed by his passive choices at some point in the future, had been planted. He needed to have his separate self appreciated and then mirrored in a way to demonstrate that an independent future was possible, even if painful emotions and results occurred. The bursting of the omnipotent bubble by his beloved pet's death and his ability to express some of his feelings and mourn her loss was a turning point that proved he could concretely survive separateness, helplessness, loss, sadness, and grief, affects that are part and parcel of the experience of regret. For Adam, this hint of regret was a developmental achievement from which he could continue to build.

Circling back to the initial queries about regret, these four vignettes demonstrate that regret can be observed in young children and adolescents, but in a variety of presentations. In Lori's case, regret initially was a painful, long-lasting affect that was a significant symptom of her clinical depression. She could not tolerate her disappointment in her fate or her shifting identity from a powerful and sexual woman in her mother's image to a rejected, tarnished, and humiliated adolescent girl. Her recovery included a reworking of her rigid fantasies and ego ideals about sexual activity and interpersonal relationships that involved a broader and kinder view of human behavior, including modulating her own persecutory judgments about herself and others. Her acceptance of the dissolution of her childhood magical thinking and omnipotent defenses by relinquishing her wish for playground "do-overs" was an important component of her occupation of a reasonably stable depressive position. Associated with that state in spite of a remnant of normal adolescent grandiosity was her relative acceptance of some uncertainty, including a vague sense that the feeling of regret might recur someday. Having survived her own internal destructive attacks, she could move on to the next stage of her life with a degree of confidence in her resilience. In many cases like Lori's, the experience of this "healthy" form of regret is a "by-product" of the psychoanalytic work as affects become differentiated and verbalized. A child's or adolescent's ability to appreciate his own pain and sorrow at not being able to undo damage to himself is a new skill.

James, like many children in treatment, may have felt caught in a loyalty conflict. As long as there wasn't overwhelming overt parental opposition to treatment, he worked hard in analysis to try to understand more of his internal and external worlds and their complex intertwining relationships. When the forces shifted, perhaps due to his clinical improvement and emerging ambivalent feelings about his objects, including the analyst, he chose to end treatment and preserve familial ties. It is possible that the beginnings of guilt, depressive anxiety, and regret had begun to emerge but, like much of his true self, had to remain camouflaged as basic attachment and practical needs were necessarily prioritized.

In the case of Serena, the analyst had to be the one to recognize and narrate the exquisitely brief moment of regret, not even named as such. It has served as the core of a reference memory as the young patient continued to learn how to avoid causing physical harm to herself, a most concrete representation of actions she might regret. For her, linking cause and effect and predicting consequences were important sequencing and regulating connections that will ground the future development of her cognitive and affective self.

For Adam, the hint of the possibility of regret motivated him to begin to consider the future for the first time in a more realistic way. Perhaps the dual assault on the narcissistic bubble by the analytic dyad stretching it and the dying pet's puncture of his emotionally deadened state allowed for a kind of awakening. In this case, his conception of regret as a possible future threat was a developmental thrust for this young man.

Both James's and Adam's pathological states did not allow either of them to be able to experience negative affects, regret being only one among them. Their externalization of these intolerable affects by projection and projective identification speaks to their own inability to manage their feelings directly, but it also raises the importance of the role of primary objects generally. In both of these cases, the parental containers were quite permeable themselves and did not allow for adequate projection and subsequent differentiation, de-intensification, and detoxification of negative affects which then necessitated more complex defenses on the part of the children with deleterious consequences (Bion, 1962b). It raises a question about the caregivers' own ability to experience regret and remorse and the role of both the lack of reflection and affective containment in the intergenerational transmission of traumatic and painful affects.

Regret is such a complex affective and cognitive state that depends on so many developmental factors. "Good enough" parents typically worry about potential harm to their children as they imagine their own potential remorse. They also innately contain their offspring's potential future regret about harm to themselves as they make the responsible safety, health, education, and welfare decisions. Over time, they can then allow their children to make gradually more important decisions as cognitive and emotional maturity allow for greater comprehension of consequences, responsibility, and complex emotional states, like regret and remorse. In these four examples, experiencing regret was a potential, and, in some cases, an actual developmental achievement that could be viewed as evidence of movement towards the depressive position.

Parents, caregivers, teachers, and mental health providers thus are the potential recipients and containers for these crucial affective experiences. Whether or not regret can be experienced during child-hood and adolescence seems to be determined, on the one hand, by the affect tolerance of the child, and, on the other hand, the ability for con-tainment, metabolism, and later reintroduction of the affect by a care-giver at a time and in a manner that the child can absorb. The analyst can therefore play a critical role in the development of the child's and adolescent's ability to experience regret in a positive manner and also in the expansion of affect tolerance and reflective functioning within the larger family and educational environments.

Acknowledgments

I would like to thank Adrienne Harris, Jill Miller, Barrie Richmond, Eric Klein and Eliana Donner-Klein for their thoughtful questions, com-ments, and edits.

Notes

1. "One of the distinguishing features of human cognition is the ability to consider alternatives to the here and now. Thoughts about what might have been are counterfactual thoughts, and when such thoughts concern better alternatives to the present they often lead to negative emotional affect. This experience is what we typically call regret ..." (Burns, Riggs, & Beck, 2012, p. 501).
2. The original Haggadah text references "The Four Sons." Contemporary versions now designate the passage using the gender neutral title "The Four Children."
3. A single gender will be used throughout this book, to apply to both.

CHAPTER TWO

Regret, resolution, and reparation in marital relationships

Joan Lachkar

A lthough a great deal has been written about remorse, reparation, loss, and mourning, little has been written about regret as a dynamic staple in the psychoanalytic literature. "Regret" connotes a deeply felt disappointment over an action or inaction whose aftermath has brought about a detrimental or disappointing outcome, sadness about something that has gone awry, or a missed opportunity. The pain of regret emanating from one's transgressions or wrongdoings can become psychologically chronic, and in some cases paralyzing, especially in those with more severe pathology. Those who have personality disorders that operate at the level of primitive defenses have a greater proclivity toward obsessive thoughts and rumination.

Drawing from many theoretical perspectives, including classical psychoanalysis, self-psychology, object relations, attachment theory, and many contemporary theorists (Grotstein, 1981; Klein, 1957, 1975; Mason, 2016; and Segal, 1981), this chapter encompasses my clinical work in the treatment of couples and attempts to integrate my views with the newer approaches outlined in this book. They are in concert with the Kleinian view that regret, resolution, and reparation occur with the diminishment of shame, envy, guilt, and other defenses.

25

In general terms, regret is a painful experience that involves wishing to undo what has been done or wishing something had been done that one failed to do. Regret involves blaming oneself for a bad or "not good-enough" outcome, a sense of loss or sorrow accompanied by grief and despair. Often other people provide the familiar mantra, "Too late to worry about it now—it's water under the bridge!" The more the event is beyond the person's control, the greater the chance for frequent rumination and obsessive thoughts to take place.

> *Things would have been better if only I had graduated college.*
> *Things would have been different if I had taken that other job, if I hadn't married so young!*
> *Why did I get an abortion? Now my fertile years are over!*

All theorists have their own voice and way of navigating around the concept of regret as they listen with their own distinct analytic ears. For example, the way a Kleinian responds to regret may differ from a Winnicottian or a Bionian. Klein might hear the regret as a move toward reparation as it occurs in the depressive position. Winnicott's (1965) assurance would emanate from the patient's true self and resolution from the ego's splitting mechanisms, whereas Bion (1961, 1967) might not justify the response until it leads to an action or recognition that the person has learned from experience—what Bion (1959, 1967) refers to as the transformation from beta elements to alpha function. According to Mason (2016), both remorse and regret are part of the mourning process and the reparation process (Klein, 1957, 1975). Both involve the legitimate desire to repair the damage one has done to the self and other. The reparation process is where one relinquishes guilt, shame, persecutory anxiety, and other primitive defenses and starts to see the other as a whole object.

Regret and remorse

According to Hoyt (1983) and Juni (1991), remorse entails deep self-reproach for what one has done. It is an exaggerated form of repentance or, as the Kleinians would say, a manic defense and not true reparation. It is where one cannot let go of the lost object and acts in a defensive manner against mourning via self-hatred and beating oneself up, avoiding punishment or reprimand from others by inflicting pain upon oneself. In contrast, regret occurs when the person not only mourns the pain caused to the victim but genuinely expresses empathy and concern. Regret is a deeper, more involved developmental process that involves working through feelings of despair, disappointment, and betrayal. Both views are consistent with the positive impetus needed for repairing, rebuilding, and moving forward toward resolution. The state of psychic regret described in this book is Klein's state of reparation.

In her book, *Regret: From Death Instinct to Reparation and Symbolization through Vivid Case Studies*, Susan Kavaler-Adler (2013), although inspired and influenced by Klein, develops her own theory of "psychic regret" that moves beyond guilt, aggression, and self-flagellation. She takes up where Klein leaves off to encapsulate the conscious experience of coming to terms with loss and grief. She moves Klein's theory away from the internal, intrapsychic world to the external, interpersonal world. This is in contrast to the split-off and persecutory dynamics of unconscious guilt that Klein refers to in the paranoid-schizoid position. Klein sees remorse as a higher form of development, whereas Kavaler-Adler views remorse as a defensive operation against unbearable pain. She offers many clonal case studies embracing such psychoanalytic methods as transference, resistance, defense, and negative transference to help patients work through the developmental mourning process to integration, a cohesive sense of self, and finally to effectuate a new experience that involves real feelings of love, compassion, and true empathy.

Kavaler-Adler views psychic regret as emerging from "developmental mourning," moving through stages of anger and negative transference in treatment to a final state of separation from the object where compassion and forgiveness for self become the replacement for aggression. Her work expands Klein's theory of guilt and loss in the depressive position by designing a developmental model for the mourning process. Her "psychic regret" encapsulates movement from the unconscious to the conscious experience of facing loss and grief. For Kavaler-Adler, regret is the "pain of compassion" (2013, p. xvii). Psychic regret takes center stage in the final stages of treatment (see the section on "Three phases of treatment" in this chapter) and leads to reparation and resolution, paralleling the depressive position.

Theorists such as Susan Kavaler-Adler and Shahrzad Siassi view psychic regret as a new way of looking at the mourning and grieving process by opening up a new, conscious space. According to Siassi

(Chapter Three in this volume), remorse is a more primitive condition than regret and reflective of a past action for which one feels unbearable guilt, whereas regret could be the product of a genuine mourning process that stops the self-blame and helps the person toward empathy with the victim. I found this distinction between remorse and regret particularly useful in the case of Tom and Rebecca.

Rebecca came into session very shaken up after discovering that her unemployed husband's gambling and financial debts had bankrupted them, leading to the loss of their family home. This was in addition to his serial affairs, drinking, and laziness. She decided to pack up her belongings and her daughters and move in with her parents. Tom had reached rock bottom. He realized that he had destroyed his home, marriage, family, and finances. When they came into my office, I had the feeling that Tom was truly sorry and sincerely meant he would never again drink, gamble, and have affairs. Momentarily, I was convinced by his weeping demeanor that he had reached the stage of regret and reparation; however, I later realized it was only a veneer. His wife was also touched, but then questioned if he really planned to repair the damage since he had not mentioned a word about getting a job or helping with the finances, even though he repeatedly told her how sorry he was. It became clear that Tom's grandiose, narcissistic self could not allow him to belittle himself to get a job or be vulnerable. Rebecca reminded him that all the while he was drinking and "screwing around," he had fabricated stories that he was working and making a ton of money.

Meanwhile, in therapy, Tom was beating his chest and sobbing like a baby. He kept apologizing and begging for forgiveness, yet never once showed any empathy for his wife despite the anguish and torment he had caused her. Although we were working through the process of psychic regret, which recently has come to my clinical awareness, I was not deceived by him and clearly recognized he was not at the stage to reach resolution or show true regret. Klein might have referred to this as a state of manic reparation.

Regret does not stand alone. It is intertwined within a matrix of many other dynamics, including shame and guilt. In analytic terms, it is fundamentally an intrapsychic experience, a reaction to a past act that is accompanied by feelings of sadness, shame, embarrassment, depression, annoyance, and/or guilt. Regret may be likened to a battle between the id and superego. The id urges one to "go ahead, do it," and the aftermath of going along with this urging often ends with the individual questioning his behavior.

Three phases of treatment

Klein's concept of the depressive position is as a final stage of treatment, in which one comes to terms with guilt, begins to show remorse, and has the desire to make reparation. Reparation is a mourning process with many stages. This mourning process is what I have come to understand as true regret. The person does not just apologize and admit wrongdoing or beat himself up but begins to genuinely feel empathy and compassion for the pain and harm that he has caused the object.

Distinguishing Klein's depressive position from the newer approaches to regret is complicated. There are no clear and concise entities, and there is a great deal of overlap. In addition, the confusion in the Kleinian conception of the depressive position has to do with the interchange between "successful mourning" and "unsuccessful mourning," which occurs when one remains relentlessly attached to internal persecutory objects and developmentally stuck in the paranoid-schizoid position. Successful mourning is not to be confused with depression (Grotstein, 1981). It is more about sadness and the ability to mourn and release feelings of guilt, as well as the desire to make reparation for damage caused to the object. Successful mourning is heartfelt and sincere, a state of sadness and deep remorse. We often see this occur when alcoholics hit rock bottom and swear to themselves and others, "Never again."

Klein's view of the depressive position is considered to be a more integrative, mature position where the individual brings together both good and bad objects, leading to whole object relations. It is a state of mourning and sadness, a coming to terms with guilt followed by integration and the desire to make reparation. According to Fairbairn (1952), guilt defends against the unbearable feeling of pain that obstructs the capacity for empathy and compassion for others, and responsibility for one's actions. To achieve reparation, Segal (1981) says one has to mourn the loss of the object to repair the damage and pain one has caused. She states that a fundamental aspect of reparation is giving up omnipotent control to come to terms with ambivalence, allowing one to achieve a better sense of reality and decreased fear of loss of the object. Reparation is where love and happiness can emerge.

Complexities in couples

In helping couples deal with grief, regret, and mourning, we must take into account the idiosyncratic nature of various personality disorders and their unique defense mechanisms. For example, narcissist and borderline patients are able to manipulate and dupe their partners and their therapist into thinking that they are truly sorry. But lurking behind this veneer of regret are many unresolved preoedipal issues. For example, for the narcissist, regret would mean admitting imperfection and letting go of the grandiose, omnipotent self. Resolution and true regret can take place only when the narcissist can embrace the idea that vulnerability is healthy and acknowledges the normal dependency needs that an intimate relationship requires. For the borderline, it would mean relinquishing hostility, pent-up rage, and envy toward the partner. Resolution and true regret for the borderline must include the letting go of aggression, which becomes the replacement for envy, rivalry, betrayal, abandonment, and persecutory anxiety. According to Freud, as cited by his biographer Peter Gay (1988), aggression can become the source of pleasure; once it starts it becomes unstoppable.

Another stumbling block to achieving reparation is the type of negative internal objects with which partners identify. Working though resistances in the final stage of treatment requires that couples get in contact with their internal objects (the exciting object, the rejecting object, the painful object, or the unavailable object). Partners may have a very hard time relinquishing their bad internal objects because they are familiar. Thus, even though they are painful, destructive, and cause damage to the relationship, partners will remain forever loyal and faithful to these bad internal objects.

In my book on marital therapy, *The Narcissistic/Borderline Couple* (2003), and in other publications (Lachkar, 1998a, 1998b, 2003, 2008a, 2008b, 2012, 2014), I have described and developed three fundamental developmental phases of treatment through which couples move. I extrapolated these phases from Melanie Klein's (1957) paradigm of the paranoid-schizoid position and the depressive position. The paranoid-schizoid position is characterized by a state of fragmentation in which thoughts and feelings are split off and projected because the psyche cannot tolerate feelings of pain, emptiness, loneliness, rejection, humiliation, or ambiguity. Klein viewed the paranoid-schizoid position as the earliest phase of development, as part-object functioning and the beginning of the primitive, undeveloped superego. Klein's depressive position marks the beginning of reparation, where one develops the capacity to mourn, tolerate, and contain the feelings of sadness, loss, and guilt. This is the phase in which resolution and reparation cohabit. The three phases of treatment in couple therapy that I describe are:

Phase One: Fusion. This is congruent with Klein's paranoid-schizoid position, whereby one "lives" inside the mental space of the other. There is no separation between self and other. This phase is characterized by blame, shame, confusion, delusion, envy, and many unresolved oedipal issues. This is where primitive defenses dominate, including splitting, projection, projective identification, and omnipotent denial. There is a great deal of gaslighting, stonewalling, and rivalry. According to Wurmser (1981), the primary dynamics in this phase are shame and envy. One cannot tolerate the success of the other, and devaluation of the other is the defense against such envy. This is consistent with what Kernberg (1992) describes about aggression: that the primarily passive person in the relationship tends to feel shame while the primarily active one feels guilt. In this phase, couples engage in what I refer to as "the dance," endless battling back and forth without ever reaching conflict resolution.

- "It was your fault that I had the affair."
- "You never apologized and just blamed me for sneaking into your emails."
- "I did apologize!"
- "You apologized but you didn't mean it. You don't show any regret for how you hurt me."

Phase Two: Twoness. This represents a movement away from the paranoid-schizoid position and toward the capacity to tolerate feelings of vulnerability. Phase Two is a transitional space that marks a glimmer of awareness of two separate emotional states and a sense that the therapist can be useful as a transitional object (Winnicott, 1965). Winnicott suggested that the infant learns to wait and to control impulsivity while intermittently making use of transitional objects. Grotstein (1981) observed that borderline patients remain forever attached to the mother's body and misuse "transitional objects" (alcohol, drugs, sex addiction), because they cannot allow themselves to develop the healthy dependency needs required for a relationship.

- "So, because you envied me and my success as the main breadwinner in our family, you feel justified in having affairs?"
- "It's all your fault; you made me feel impotent and less than useless."
- "I didn't make you feel useless. It's you that feels useless! So to prove your manliness you had to go out and fuck other women?"
- "I never realized it was because I felt inadequate. I always thought that I was having these affairs out of revenge. I needed some excitement in my life."
- "That does not justify you betraying me!"
- "I'm sorry, honey. I regret I did that."
- "You say you regret it, but I don't see you doing anything about it!"

Phase Three: Sadness/Mourning. This final phase is the focus of this chapter. It begins the healing process and is characterized by a state of reason that occurs when one comes to terms with shame and guilt and begins to feel regret, remorse, and a desire to make reparation. This marks the beginning of the depressive position, the interdependent expression of separateness, the capacity to come to terms with guilt and past transgressions. Not everything is seen in terms of black and white in this state, in which there is more tolerance, guilt, remorse, self-doubt, frustration, pain, and confusion. One assumes more responsibility for one's actions. There is an emerging willingness to express sadness, regret, and remorse and to repair the damage that has been done to self and others.

- "So how can you show me you're sorry?"
- "I will tell the woman I had the affair with never to contact me again. I realize now how much I love you and the kids and don't want to do anything to cause any further pain or damage."
- "How can I trust you or believe you?"
- "Look, I've blocked the phone, I stopped gambling, and I'm sending out resumes to find better work to help support our family."

Resolution

According to Grotstein (1981), the depressive position is where resolution of splitting defenses occurs and reparation begins to take place. In conjoint therapy, we see this as moving away from shame, endless rivalry, and persecutory anxiety toward a desire to reach conflict resolution. Although resolution is not a specific analytic term, it does make reference to the effort to problem solve and find a solution. Short-term, goal-oriented conjoint treatment and mediation help individuals to reach resolution.

Ironically, not all couples come to therapy to problem solve. Couples going through the mediation process in divorce are more prone to reach resolution because the primary goal is negotiation, and both part-ners know—but not necessarily admit to themselves—that there is an ultimate end to the process. Exasperated mediators report frustration when the mediation process is drawn out for years on end. Resolution is more of a behavioral consequence than an interpersonal or intrapsy-chic one. Many couples think their battles are over money, sex, children, and custody arrangements, but the arguments are really are about con-trol, domination, victimization, rivalry, and unresolved oedipal issues (Lachkar, in press).

Shahrzad Siassi's 2013 book, *Forgiveness in Intimate Relationships*, addresses the relinquishing of the rage and anger that occurs when, transferentially, the analyst accepts and survives the destructive attacks of the patient and thus neutralizes the path toward paranoid expecta-tions and attachment to painful affects. This applies to couple therapy as both partners can identify with the analyst's ability to tolerate their out-of-control outbursts, which facilitates self-reflection and helps them toward understanding instead of judgment. As such, the partners enter the final phase of treatment and embrace acceptance. Reparation, a concept highly developed by Melanie Klein (1957), is a hybrid, ego-involved effort to address the damage one has done, accompanied by a desire to repair this damage and make amends for one's actions.

How different personality disorders handle regret

For the narcissist, the capacity to feel regret and make reparation is extremely difficult, mainly because of the narcissist's inherent lack of empathy and the feeling that everything is an attack on his specialness. Feeling regret means facing some imperfection within the self, which is in opposition to the typical narcissist attitude of being perfect. For the borderline, the capacity to regret and make reparation is also difficult because it means relinquishing control and letting go of the idea that he has power and domination over another human being. It also means being exposed to shameful feelings that are defended against by retaliating against the other.

Many question if narcissists and borderlines have the capacity for regret, and it is always questionable if patients with severe narcissistic and borderline pathology can ever reach Phase Three of treatment, in which reparation takes place. Narcissists have extreme difficulty summoning remorse for the person they have wronged because they are lacking in empathy. The borderline who is caught having an affair may also experience regret or remorse. But, like the narcissist, the borderline does not relate to the pain or injury he has caused or feel for the person who has been wronged. Rather, the borderline's expression of regret or feeling of remorse stems from a threat to his sense of power—the letting go of control, shame-blame, attacking, and victimization defenses. The borderline will instead project the wrongdoing and hence accuse the other of causing the problem.

Other personality disorders have their own ways of experiencing regret or remorse. For the obsessive-compulsive, these feelings constitute a wound, marring his or her perfectionistic, emotionally compartmentalized world. For the depressive, feelings of regret or remorse evoke persecutory anxieties. For the antisocial or psychopath, expressing regret or feeling remorse occurs only if he is caught and involves no thought of others. One should think of these reactions as pseudo- regret or remorse because it is too late in the game to come "clean" (Kernberg, 1992). Bernie Madoff, who pulled off a massive Ponzi scheme that cheated people out of millions of dollars, is a good example of an antisocial personality who only felt remorse because he got caught. He felt nothing for the victims who fell for his charade of being the "loving Uncle Bernie."

Within the context of various personality disorders, each has its own unique defenses and resistances that obstruct the attainment of resolution. For the narcissist, it is the need to avoid any threat to his sense of entitlement and to maintain a sense of specialness. The borderline must guard against regret because it means letting go of the role of victim and impairing the shame/blame defenses that he has carefully built up. For the obsessive-compulsive, experiencing regret and reparation means being open to emotionality and messing up his antiseptic, perfectionistic world. For the depressive, regret for any wrongdoing exacerbates persecutory tendencies that manifest as self-blame and self-hatred.

To put all these dynamics into suitable perspective and relate them to therapeutic goals, let me set out a template of a narcissistic/borderline relationship and detail the basic dynamics of these two personality types. In my book, *The Narcissistic/Borderline Couple* (Lachkar, 2003), I describe what happens when these two oppositional types join together and how each partner stirs up some unconscious, unresolved issue in the other. Together, they do what I refer to as "the dance"—engaging in circular, never-ending, destructive interactions. The psychodynamics of this couple include: shame vs. guilt; envy vs. jealousy; greed; splitting, projective identification, and dual projective identification; dependency vs. omnipotence; control/domination/victimization; and competition/ rivalry (unresolved oedipal conflicts).

Projective identification is a process whereby one splits off an unwanted aspect of the self and projects it onto the object, the partner, who identifies or overidentifies with that which is being projected. In other words, the self experiences the unconscious defensive mechanism and translocates it onto the other. Under the influence of projective identification, one becomes vulnerable to the coercion, manipulation, or control of the person doing the projecting. I extended the term "projective identification" with one I originated, called "dual projective identification," a two-way process that lends itself to conjoint treatment. Each partner projects a negative feeling onto the other, who then identifies or overidentifies with the negativity being projected: the splitting of the ego.

The two developmentally arrested personalities engaged in these beleaguered relationships bring archaic experiences embedded in old sentiments into their current relationships. I refer to these archaic injuries as a "V-spot," or "vulnerable" spot (Lachkar 2008a). The "V-spot" is a term I devised to describe the most sensitive area of emotional vulnerability that becomes aroused when one partner hits an emotional raw spot in the other. It is the emotional counterpart to the physical "G-spot." The concept of the V-spot became apparent to me as I treated couples who were highly affected by early childhood traumata. Each person has an individual V-spot, the epicenter of highly charged emotions. With arousal of the V-spot comes the loss of sense and sensibility. Everything shakes and shifts in this emotional earthquake, including memory, perception, judgment, and reality.

Even the most innocuous remark or action can trigger a volatile response, which is actually a defense. Reactions stemming from an ignited V-spot will differ, depending on the personality types involved. Narcissists will withdraw, borderlines attack, obsessive-compulsives will clean and wax. It behooves therapists to first break through to V-spots in order to get to the depressive position and move toward reparation. Even though the narcissist and the borderline have their own qualitative distinctions and defenses, they have one thing in common— the proclivity to blow at the slightest provocation. Marsha Linehan (1993) describes the borderline as tantamount to a third-degree burn center patient, who experiences agony at the slightest suggestion of betrayal or abandonment. The narcissist will blow at any hint or threat to his sense of specialness.

Without the work of Melanie Klein (1957), I would not have been able to understand the in-depth interactions of couples such as the narcissist and the borderline. Klein's concept of projective identification provides us with their movement not only between her two positions but between their psychodynamic interactions. We begin to see how someone like a narcissist pathologizes or coerces someone like a borderline into becoming the needy and demanding one, and how someone like a borderline, who already has a thwarted sense of self, will identify or overidentify with the narcissist's negative projections. Klein's contributions are invaluable in helping individuals face internal deficits, distortions, and projections, and helping therapists understand the tangled web that couples weave.

The formulations of Fairbairn (1952), Kernberg (1980, 1992), and Grotstein (1981) also provide us with a meticulous understanding of the flow within marital relationships. These are movements between internal and external objects. For the narcissistic/borderline couple, these dynamics include shame, guilt, envy, jealousy, splitting, projection, projective identification, paranoia, and persecutory anxiety. Within the complicated and convoluted dance of the couple, they help us see how certain dynamic mechanisms of the narcissist (grandiosity, entitlement, guilt, withdrawal) arouse states of unworthiness and nonexistence in the borderline such as shame, blame, envy, abandonment, and persecutory anxieties (Lachkar, 1998a, 1998b, 2004, 2008a, 2008b, 2012, 2014, in press).

I devised the term "couple transference" to describe what happens during treatment when the couple jointly projects onto the therapist some unconscious fantasy. Couple transference refers to the mutual projections, delusions, and distortions or shared couple fantasies that become displaced onto the therapist. The therapist might point out: "Now you are doing the same thing with me that you do with your husband!" Or a borderline husband might say to the therapist: "You're acting just like my wife—selfish, greedy, and only caring about yourself." Couple transference interpretations are derived from the analyst's experience and insights and are designed to produce a transformation within the dyadic relationship. The notion of the "couple/therapist" transference opens up an entirely new therapeutic vista, a transitional space in which "real" issues come to light.

Working through the therapeutic phases

I have choreographed the movements of the narcissistic/borderline couple as they traverse through the three treatment phases towards resolution. These movements are also applicable to other types of couples, for example, the obsessive-compulsive who hooks up with a histrionic or the passive-aggressive whose partner is a caretaker type.

Phase One is a state of oneness (fusion/collusion) in which one partner lives internally "inside" the other: "I am you and you are me!" I refer to this phase as the shame/blame/attack phase. Complaints run amuck, emotions are out of control, and V-spots are erupting everywhere! It is a phase in which attacks against the other are relentless, with each partner insisting the other is at fault for all the shortcomings in the relationship. For the narcissist, the constant attacking results in withdrawal; for the borderline, it becomes all about revenge and retaliation. There is much stonewalling, blaming, and shaming, and often envy or rivalry, even to the extent of putting down the accomplishments of the other. It is a phase during which couples live intrapsychically—inside the emotional space of the other—a state of fusion where there is little differentiation between self and other. Moreover, there is little awareness of the inner unconscious forces that invade and intrude upon their relationship. Instead, primitive defenses such as splitting, projection and projective identification, magical thinking, and denial take center stage. Needs and feelings are often attacked and blown out of proportion. When there is so much blaming and attacking it is hard to know what the real needs are. However, during this phase, the therapist has the opportunity to filter through the complaints to determine which are normal and legitimate complaints as opposed to those that are used for evacuation: "Tell us what to do. Should we get a divorce or stay married?"

Phase Two sees the emergence of two separate emotional states. There is more tolerance for ambiguity, less fighting about who is right and wrong. Instead the partners have budding insights into unconscious motivations (the internal object). It is the beginning of bonding with the therapist and a weaning away from parasitic dependency and the bad internal object toward mutual interdependence.

One of the most important therapeutic goals is helping partners move through the various therapeutic stages until they reach what Melanie Klein (1957) refers to as the depressive position, or what I describe as *Phase Three* of treatment. This phase marks the emergence of separate dependent and interdependent mental states, as well as a budding ability and willingness to feel sad and express remorse and regret, allowing for reparation to occur (Klein, 1975; Lachkar, 1998a, 1998b, 2004, 2008a, 2008b, 2012, 2014). This is a state of mourning and sadness, involving feelings of loss and vulnerability as one comes to terms with guilt and begins to face up to all the wrongdoings and transgressions of the past. Even though the couple in therapy has not yet attained complete resolution on any issues, there is the desire to "repair" the damage, to embrace guilt, mourn, and take responsibility for all the transgressions that have occurred. Each partner comes to terms with uncertainty, ambiguity, and healthy dependency needs. It is a time to heal and listen nondefensively to one another's hurts. There is also an attendant diminishment of oedipal rivalry.

On a precautionary note, oftentimes therapists, as well as patients, confuse sadness and states of mourning, which are normal and healthy feelings, with depression. One man came to session angry, feeling that treatment made him feel worse: "I think I'm regressing. I've never felt so sad in my life. I'm depressed all the time and feel bad about myself and what I've done to others." My response: "You feel sad and mournful because you are coming to terms with all the wrongdoings you have committed and want to make reparation for them. This regret and remorse is all part of the healing process."

When working with couples, the first thing I look for is the most dominant feature in each partner. In the example of the narcissistic/ borderline couple, the narcissist is the partner dominated by fear of the loss of specialness and entitlement, whereas the borderline is the one dominated mainly by abandonment anxiety and betrayal issues. While the narcissist seeks to be the special child of God, the borderline is busy just trying to prove that he or she exists. The narcissist is the entitlement lover: You know when you are around narcissists because they are all and only about themselves. They believe the world owes them something, and when they feel they are not properly mirrored will withdraw or isolate themselves. Narcissists cannot tolerate criticism. They place the highest value on such things as success, fame, physical beauty, wealth, material possessions, and power. They also exhibit self-love to the exclusion of the needs of others. One can imagine how this arouses feelings of unworthiness and abandonment in the borderline partner, who already has a thwarted sense of self.

Narcissists lack empathy and consideration for the needs of others. They are perfectionistic, self-righteous, and feel they are superior to others. They cannot tolerate their own dependency needs and unwittingly project their needy selves onto someone like a borderline partner: "You're the needy one, not me!" Narcissists are continually seeking out others as narcissistic supplies or self-objects that affirm and collude with their grandiose fantasies. They have a tit-for-tat attitude and a fighting, competitive aspect, whereby the partner becomes the oedipal rival. In court battles, narcissists are the ones who want all the visitation rights, total custody, or demand outsized child support and alimony payments. They take advantage whenever, wherever, and with whomever they can.

Many have affixed the term "as-if personalities" to borderlines, who tend to subjugate or compromise themselves. They question their sense of existence, suffer from acute abandonment and persecutory anxiety, and tend to merge with others in very painful ways in order to achieve a sense of bonding. "Better to inflict and feel pain than to endure the emptiness of the abyss. Then at least I know I exist!" Under close scrutiny and stress, borderlines distort, misperceive, and turn suddenly against self and others, attacking, blaming, finding fault, and seeking revenge. They are impulsive, reckless, have self-harming and suicidal tendencies, and exhibit extreme self-sacrificing behavior (Kernberg, 1975). Borderlines also exhibit poor reality testing, poor impulse control, and lack a self-regulatory mechanism, which means that their feelings are often disproportionate to the reality of their environment. Any hint of abandonment or betrayal can trigger an intense outburst of rage and revenge—a desire to get even, or teach the other a lesson.

Borderlines are the victims, the scapegoats, and when betrayed will spend the rest of their lives seeing ways to retaliate at the expense of self until they reach their final destination—revenge! In court custody cases, borderlines are the ones that will sacrifice themselves, their children, their families, their finances, and do whatever is necessary to get even with those they perceive have betrayed or abandoned them. It is not unusual for borderlines to keep their spouses as a courtroom hostage. Borderlines have an exquisite false self and can dupe the most seasoned therapists and court officials with their façade of being the poor victims, the betrayed, abandoned ones. In an attempt to defend against shame, they are determined to win and prove their self-righteousness at any cost. They may appear intelligent, charming, and genuinely concerned about the family. However, behind this façade the borderline schemes to coerce the other into the role of "bad parent."

The affair

To tell or not to tell, that is the question.

One cannot talk about regret and remorse without addressing one of the most life-shattering scenarios that gets revealed in conjoint therapy: cheating and infidelity. In the back of every therapist's mind is the fear that lurking in the shadows is the discovery of "the affair." Common reasons for an affair include that the unfaithful partner: falls madly in love with someone else, feels something is missing in the relationship, acts out of revenge or anger and has a one-night stand, needs the adulation and attention of many different people, is perverted and looks for excitement in lieu of love, has lost contact with his or her inner passion and craves excitement as a superficial substitute.

The revelation of the affair puts both therapist and the victim of the affair in a most compromising position. After the revelation, there is the problem of how to deal with the initial shock of the cheated-on partner and the disbelief, grief, anger, and distrust that follows. Then there is the determination of how best to explore the reasons for the affair, how to deal with the threats of divorce, and/or how to begin the reparative process and reestablish trust between the partners. At the beginning of conjoint therapy, the therapist should let the couple know that everything that happens outside of session can be shared during therapy, except when the therapist's discretion suggests otherwise. Some therapists terminate treatment with the idea that it has been contaminated by the knowledge of the affair. My goal as a psychoanalytically trained therapist is to use the affair as a venue for emotional and psychological exploration, as illustrated by the following case.

Case of Adele

In this case, we see the entire array of psychic regret. Adele, a thirty-year-old woman, has been married for six years. She and her husband have a new baby, whom they cherish. When Adele found out about her husband having an affair while she was working, she was so shocked that she could hardly speak. She came into session alone, shaken up and obviously severely traumatized. We agreed we first should work together for a while and eventually invite her husband into session. After many sessions together, we discovered that unconsciously, Adele was reenacting a very familiar scenario. As a child, she recalls always being the caretaker for her family. Her father was an alcoholic, and as a young girl, she was put in the position of caretaker for her mother, and later had to help support the family. She was the little girl who grew up much too soon. She recalls never having a childhood, always having to be perfect. But, what is more significant, Adele never got the chance to mourn the loss of her childhood. Unconsciously, she ended up marrying a man like her father—"lazy, a loser, good for nothing!"

Adele: Everything was perfect. We have loving and supportive families. We were childhood sweethearts. I know I am the love of his life—the one and only. When we are together, he cannot keep his hands off me. There isn't a day that goes by when he doesn't call me to tell me how he can't wait to come home to me and our baby. I don't know what got into me but for some reason, I decided to check his emails. I was stunned. For two years, my husband has been fucking another woman! How is this possible? How can a man who loves me so much suddenly be having an affair? Where is his conscience to come home and sleep with me and act as if nothing happened? Of course, I checked out the other woman, only to find someone who is the complete opposite of me—passive, compliant, needy, and dependent. I am the alpha woman, independent and self-sufficient. I don't need anything from anybody.

Therapist: What I am about to say in no way validates your husband's betrayal, but we do need to look at the dynamics in your relationship—how your husband loves you, but at the same time may have felt very threatened by your independence and inability to depend on him.

Adele: I didn't realize it, but I guess he must have felt that with all my strong attributes, I was just castrating him and cutting his balls off. I don't know if I will ever take him back or forgive him. But if do, I guess I will have to take some responsibility for making him feel like a nothing.

Therapist: I think this affair has brought to the fore some very real issues such as dependency and feelings of self-blame. You say your husband used to get upset when you never needed anything from him.

Adele: But I really didn't need anything from him. I am very self-sufficient, and when I do ask him to do something, he screws it up.

Therapist: So in a way, you married a "baby husband"—someone like your father.

Adele: Yes, he is like my father. My mother could never depend on my father; she ended up depending on me!

For a short while, Adele was very appreciative of my compassion and willingness to explore her part in the affair to help bring meaning out of the senselessness. In time, I brought up the concept of identification with internal and external objects. At this point, there was a switch in her attitude. She started to get very snippy and abrupt and had difficulty taking in my interpretations. This was the beginning of a negative transference or what I refer to in couple therapy as "the couple transference" (Lachkar, 1998a, 1998b, 2004, 2008a, 2008b, 2012, 2014).

Therapist: You know, Adele, there can always be an external betrayer. All of us can get betrayed at any time and unexpectedly. We can't control that, but we can control our "internal betrayer."

Adele: What are you accusing me of? Are you saying I'm betraying myself when he is the one who violated me?

Therapist: I'm not talking real time. I'm talking in analytic terms. There does seem to be an internal part of you that has identified with a mother who enabled your father, who never stood up to him and just allowed him to drink and ignore his family.

Adele: This is bullshit!

I was beginning to see that Adele was transferring her rage from her mother onto me.

Therapist: Adele, it is important for you to get angry. For many years, you have been this perfect wife and perfect daughter, always doing the right thing and in control of the situation.

Adele: I don't mean to lash out at you. I guess I am angry that she never did anything to protect me or even made an effort to stand up to him.

Therapist: Allow yourself to get angry. You don't have to be the perfect child or be the caretaker for me.

Adele: I always worry that I will hurt your feelings.

Therapist: That's probably what happened with your husband. Instead of calling attention to his behavior that annoyed you, you just let it slip by the way your mother did with your father.

Adele: You mean how he always makes jokes and expects me to laugh.

Therapist: Yes, stuff like that.

Adele: Yes, there is a lot more I did that I didn't tell you about.

Therapist: We need to stop now, but in a few more sessions we will invite your husband in.

Many sessions later, Adele's anger and rage continued to mount. She got angrier and angrier, more enraged with me than with her husband. Later in the transference, she began to see that she not only identified with her mother but "became" her mother. This was coupled with the idea that I had too many expectations of her and was making unreasonable demands by abiding to therapeutic boundaries such as time and payment. My continual interpretations let her know that this was not a dreamlike or storybook relationship but very real. Yet, I could understand how she felt that I was like her mother when I made demands on her even though it was obvious that I didn't depend on her. Having put herself in her mother's shoes, after a while, Adele began to feel sorrow, empathy, and compassion for her. This was the beginning of Adele's regret and the start of the mourning stage. She was now ready to invite her husband into the sessions.

Adele also was ready to accept some responsibility for the problems that occurred in her marriage. Her husband regretted his infidelity because he sincerely loved his wife and their baby and did not want to hurt her or to jeopardize their relationship. The therapeutic challenge here was to help the unfaithful partner concretize his regret for the spouse he had emotionally injured. These are sensitive moments

because as the therapist mirrors the person who had the affair by enumerating reasons why this may have occurred, there still must be no
hint of the impression that the affair is justified.

Conclusion

In this chapter, I have discussed the interlocking dynamics of regret,
resolution, and reparation. As a marriage and family therapist and
author of numerous books and publications, I have taken the liberty of
using as a template the starring couple in my first book, *The Narcissistic/
Borderline Couple*. Inherent in this work are typical aspects of conflict that
are common in couple therapy and can be abstracted to many different
types of couples, including one common area of conflict that is the most
earth-shattering of all—the affair. In addition, I discuss the three phases
of treatment through which couples move, as well as the dynamics
involved. In the final stage of treatment, couples come to the realization that words are not enough: "I'm sorry," "I will do anything you
want me to," "I promise," "I love you!" are meaningless unless they are
motivated by sincere regret. Through many years of clinical practice,
sharing the journey of couples in conflict, I appreciate that the concept
of regret is a transformative experience, moving from part object thinking to wholeness and integration and away from shame, envy, and guilt
toward feelings of love, compassion, and the desire to repair the damage that has been done. Couples are most grateful when they hear these
final words: ACCEPT, FORGIVE, and JUST LET IT GO!

CHAPTER THREE

The trajectory of remorse to regret in old age

Shahrzad Siassi

Regret is a universal human experience. In old age when the prospect of second chances are almost gone, one is left with the anguish of facing lost opportunities, declining potential, and the real or imagined consequences of one's actions. The advent of old age necessitates a life review that may entail a mourning process and working through not only lost chances but also a reassessment of an unrealistic idealization of the past, such as "what if ... fantasies" (Akhtar, 1996) like those articulated in Robert Frost's poem, *The Road Not Taken*. For some, the manic "omnipotentialities" of adolescence and the idealistic optimism of youth harshly juxtapose with an ego-depleting nostalgic focus on decline, irreversible losses, missed opportunities, and a negative and unfavorable review of the past which generates deep regret and a perverse failure of optimism (Landman, 1987). The present becomes payback time for a mindless, foolish, self-centered past. Youth, the magic age of happiness, is long over and pessimistic memories and feelings of loss and sadness prevent the mobilization of the robust mind-set and attitude that give one the ability to face and cope with the challenges of this last phase of life. For others, insight and awareness arrive late and appear only when the manic defenses of filling one's life with endless empty activities and gadding about are no longer possible and

45

one comes face to face with agonizing reflections and a philosophical assessment of an unexamined life.

Regret in old age can fill the mind with resentment, feelings of desolation, and endless rumination if one cannot come to grips with the inability to amend. Fortunately, for some, they can die contented, because self-recrimination over things they either did or did not manage to do is tempered by the satisfaction gained from what they included in life. Additionally, a minimized expectation of accomplishment in the materialistic sense and less possibility of regret in the time left before dying accompanies a diminished capacity to do certain things. The heightened wish for peace and tranquility runs parallel to the diminution of the aggressive competitive ambitions and restlessness of youth and gradually helps the elderly to seek peace both internally and in relationship to others. Thus, old age, for many, is also associated with the emergence of wisdom and the ability to reflect upon the past, review life, and sort out the inevitable mistakes and their consequences. For some, it could bring a more resigned attitude vis-à-vis their limitations, mitigate the ravages of regret, and allow them to review their past and reconcile with what cannot be changed, to mourn losses and to confront sorrows, unfulfilled dreams, and ambitions, and thus facilitate a vital involvement in old age. It is this wisdom gained from aging that also allows a more realistic assessment of life and enables the psyche to move in the direction of pride in accomplishments perhaps previously eclipsed by nostalgia. Yet, the time to change has passed when death lies on the horizon. One has to accept the reality of aging, face and mourn the pain of loss, settle for the "good-enoughness" of one's existence, and find solace in the birth of a more reflective and tolerant conservatism. This hallmark of a mature philosophical outlook of this age is ignited by the depressive position qualitatively at a different level due to a tragic recognition of the inherent presence of hatred and destructiveness that appears side-by-side with goodness in man, facilitating resignation to the limitations and imperfections of mankind in general (Jaques, 1965). The prospect of limited time can also create a new focus and lead the mind to work through both past losses and future decline with a new freedom from inhibitions as one becomes more reflective and perhaps more appreciative of the depth and complexities of one's feelings.

For many, without the emergence of a depressive crisis which calls for the reworking through of the infantile depression and the recognition of death and human destructiveness (Jaques, 1965), regret in old age perpetuates regression into self-blame, disappointment, grief, and pessimism, and gradually morphs into remorse, deflating the hope out of the psyche. Generativity turns into stagnation and the potential for reinforcing ego integrity is taken over by despair (Erikson, 1950). This emerging philosophical outlook can turn despair into a sense of peaceful acceptance of the past through a meaningful appreciation of one's earlier limitations and constraints, rescue the present and future from the wasteland of unbearable remorse, and generate a new intensity to live life as fully and genuinely as possible. Thus, corrective actions are not about the past but the future, and they give a new sense of vibrancy to a life imagined as a downhill slope. The continuity and sanctity of life is maintained despite the real challenges and inevitable devastations of aging.

Theoretical considerations in distinguishing remorse from regret

Regret is a complex concept with both cognitive and emotional components and although, for the most part, a conscious experience, it has an underlying dynamic that overlaps with other psychoanalytic concepts such as remorse, guilt, atonement, reparation, mourning, and forgiveness. In everyday language, regret and remorse are often used interchangeably. Salman Akhtar's (2009) distinction between the two in his *Comprehensive Dictionary of Psychoanalysis* is useful but could be further expanded. Akhtar points out an important distinction: "'Remorse' involves feelings about how one's actions have affected others, while 'regret' involves feelings about how one's actions affected oneself" (p. 244). I would like to add that regret is not limited only to the self-harm of actions or inactions, one can also regret one's failure as a good parent; therefore, regret has both intrapsychic and interpsychic components; one should be clear about the dynamic of regret in interpersonal relationships distinguished from remorse. I believe a distinction between the two should focus on the archaic and primitive qualities of remorse in contrast to a certain conscious tolerance of events for which one is regretful. Another way of conceptualizing these two overlapping concepts is to consider the way the psyche comes to terms with their pressure. Remorse is assuaged by atonement whereas regret in the interpersonal domain propels the psyche toward mourning and repair in reality. In order to distinguish this kind of regret from regret for lost personal opportunities, I identify this kind of regret as interpersonal.

Whereas remorse encompasses some form of regret, regret can exist without remorse. That is—if a person feels remorse for having hurt someone, he also regrets the action albeit with an extreme sense of hopelessness to emerge from it, but if he regrets certain actions or inactions, he does not always need to feel remorseful about them. Akhtar's sharp distinction of remorse as more object-related and regret as more narcissistic is blurred in the experience of regret in interpersonal relationships in that it shifts the focus from the self to the hurt party quite consciously, unlike remorse which oscillates between a minimal focus on the hurt party to the self with vengeance because of the unbearableness of guilt. The experience of conscious regret is a developmental accomplishment (Kavaler-Adler, 2013) that brings the individual out of the archaic mode of narcissistic self-flagellation observable in remorse. In conscious regret, the focus is primarily on the hurt party; the unbearableness of guilt in remorse brings back the focus to oneself through self-reproach, self-loathing, and a narcissistic preoccupation with oneself. This is the case because preoccupation with the hurt party is not out of concern but in the service of one's archaic superego preventing the experience of true regret. In fact, on an archaic level, the hurt party could be loathed and despised for causing so much pain; in that sense remorse could be conceived as *anti-object relational* and interpersonal regret as *object relational.* In remorse, the self-reproach can become so narcissistic that any focus on the pain of the other is minimal as it shifts back to the self in danger of annihilation. The proto-experience of regret does not stem from concern for the other but represents regretting the unbearableness of events for a fragile psyche filled with aggression that can only beat itself. This is an observable phenomenon in analytic work, and in my case presentation, I demonstrate the trajectory of initially bypassing regret through remorse to the dawning of a glimmer of regret for oneself and for the other thanks to the burgeoning capacity for concern as analytic work progressed. Just as the goal of analysis is to help the patient move from a paranoid-schizoid orientation to a more depressive one, when it comes to remorse and its primitive atonement solution, the patient has to be helped to tolerate his guilt and enter into a realistic assessment of himself and his environment before reaching the capacity for regret through mourning and repair.

Although the degree of the experience of remorse and regret about the same action varies among individuals, generally regret, because of its predominance of sadness over anger and self-loathing, has a depressive bent and appeals to mourning. Remorse, far from being object relational, is focused on the self and the creation of the closed loop system which turns it into a narcissistic angry experience entrenching the individual in a paranoid-schizoid position and cutting the person off from reality. Despite their common roots in narcissistic self-evaluation, regret in interpersonal relationships belongs to the healthier narcissistic sense of self.

The experience of regret/remorse can be traced back to the Kleinian notion of reparation (Klein, 1975). What sets off the wish to repair in adulthood is an experience of regret/remorse embedded in the first experience of the child's awareness of the other as a whole person in the depressive position; however, the wish for reparation purposes to mend the fantasied damage, destruction, and fragmentation of the object. Unlike the adult conscious experience of regret, however, Klein's notion of reparation is rooted in the rudiments of the child's unconscious fantasies of remorse for his aggression and early sadism and destructiveness that are conceived as having harmed the significant well-meaning other. It is the experience of guilt (the unconscious wish to harm)—that is, remorse (fantasy that one has already harmed) (Freud, 1930a)—that is counteracted by the wish to restore and repair the wholeness of the object (mother). We can nevertheless observe that the distinction between the wish to harm (guilt) and the actual harm (remorse) is blurred because, at an unconscious level, wishes and deeds are the same. Simultaneously, the distinction between the narcissistic dimension of feeling bad because of one's aggression, and the object relational aspect of feeling bad for having damaged the other collapses. At such an early stage, the wish to repair while heralding the onset of the depressive position (awareness of the object) is simultaneously ushered in by the child's wish to gratify his dependent longings on the object (anaclitic needs), necessitating the safeguarding of the wholeness and sanctity of the mother for his own survival as well (the self-preservative instinct). Thus, a clear-cut distinction between narcissistic concerns and object relational needs of the child so early in the development is not tenable because the self-preservative instinct and the anaclitic needs of the child are always in the background, as there is a progressive need to relate to a whole object capable of taking care of these needs. Simultaneously, the distinction between the experience of regret and remorse collapses in the Kleinian notion of reparation. The child's narcissistic need for a whole object (for his own survival) coincides with the dawn of his ability for concern and wish to repair what he has destroyed. We can see that at such an early stage, the distinction between these overlapping concepts guilt/remorse/regret in relation to reparation is almost nonexistent or at best very murky. With the metabolism of anger in the matrix of the mother and child interaction, what feels good narcissistically is also good for one's relational needs. Not only is there no distinction between wishes and actions at the unconscious level, there is great overlap between one's own self-preservative (narcissistic/anaclitic) needs and development of concern for the other (relational needs). The child's wish to repair could emanate from his bad feelings for having hurt the object, as well as his growing awareness of his narcissistic need for a whole object that needs to be preserved in order for him to rely upon it and survive. Thus, both remorse and regret have narcissistic as well as object relational components because one cannot separate the bad feelings associated with one's damaging aggression to others from how one feels about one's destructive self.

Yet, in adulthood, regret is a more frequently shared and familiar experience than remorse. It appears that one's relation to oneself, that is the person's existential concerns especially in old age, can control and influence all the other experiences, including remorse. Regret, with its narcissistic component, the failure of one's expectations from the self, is an existential concept rooted in the inevitability of the human condition and some vague awareness that it is part and parcel of being human and imperfect. It is an experience that has the potential to propel the person to settle for his limitations and find meanings in tolerating the pain of falling short.

Just as the experience of forgiveness overlaps with the mourning process, the experience of regret is intertwined with mourning, and just as a successful mourning process leads to the ability to forgive oneself, mourning past losses could free the person from unrealistic regret and allow him to make peace with justified regret. In both situations, the individual is endowed to move forward and not be held by the past. Simultaneously, just as the inability to mourn could hold the person in a state of unforgivingness and keep him hanging on to grudges and primitive defenses, the refusal to mourn for what one feels regret about could easily be in the service of and perpetuation of sadomasochism. However, as I have previously demonstrated (Siassi, 2003), the unconscious wish to forgive dovetails the mourning process and, for the most part, emerges after the mourning process. A successful mourning process leads to a reorganization of the personality on the basis of more object relational concerns rather than narcissistic ones. The conscious experience of regret overlaps with mourning and forgiveness. The mourning process for loss could be a stepping stone toward forgiveness, that is, the wish to be forgiven (usually intrapsychically by oneself) as one comes to terms with the limitations of making amends and the inability to change what can no longer be changed. By mourning the losses and tolerating one's vulnerability vis-à-vis the awareness of guilt, the self-blame and misplaced anger and destructiveness toward the world and others diminish and one experiences the same shift of affect that is the hallmark of the dynamic of forgiveness. Through understanding and contextualizing the negative feelings, the capacity for concern for oneself and others sets in.

In contrast, the experience of remorse is tightly entwined with atonement and its potential pathological slippery slope toward masochistic tendencies, which Rosen (2009) has aptly demonstrated by breaking down the word itself into "at-one-ment," that is, the shared identification with the aggressed. Rosen demonstrates how in atonement, in response to remorse, there is a wish to first become one with the victim in his suffering before consciously restoring the damage. He points out that at the extreme, the atoner could fantasize that his suffering itself is sufficient to repair the victim, as though through suffering, the aggressor is extracting the pain of the other and putting it on himself. This happens when, due to the primitiveness of the harsh archaic superego, the ability to tolerate guilt is absent. Nonetheless, in its benign form, atonement does not need to be a masochistic exercise. Instead, through empathy, compassion, and a capacity for acknowledging and tolerating the guilt, a mourning process, both for the victim and oneself, can result in forgiveness of oneself and the wish to be forgiven by the aggressed.

In this chapter, I will discuss the case of an elderly man that highlights the transformation of remorse embedded in extreme hopelessness and self-loathing—for the unconscious purpose of assuaging guilt—into a conscious experience of regret for the past but hope for the future. While the patient's remorse served no purpose other than mindless self-beating to alleviate an archaic guilt emanating from a disavowed anger, the gradual dis-identification with a sadistic mother gave way to the creation of space for reflection and tolerance of guilt so that he was able to express genuinely his regret for having harmed himself and his intimate others. Now conscious and mindful of his developmental arrest in a terrorizing childhood devoid of any meaningful parenting, his regret was accompanied by a newfound ability, through identification with the analyst, to make sense of the devastating implication of his vast maternal and paternal deprivation. As he became more empathic with the growth-impeding circumstances of his childhood, paradoxically he became more capable of shifting his initial focus from himself to those he had hurt, namely his daughters. While his experience of remorse was a dead-end doomsday experience, his conscious experience of regret was expansive and even though the past painful consequences were no longer retrievable, with acceptance came a degree of hopefulness that motivated him to reach out in his declining days and take the risk of intimacy and make amends.

In this case, the investment in remorse had blocked the experience of regret and prevented the person from entering into a genuine experience of mourning for the losses of the past. I will explore how by hanging on to the bad object of the past through primitive identification, the patient was unable to overcome narcissistic resistances that had blocked him from entering into a mourning process, the stepping stone to the experience of regret. In a refusal to mourn and forgive, the familiar self-debasement observed in melancholia is replaced with the abasement of the object, transferentially, the analyst. In the inability to fully experience regret, one is attached to negative affect through sorrow, sadness, despair, and self-debasement, as well as abasement of others.

Remorse as a defense against unbearable regret in intimate relationships

The first time I opened the door of the waiting room to greet my new, Caucasian male patient, Mr. C, an elderly man of seventy-nine, I was struck by two things: his emaciated gawky body and his strange unhealthy dark skin that contrasted sharply with his penetrating large blue eyes. Soon my initial puzzlement and shock about his unusual appearance gave way to discernment as he started telling me about his extreme anxiety, his co-dependency, his painful loneliness, and his twenty-year HIV-positive status. He stated that he was intermittently in analysis and therapy for many years and since his last disappointing attempt at CBT, he took the advice of a colleague, a past patient of mine, and came to see me.

Mr. C was a highly educated man who twenty-five years ago left his career in law for psychology. He had a full practice, including training groups for many years, but was not doing well currently because his particular orientation was no longer popular. Mr. C. was twice divorced with three daughters from his first marriage that came to an end some fifteen years prior due to his unfaithfulness and subsequent contraction of HIV during a confused promiscuous period in his life and experimentation with bisexuality. Despite his HIV, he married the woman with whom he had an affair and who was not threatened by his illness. Together, they continued a reckless lifestyle of drugs and nightly weed-smoking. The marriage lasted five years; for the past eight years, Mr. C was single and unable to start any desirable relationship with women supposedly because of HIV and old age, which made him feel like a pariah despite his extremely good looks. He expressed a lot of bitterness both about his current condition, as well as his mindless sexual adventures that had cost him his health and family. However, his expression of regret appeared more like a figure of speech and did not embody any deep sense of sadness for himself or those impacted by his actions. Instead, Mr. C was extremely anxious, remorseful, self-absorbed, and angry at himself and at the world. His remorse was tightly entwined with self-flagellation, extreme hopelessness, and immense self-loathing. The purity of sadness and sorrow that one encounters in healthier forms of regret was missing in his communications. Instead, his sadness was polluted with considerable "why?" protests, and the result was extreme bitterness, anger, and a readiness to accuse both himself and the world for his feelings of misery.

Mr. C was the youngest of three siblings. His mother kicked his father out of the house when the patient was only three and put herself in charge of raising her children with an iron fist, extreme coldness, and hostile distance, in an atmosphere of terror and fear. Instead of physical punishments, Mr. C's mother was an expert in playing mind games that would give Mr. C the illusion of freedom of choice but was meant to make him doubt any choice different from hers. Her questioning of his choices and the scary scenarios related to this questioning broke his confidence and pressed him to surrender to his mother's opinion out of fear. The result was an extreme dependency upon his mother and a total loss of the ability to decide, to trust his judgment, and to have a mind of his own or any sense of self.

During our first few sessions, Mr. C gave me a clearer picture of his past by sharing some of the most egregious, sadistic qualities of his deceased mother who nevertheless was still alive, omniscient and omnipresent in his life, someone he could not let go of without extricating the love and approval he never got from her. In short, he was entrenched in an acute sadomasochistic relationship with her and unable to let her go and become a free agent. If he ever felt good about life, the fantasy of his mother's dissatisfaction with his good feelings made him anxious. He once commented, "I don't let anything good in." Despite his extreme hatred and loathing of her, he needed her approval and was petrified of his anger toward her—a classic sadomasochistic scenario of abused children and their abusive mothers. He felt as if his mother had lured him and his siblings into doing everything she wanted with the unspoken promise of "Maybe someday I will like you." He found himself still chasing after that someday. With such a preoccupation with keeping his hateful feelings toward his mother at bay, he knew that he could not focus on anybody else's problems and accused himself of using people to take care of his neediness and loneliness. He corroborated his own narcissism as he recalled what his older daughter had conveyed to him—that he simply could not get it, meaning he was unable to empathize with or understand her feelings.

I found the sessions with Mr. C heavy, exhausting, and dreadful because of a sense of being put upon by his unspoken demand for me to take care of his anxiety, sadness, and neediness, which unbeknown to me was pushing me to work considerably harder than usual. Initially, I was encouraged because he felt bolstered by some of my illuminating comments and interpretations he felt were right on the money; however, there was little carryover to the following session. When he had a bad day, he would exude such a degree of disappointment and hopelessness that I felt like throwing in the towel. Every session would start with a different version of "I'm a wreck" and a subtle but urgent demand to extract something out of me in order for him to feel better. And I, in turn, initially felt compelled to oblige so he would not cast me in the same light as his cold sadistic mother. Despite my conscious best effort not to do that, within the transference–countertransference interplay, soon I was very much cast as such. It started with a barrage of accusations against me for not being empathic enough, being in my head with my interpretations, and not understanding how hard it was for him, not looking at him all the time, and not sitting close to him, avoiding him.

Despite my awareness of the transferential nature of his accusations, I started listening closely and wondered about the impact of my own conscious negative countertransference and if there were some validity to his complaints. I found myself trying very hard to come up with very insightful interpretations that made him feel well understood, but my delivery was devoid of ease and spontaneity and he would catch me not looking directly at him but elsewhere. I found myself getting defensive when he started confronting me with this bizarre behavior that was also very unfamiliar to me. The more he attacked me for my shortcomings and failure of closeness and demanded it, the more I felt under his tyranny and could not be moved by a genuine wish for closeness or be the usual warm and easy person that I experience myself with other patients. I noticed how the sadomasochistic relation with his phantom mother had pervaded our relationship. In one session, after a heavy criticism of my cerebral style, he shifted to expressing his anger toward his mother by wishing to punch the wall but he found his arm was weak and lifeless. I told him how much this fantasy was also present between us and suggested he wanted to punch the wall that I was looking at while giving my interpretation to him. He felt relieved and validated that I could be empathic with his rage and direct it to myself. He commented, "I hate her so much that I'm afraid that if I let it out I will hate everyone; like the time I took out my anger on my children." Then he retreated and reported he felt he was distracting himself by entertaining the thought of going to the gym after the session. I commented, "It does not sound so random to me. Perhaps you're going to get those weak, lifeless muscles strong enough to make a huge hole in the wall and teach me a lesson." He regressed and exposed his ambivalence and undoing by claiming that he would feel lost and helpless in the gym. He then associated his current behavior to how he would avoid his mother's gaze when she was giving him directives to do things in order not to annoy her with his neediness for love and affection, simultaneously fearful that if he did look at her, she'd pick up an indication of his hatred for her. Suddenly, I realized that in my own countertransference, I had reenacted this aspect of the relationship with him in reverse. Annoyed by his extreme tyrannical demanding and accusations, I felt under attack like the "little boy C" who would not dare to look at the mother and robotically tried to please her. In this reversal, I was dutifully assisting Mr. C (interpretation) while maintaining distance from him in this compromised way of avoiding my hostility and anxiety.

In this role exchange, he had assumed the role of the sadistic mother who was set to be critical enough to stir up fear and trembling in me so that, like her, I avoided any warmth and closeness in the relationship. In this enactment, he was also conveying to me firsthand how he must have felt with his mother, robotic, dutiful, and distant, and that was how he was experiencing me, another version of himself with his actual mother. Acting on this realization, I shared my observation that this role exchange gave me a pretty good understanding of what it was like to live with that mother and simultaneously appreciating how furious he must have been with me for becoming a version of her—cold, cerebral, and avoiding his need for closeness. He started crying and felt grateful that he could enact his mother's sadism without me breaking or turning against him, instead feeling more empathic and genuinely closer to him. As he was leaving, he said that for the first time, he felt hopeful and felt safe with me. He started the next session by telling me that he did not want to push me away. Despite his trepidations, he had largely overcome his negative maternal transference in our work and his relentless childish quest for the love of the sadistic mother had diminished greatly.

Therapy continued within a background of a warm, positive transference periodically disrupted by his angry protest for my occasional misattunements. He claimed that he did not remember everything I said outside of the session, but somehow it stayed with him. I commented that he could now hear the music more than the words. He started crying and told me now he felt vulnerable, that something might go wrong and he'd lose me. I responded that his worry is the fantasy of losing me if his anger flares up again, that it will destroy me and the relationship. He felt increasingly more secure and relieved that his anger, despite its intensity would not annihilate either one of us. He was able to tell me that he missed me and could think about me between the sessions. He said that of all his ten therapists, I was the only one he trusted, and he no longer complained about the fee depleting him. Instead he was thankful and felt it was well earned.

Gradually, there was a new quality to his sadness, and as he took me back to the darkness of his childhood, he began an intermittent process of mourning, recalling all the sadistic actions of his mother whose goal it was to destroy the confidence of her children and prevent any genuine moment of happiness or carefreeness in the house. Tearfully, he remembered the toy soldiers that he had received for Christmas when he was nine and how excited he and his brother were to imagine war scenarios together in order to play with each other for the first time. Alas, as soon as his mother heard the cheerful, excited voices coming from their room, she walked in and demanded that they give her back the toys so she could give them to less fortunate children. The gradual recollection of similar sadistic memories of his childhood became a bit more bearable as he felt he was not alone in those dark painful places of his past. He wrote letters to his dead mother enumerating the emotional wounds she inflicted on him and his siblings and read them to me. He could articulate how he wanted to be held like a little boy without shaming himself. There was a genuine authentic quality to his sadness, and it appeared that rather than relentlessly chasing the sadistic object, he was experiencing a lot of empathy for himself in his identification with me as the good mother who had survived his wrath and was devoted to his development and growth.

Although he was less anxious in his interactions with his friends, a constant source of anxiety and extreme pain was the inadequate relationship he had with his three daughters. In his remorse, he was so self-punitive and expected so little that he could not imagine anything that could justify some kindness coming from them to him; simultaneously he was furious at them and preoccupied with fantasies of revenge such as dying and rejecting them when they'd visit him on his deathbed. His remorse about his past insensitivities and parental failures toward them was such that, on the one hand, he felt no sense of entitlement as a father to be treated in any decent way, and at the same time he was so needy for their love and so angry for not getting it. In his self-reproach, alluding to their constant accusations that he was uncaring, he had found proof of his unworthiness as a father and had completely lost any hope for relationship with them; thus his remorse with its closed loop had abandoned him to hopelessness and despair. He had a minimal relationship with his oldest daughter and her daughter, his only grandchild. Periodically, they'd meet in the park so that he could see his granddaughter. But lately, his daughter had given birth to her second child and was totally absorbed by health issues of her own and the newborn in the aftermath of the delivery. My patient had only received a birth announcement and when he had called to visit her, she had explained her dire situation and had asked him to be patient and give her some time. He was devastated that he was the only one who had not seen the child and felt a huge narcissistic rage thinking that everybody else had this privilege except him. Concurrently, he felt all rights were taken away from him after his unfaithfulness and the divorce especially, since one of his daughters had discovered his love letters and found out about his affair prior to divorce and called him a liar. Now, being a liar was added to the list of their accusations of him. He felt totally defenseless.

What was clear was that throughout his experience of remorse and self-beating, his focus was only on himself and how his actions had alienated his daughters from him, and since he could not ever have them back in his life, he was washed up and finished. In other words, he focused on them only in terms of the consequences of his mistreatment of them; it was his deprivation and alienation from them that he perceived as his punishment. Through this scenario, his punishing daughters were cast as tormentors with whom he had no rights, just as he didn't with his mother. In his huge unconscious rage toward them as his tormentors, he could no longer experience them as his daughters. There was no apparent concern about how they had been affected by his reckless behavior and the damage he had caused them. Casting them as such, he had no access to tender paternal feelings that could lead him to wonder how his mistakes had hurt and impacted them. The fact that in their anger they had deposed him from the status of a father had stripped him of all paternal feelings and his ego was so badly demolished that he could not imagine himself worthy of any form of reconciliation.

Realizing that before he could come closer to empathizing with others, he had to come out of his relentless self-loathing and inability to empathize with himself, I commented that he treated himself as though he had been worse than a molester and had damaged his daughters beyond repair. In one session, while he was expressing his total despair about the impossibility of ever having a relationship with his daughters because of their accusations, I asked him why was he so adamant to take in all their accusations and assume he had not brought anything to his daughters' lives. For the first time, he was able to talk about the different ways he was a good father to them; for instance, the only time he stood up to his own mother was when she attacked his older daughter. For the first time in his life, with an inexplicable courage, he was able to shout at her, put her in her place, and warn her not to ever mistreat his daughter again. Another time, in his sensitivity to rejection, he became very protective of his middle daughter who was not his wife's favorite, making sure she got adequate love and attention from him. Despite his dire financial situation, he took full financial responsibility for his youngest daughter's education. He knew he had a short temper with them but was also aware of having been very protective of them. I suggested that he was beginning to change his distortions and acquire a new ability to consider all the facts of his paternal relationship and establish a realistic assessment of his fathering, and mused that perhaps he was getting in touch with how much the banishment he was experiencing was self-banishment. His resistance continued as he could not take in my empathic comment and remained remorseful because he had completely screwed up his life and had no options to pay the price of suffering. I commented, "You seem to be more comfortable in your lonely dark place of self-beating rather than tolerate other feelings of your anger at them and your regret for damaging those you love—as though your self-beating is the only way you can deal with your guilt. Perhaps, this is what your daughter meant when she said 'You don't get it.' I feel it's not that you don't get it, but rather it is too painful for you to get it." He looked puzzled and for the first time became curious about his self-beating.

When his daughter called to tell him one more time to be patient regarding visiting her and the newborn because of her continued health issues, he was somewhat relieved but still felt totally at the mercy of his cruel daughter. I suggested that the way he sees his daughters is no different from how he saw his mother who had the power to make or break him leaving him without having a voice. He did acknowledge that he felt marginalized and therefore furious at them for putting him in touch with his worst fears of abandonment. I felt that as long as he unconsciously and understandingly mistook them for his mother, there was no hope of coming out of the situation. I added that he had simultaneously deprived himself of feeling like a concerned father by recreating the sad scenario of his childhood interactions with his mother. He protested that he could not do anything about their hatred of him and that his older daughter had called him a pathological liar. I said, "And that should make you feel angry!" He responded that he felt like all rights of being angry were taken away from him because of his misdeeds. I suggested that by turning his daughters into his mother, he had finally arrived at his most scary fantasy—that his mother was right to withhold her love from him, and now his daughters were too. I added, "They're not your mother, they're your children. Perhaps you can change your focus away from how much you hate them for representing your mother who has finally in reality banished and abandoned you through them." He continued his refrain that he had failed as a father and that there was not much he could do about changing anything. I spontaneously blurted out, "How about sending your daughter or grandchild a gift?" He looked at me with surprise and asked, "You think so?" I responded, "What do you think? Isn't that what fathers do?" He said it never occurred to him. While in the throes of his narcissistic regression, he could not see himself as a father capable of feeling for his daughters or acting like one.

My comment came spontaneously from a place of wanting to snap him out of his self-preoccupation and wake him up to his potential fatherly presence in his daughters' lives. This was the beginning of his insight into his narcissism and the closed loop that his extreme remorse had created. For the first time, he became aware that this closed loop of guilt, punishment, and revenge did not allow him to see the reality of the ban he had put on his fatherhood and his ability to shift his focus on them. I also conveyed that in his regressed state of feeling at the mercy of his mother, projected on his daughters, his paternal aptitude was completely sapped. After receiving the gift, his daughter had an hour-and-a-half phone conversation with him. Despite some positive headway with his daughters, his despair and hanging on to remorse continued. I suggested, "As long as you don't give yourself the right to be angry at them and continue treating yourself as someone who does not deserve to be in their lives, your suffering will get you nowhere."

During this time, his anxiety was back and with sadness he reported that he had resumed his marijuana smoking as he had a very hard time dealing with his daughters' rejection of him and that he had hidden it from me. He reported that despite progress with his daughter, his anxiety was on the rise and he was unable to self-regulate as he felt as if he were in free fall. It became clear that his investment in doom and gloom was his way of keeping close his sadistic mother who could not tolerate any genuine happiness and joy in his son. He blurted out, "If I give up the anxiety that keeps me vigilant, I'll feel terror." I said, "Then you become motherless. You'll lose your link with your mother. It seems like the pain of anxiety and constant vigilance is a small price to pay not to be totally abandoned by her." He began crying like a baby and whimpered that he did not want to let go of his mother, that he felt like a baby without her, like a leaf in the wind without her presence in his world. Immediately, he switched to the scathing letters that his daughters had sent him in the past. I drew his attention to the shift and how much perhaps he wanted them to feel abandoned by him. I told him that he is so afraid of his anger toward his daughters/mother that he has to create the terror of his own abandonment in order not to feel it.

A few weeks later, he was reporting that while he was joyful for remembering me outside the sessions he was also apprehensive. He confessed that sometimes, he tells himself that the therapy is not working, but that this is a fleeting thought. His association led him to a multitude of incidences with his mother, for instance, when she could not tolerate his sad or anxious feelings, she would demand that he put on a fake happy face; yet she was determined to destroy all his genuinely happy moments. He also realized that he was petrified by the extent of his dependency on me which made it hard for him to surrender to the work. As he explored his fears of abandonment, he also got in touch with his anger for getting so little of me at the time that he was becoming more needy and dependent. I empathized with his frustration and wondered if he was worried that he was not in my mind outside of the sessions. Assuming that I had so many better things to think about than him in his absence, he expressed his anger but then acknowledged that he carried me outside of the sessions and felt good about it. I suggested that he must have unconsciously realized that he is in my mind as well to give himself permission to hang on to me in my absence. He agreed.

In the course of several months, as he was allowing himself to be dependent and identify with me, his anxiety became more bearable. During an episode of what appeared to be a readiness to feel regret, he cut his trip to the mountains short in order to see me. The thought that his daughters were not talking to him while his friends' children were on good terms with them became unbearable. He came to see me with the hope that I could fix things for him. He added that he needed to see me to get my empathy with his sadness, and even though he wished that I was a miracle worker, he knew the work should be his. I remarked that he came to me in order to receive the empathy that he could not give himself. While he was talking about the miracle of getting his daughter back, perhaps there was also the little miracle of making me the model for what he wanted to be, an empathic person with him and his suffering. It was clear that despite his best intentions, he could not shift his focus on the pain of his daughters and wanted me to be a model for him as an empathic father. In the session, he was able to experience shame for his reckless years when his children were still at home. He could conjure up their faces, their vulnerability during his outrage. It appeared that the shift had finally happened, and he could feel like a father focused on his daughters and not on himself and his hopelessness. When he finally heard from his older daughter and got a surprise call from his middle daughter, he felt gratified and felt like this was enough of a boost to become hopeful. Simultaneously, he was able to link this new awareness to his masochistic use of marijuana that was not helping him with his anxiety and instead was a way of denying his aging, lost sexuality, and loneliness. He wondered why he had gone back to it when he was starting to feel better.

As he acquired new insights about self-sabotage, his infantile need for his sadomasochistic relationship to his mother diminished. His mourning process picked up again as he was able to hang on to me as a good mother who was empathic and nonjudgmental. Gradually, he could feel like a concerned father to his daughters. He was working toward mustering up the courage to invite his daughters to family therapy in order to listen to them and resume his fatherly role with them when, during my vacation, I heard news of a serious accident that had put him in ICU fighting for his life. He asked to see me and when I went in, he was surrounded by his three daughters, his ex-wife and his granddaughter that he was so eager to see. I later found out that, all this time, his children were under the impression that their father was too involved with himself and not interested in seeing them and in order not to get hurt they kept their distance. Little did they know how much he was afraid of them, as he was of his mother, and the only reason he did not make any attempt was because he had taken all rights of fatherhood away from himself. Sadly, after two weeks of struggle with his injuries, Mr. C's compromised immune system gave up, and he died peacefully with some regret but no remorse. His past soothing fantasy of revenge at his deathbed, rejecting his remorseful daughters and reversal of his condition, was turned into a reality of reconciliation and correction of misunderstanding. In their eulogies, each one of the daughters shared wonderful touching memories of his care and protection.

In our last session before we parted, Mr. C told me that he was thinking of his friends and himself differently. He was not using them as a relief from loneliness but was more in touch with how much their time was mutually rewarding, and instead of bombarding himself with self-doubt and fears, he found a new sense of enjoyment without fearing his mother would take it away. He was able to think of them while he was away from them. Our work remained incomplete but the movement from remorse to conscious regret for missed opportunities and outright mindlessness of the past had begun. The mourning process had freed him from the closed loop of remorse, and to a great extent he was heading toward reality and a world in which his mother was no longer the major player.

Discussion

"The etymological root of regret both in German *gretan* (to weep, lament) and old French *regretter* (bewailing the dead) to lament, alludes to an embedded mourning process" (Wiktionary). "The Latin root of remorse goes back to the old French *remors*, and to medieval Latin *remorsus*, as well as Latin *remordere* with *re*-expressing intensive force +*mordere*—to bite" (Oxford Advanced Learner Dictionary).

While the word "regret" with both its German and French base emphasizes the lamenting and weeping for the dead, the word "remorse" is associated with biting with intense force. The etymological roots of the two words in and of themselves can tell us a lot about the differences in the dynamics of these experiences: how the psychological self-biting in remorse is emblematic of its defensive nature, not allowing the psyche to feel the actual pain in reality and instead resorting to self-made pain of self-biting to prevent mourning for the actual loss and pain caused by one's action. The sadistic omnipotence in remorse is reflective of the primitive superego biting and chewing the ego to such an extent that its reality testing function is disturbed and the actual pain caused to the other and the need to rectify it is removed from the picture. A closed loop of anger at the self, guilt, and self-punishment distances the individual from the possibility of mourning loss and freeing up the psyche for repair.

More often than not, people relish the thought of being their own harshest critics and assume that their brutal attitudes toward themselves regarding any wrongdoing is indicative of their high moral stance rather than seeing it as an impediment against an organic morality grounded in reality in order to rectify the harm. This is the mentality behind remorse preventing the individual to shift the focus from self-punishment to acknowledgment of harm done to the other with the possibility of putting guilt to the good work of repair. True sadness is about recognizing and accepting loss, whereas depression is about denying the loss—in this case, Mr. C's denial of the fact that his mother could never love him. There was, therefore, no purity to Mr. C's experience of sadness. He was anxious and depressed and mired in a closed system of preserving and internal relationship with a dead object whose love he still wanted to extract. Enforced by repression, this closed system removed him from an affectively meaningful interaction with the world of the living. Mr. C felt scared and anxious because he believed there was something dreadfully wrong with his environment (projection of his childhood to the present). It was only when he accepted the full tragic implication of having been a baby with a sadistic mother incapable of love that he was able to renounce his relentless, stubborn attachment to the bad object and started the mourning process. Only then was he able to feel the purity and the full brunt of his sadness and loss and began mourning a badly damaged life and irretrievable losses. His narcissistic rage toward his hurt daughters was a reflection of the neurotic guilt that had become the travesty of moral guilt. As he took more responsibility in their alienation from him, his paralysis and fear of reaching out to them diminished.

Mr. C's burgeoning regret emerged only after his identification with the empathic stance of the analyst who was contextualizing his actions and sensitizing him to the dire consequences of his deprived and sadistic childhood. Gradually, he was able to better assess the reality of his limitations as a father, and his harmful actions were mitigated by the memories of his fatherly presence and fierce protection of his daughters at various times. In due time, his primitive self-beating gave way to empathy for himself and with new understanding he became more consolable and capable to move away from self-biting of remorse to interpersonal regret for the impact of his actions on his daughters.

In this case, the manifestation of regret as a movement from apprehension, guilt, and remorse and finding the capacity to focus on the other's pain demonstrates the true meaning of regret as lament with an embedded mourning process. When Mr. C began working with me, he was only sad for himself for not having had an adequate mother who could love him, and his daughters' unconscious representations were that of his mother who refused to love him because of his inherent badness, manifested in his reckless behavior. Developmentally, there was no capacity for empathy for himself or for his children. He was a baby without a mother, lost in oblivion desperate for the love of his "mommy" projected onto his daughters. He was thus removed from any meaningful interaction with the world outside, the world of living versus the dead world of his mother that had engulfed him and was not allowing him to live his life. Initially, this love had to be extracted from me in the transference with the rage of a hungry neglected child. The raw unprocessed anger needed to be first directed toward me, contained and processed for his own digestion and metabolism before he could take in the empathy and love of a mother in me. The intense biting wounds of remorse which constituted his atonement were used for the sadomasochistic purpose of satisfying his fantasy bloodthirsty mother who would relish in his suffering. In this case what stood out most for me in my interaction with Mr. C was the fearsome infantile quality of his world, conjuring up the unthinkable, not only a baby without a mother, but a mother set to destroy him because he failed to be a good slave. The constant projection of this dreadful scenario into the outside world created the powerful overwhelming anxiety that he would bring to the sessions and which for a while paralyzed me. It was only after I survived the full expression of his rage that he was able to let go of his mother and find safety for turning his maternal longing onto me. The gradual deepening of his relationship with me allowed him to fully appreciate the implications of his childhood trauma and only after mourning his own losses was he able to regret the pain he had inflicted on his daughters who no longer were stand-ins for his mother. In his regret, Mr. C was lamenting the irretrievableness of an essential attachment to a mother who could not love him, but he found hope in repairing the broken ties to his daughters who, unlike his mother, were willing to listen. His neurotic paralyzing guilt was a travesty of moral guilt because he was blocking himself from taking the necessary action to mend the harm; he needed to repair the harm done by accepting responsibility and taking the risk of intimacy. Then, he could gradually move toward experiencing himself as a caring father regretting his past conduct and mustering up the courage to listen to the pain of his daughters and tolerate their real rage and anger at him for letting them down without falling apart. For the first time, he was concerned about his daughters who were not in a relationship and was able to express his worries about their future.

Conclusion

Faced with a serious illness, the financial threat of a dwindling practice with professional skills that were no longer in vogue, loss of sexual capacity, fear of the inability ever to retire, awareness of his own aging, illness, loneliness, unmet dependency needs, failed aspirations, unfulfilled life, and, most important, the inevitability and anticipation of death, Mr. C's lifetime anxiety and depression had exponentially heightened when he started therapy with me in advanced age. I was very much aware of his vulnerability and breaking point, due to his crisis at this period of life while cognizant of the fact that he was someone who had coped poorly most of his life and was full of remorse about his unfulfilled and unexamined life that was fast coming to an end. This awareness, on both my part as well as his, created conditions in therapy that were different than working with the non-elderly. On his part, the awareness of his limited time made him a very serious patient, eager, engaged, and hardworking. As for myself, I was very cognizant that the role of analysis for Mr. C was not an extensive character change but to help him make necessary adaptive changes to gain the most out of his environment in his few remaining years. Once the negative transference was worked through, I did not wait for Mr. C to develop the essential insight to make the first move toward reconciliation with his daughters. Instead I made a suggestion to take steps which eventually led to something that should have happened a long time previously, a family therapy that was very promising had it not been for his unfortunate sudden death.

Sandler (1982) calls attention to the threats of object loss that remain as latent dangers throughout life and exacerbate in old age if adequate mourning for losses has not taken place. Throughout childhood, Mr. C was not permitted to feel sad or anxious and was encouraged to deny his pain. Therefore, he had never mourned his accumulated losses and when he was able to do so finally, the atonement associated with his self-biting remorse gave way to the lament that paved the way for the first signs of forgiveness of the self and regret for others.

PART II

CULTURAL REALMS

CHAPTER FOUR

The poetics of regret in repetition, mourning, and reparation

Ingrid M. Geerken

W e often feel sorry for acts we have either done or failed to do, whether the object of regret is miniature (the breaking of a vase), or gigantic (the killing of a person). Regret has primarily been thought of as obsessive repetition in the service of the death drive, or the repetition compulsion. I will argue here that creative, developmentally oriented regret requires an agent who accepts responsibility, even in the case of an unintentional act. The spur of regretful conjectures that provoke a provisional state of turmoil in the mind will ultimately set the conditions for mourning and working through that are prerequisites for internal and external reparation. Regret is essentially generative of narrative. It is an emotion that engages the mind in a story-making process that seeks to correct a past experience. Regret can be formulated mentally and verbally through the conditional phrases "If only ..."; "I wish I had ...". In imagining what might have or could have happened, how things could have gone differently, we rewrite the past and invent a new future.

Regret, as a simultaneous expression of a wish and a grief, *is a special kind of counterfactual thinking* that is connected to dreaming, grieving, and thinking. As an expression of the conditional—"if only ..."—regret is an act of the imagination that involves a special kind of agent. This agent dreams as a defense against loss. Similarly, Freud's (1899a) dreamer, suffering from regret (in a situation of unfulfilled desire), produces a hallucination that both disguises and fulfills a wish. Bion's (1962a) dreamer is active not only at night, but dreams all throughout the day. In his mind, dreaming *is* thinking. This concept is later used by Civitarese and Ferro (2013) to construct a model of the mind whose foundation is made up of reveries (a kind of daydreaming) and, using narratology, privileges the use of metaphor. Regret involves an *excess* of the imagination that exceeds normal boundaries of time and space, even of the individual mind. A thinking agent, in this case one full of regrets, is engaged in a symbolic activity that substitutes for and replaces the missing object. This involves a kind regression in which parts of the lost object are reassembled into a structural form. The agent experiencing regret, in a moment of disequilibrium, does and undoes the scene of regret, which is then repetitively re-bound in pictograms and in the narratable.

The conjectures of regret that occur in the imagination appear in ingenious ways in narrative. In *The Interpretation of Dreams*, Freud (1900a) recognizes the generativity of regret by making it the impetus for a dream: he writes that a dream "is a reaction to an experience … which has left behind it a regret, a longing, a wish that has not been dealt with" (p. 157). The representational strategies in what I call "regret narratives" are analogous to those described by Freud as dream work: condensation, displacement, dramatization, secondary revision. Attention to the formal aspects of regret narratives alerts us to the presence of regret so that the affect can be mobilized in formal structures to be used in the service of development and in the resolution of a painful psychological conflict.

The formal and structural aspects of regret narratives (as part of the dream work) play a crucial part in working through, but do not receive enough attention in an analytic context. I argue that an analyst should be *as* aware of the formal properties of a session as to its content. The content of a session is, in fact, inseparable from its form. In clinical work, this relation is analogous to Bion's (1962a, 1970) concept of the relationship between the container and contained. In my formulation, the container is always under construction as the raw material (what is being contained) takes shape. The active process of reassembly, what Ogden (2005) describes as "the gathering of bits" (p. 96), occurs within the larger frame of the analysis and is analogous to a "Chinese box" structure. In literature, the Chinese box refers to a frame narrative, a story that takes the form of a narrative inside a narrative. Close atten-tion to the formal and structural properties of regret narratives can help analysts intervene in ways that facilitate the working-through process in accordance with the repetitions *particular to and consistent with the forms* emerging in the treatment.

The philosopher, Amélie Rorty (1980), has described how regret, and the closely allied emotions of shame and guilt, produce "filmic" remembrances of the painful event. Although all three emotions gen-erate "obsessive imagistic replays," regret has a "freer play" in the imagination: "[T]he action's long-range consequences are explored, the possible preventive alternatives are investigated" (p. 498). In *Beyond the Pleasure Principle*, Freud (1920g), perplexed by the literal nightmares and flashbacks of battlefield survivors, emphasized the negative aspect of this kind of repetition as a "traumatic neurosis" that "emerges ... as the unwitting reenactment of an event that one cannot simply leave behind" (cited in Caruth, 1996, p. 2). In regret narratives, these trau-matic repetitions are made available to the mental work of elaboration so that they become, to use de M'Uzan's (1969) concept, "the same but not identical." These reproductions can then function as a kind of "transitional object" (Winnicott, 1953), later described by Bollas as an adult experience of being "held" by an aesthetic object (1987). In clinical work, a patient might come to analysis precisely because her regrets have become fixated or stuck and are not available to the work of elabo-ration and mourning. In successful cases, regret will be linked to a drive towards reparation as described by Melanie Klein (1937) and which is paralleled in a text by an aesthetic resolution.

By studying literature and film, we can see how regret narratives that are successfully worked-through have different structural elements than the failed or incomplete attempts that lead to unhappy outcomes in real life. Our aim here will be to imagine interventions that mobilize the conjecturing energy of regret to bring about a creative resolution to a painful mental dilemma. I will begin with a description of the *poetics of regret* (the study of linguistic techniques and aesthetics) as expressed in my research on the structure of regret narratives.

Regret: martial, marital, mortal

Thus far, my work has produced an account of regret as an affective state and as a structural feature of narrative and poetry. One of my discoveries is that regret is unique in the study of literary emotions because it represents a feeling that is itself a mode of analysis; moreover, that feeling may be expressed formally, in the aesthetic arrangement of the work. My study of regret is divided into three parts: *martial, marital,* and *mortal*. In each part, I display how the structure of regret in literary works varies according to its object (war, marriage, and death, respectively). Each type of regret—over killing, over marrying, over death or dying—has specific features, though regret also has certain properties that remain constant across its forms. I intend to lift the poetics of regret into a viable category of literary description, as well as describing how regret can function as a psychological construct. These concepts can be clinically useful in understanding and working with the regrets of our patients.

I will be using three main theoretical ideas: *agent-regret* (from philosophers Amélie Rorty, 1980, and Bernard Williams, 1981); what I call *surge of affect* (a rush of emotion and an upswell of aesthetic energy), and *reparation* (as described by Melanie Klein, 1940). In sketching out the poetics of regret, I investigate the ways regret affects different features of narrative, such as plot, language, and rhetorical figures. As examples, I will refer (in a condensed form) to three exemplary literary texts: Conrad's (1900) *Lord Jim* for martial regret; Eliot's (1871) *Middlemarch* for marital regret, and Brontë's (1847) *Wuthering Heights* for mortal regret. In particular, in the clinical realm, I link my work on regret to that of de M'Uzan, who, as the founder and most prominent exponent of the Paris school of psychosomatics, first coined what is now called "mentalization" (Scarfone, 2013).

Martial regret

In *martial regret*, I center my analysis on an act of killing that remains unjustified. This usually occurs in proximity to the legitimate injury of war, and produces in the agent a state of *moral emergency*. For example, Conrad's Jim abandons ship when 800 lives are at stake; Coleridge's (1798) ancient mariner inexplicably kills the bird of good omen, and Billy Budd (Melville, 1924) strikes and kills the master-at-arms on his warship. Martial regret is typically centered in one sensational scene that isolates the agent and appears fated. *Agent-regret* is distinguished by an agent who is made to bear a special moral relationship to the past action: one that is not, for example, absolved by a legal sentence.

By sidestepping Jim's conviction by a court of law, Conrad emphasizes Jim's ethical relation to his regretted act of jumping ship. The duty of the soldier is at issue here. As Siegfried Sassoon writes, "Soldiers are dreamers" (from the epigraph in Tim O'Brien's *Going After Cacciato*, 1978): Jim's state of hyperarousal makes him susceptible to the free play of the regretful imagination.

What I call *surge of affect* is an emotional upswell and an explosion of symbolic energy. Even as the agent dissects the scene of regret, he is improvising alternatives that would have avoided or revised the regretted outcome. These hypothetical alternatives are encoded in the text as subplots, parallel plots, and fantasies. Contemporary studies on traumatic memory can elucidate the structure of *Lord Jim*, which is replete with flashbacks, hallucinations, and conjectures. Jim's jump is embedded in the text as what Turner calls an "image schema" (1996, p. 16) that is triggered again and again when the coordinates of his original mistake are repeated in the plot. A "good-enough" reparation will depend on the agent's capacity to create a repetition which transcends its first occurrence and, in so doing, transforms the world—as Conrad's Jim says, "Someday one's bound to come upon some sort of chance to get it all back again. Must!" (p. 174).

Marital regret

In *marital regret*, I take up what George Eliot termed "the great home epic" and describe three strategies for regretting one's choice of husband or wife (1871, p. 832). The *surge of affect* produced by marital regret creates multiple versions of the original pair, causes the proliferation of suitors, and dramatizes the melodramatic (but not always taken) options of divorce, adultery, and murder. The contemplation of a crime of passion becomes essential to the denouement of marital mistake, and protagonists such as Dorothea Brooke, Isabel Archer, and Jude Fawley face a moral trap in the marriages they make. In these novels, marital regret becomes an economical way of describing the plot; it functions as what Freud (1900a), in his work on dream interpretation, calls a "stimulus of increasing insistence" (p. 218), and is responsible for the many versions that appear of that theme.

Although *Middlemarch* was published in 1870–1871, approximately ten years after the establishment of the Divorce Court, Eliot precludes the possibility of using such legal remedies by setting her novel in the

1830s, in the years just before reform. In marital regret, the deliberative process that precedes the decision to marry does not lessen what Isabel Archer—in James's (1881) *The Portrait of a Lady*—calls the "grave risk" of marriage. Rather, the marriage contract becomes both a personal, ethical dilemma and a matter of public importance. In *Middlemarch*, Eliot's aesthetic "web" is reflected not only in the marital intercourse between Dorothea and Casaubon, but in the interconnectedness of plot lines; it is Dorothea's act of empathy towards her rival, Rosamund, that ultimately enables her reparative marriage to the political reformer, Will Ladislaw.

Mortal regret

In *mortal regret*, I examine four different acts that express reparative responses to mourning. In each, the agent takes as its objective the resurrection, or restoration of the lost loved one—whether by attempting bodily re-membering (Shelley's *Frankenstein*, 1818); by playing dead—what I call "corpsing"—(Dickinson's and Rossetti's poetry); or by the "live burial" of a son or lover (Emerson's *Experience*, 1844; Brontë's *Wuthering Heights*). Elegy, too, can express mortal regret, as in Hardy's volume of poems upon the death of his estranged wife (*Poems of 1912–1913*). In these texts, reparation—the wish to restore the past or revive the dead—collides with the limits of human will confronting mortality. The grieving agent, avoiding mourning, attempts to resurrect the dead through the force of longing. These attempts at revitalization— which are paralleled in the author's own act of creation—are necessarily flawed and bring forth ghostly or hybrid forms that exist at the boundaries of the animate.

In her novel, Brontë vividly imagines a passionate love between Heathcliff and Catherine but must then resolve the problem of the heroine's death halfway through the novel; she does this by reproducing Catherine both in the body of her daughter, Cathy, and in the spirit that haunts Heathcliff until his own death. Corpsing is the self-conscious attempt to play dead accompanied by the paradoxical attempt to represent that state. Using this technique, Dickinson can begin a poem by saying (remarkably) "I heard a fly buzz—when I died" (#465). By making life-in-death an imaginative possibility, mortal regret extends human agency to its furthest limit—beyond mortality. In *Wuthering Heights*, Brontë revises the form of the elegy and rejects the Christian afterworld by foregrounding the inadequacy of such conventional forms to assuage vehement grief, and by making spectral substitutions for the Christian afterlife.

My theory of regret calls our attention to well-known features of these novels, as well as making us see these attributes with fresh eyes. It has been noticed, of course, that the second half of Lord Jim is an attempt by Jim to both flee from and atone for his cowardice in the first half, that there are multiple subplots of marriage in Middlemarch, and that Wuthering Heights is haunted by generational repetition. However, these facets are taken to be individual plot developments, and there is no current theory of fiction that might see these as permutations of a single problem, plot functions springing from a powerful authorial compulsion. I argue that such plots are best seen when they are conceived of as the acting out of a poetics of regret.

At the same time, critics have consistently struggled to account for certain incongruities in the structure of all three novels, including the following: Conrad's conversion in Lord Jim of the deeply psychological plot of "Patna" to the heroic adventure story of "Patusan"; Eliot's choice of the bohemian figure of Will Ladislaw as a second husband for Dorothea; and Brontë's resolution of the marriage plot with an arguably less compelling second generation. I argue that these features are not flaws, but, rather, representative of the necessarily incomplete state of a reparative resolution. Patusan, assembled out of the bits and pieces of the first half of the novel, is an expression of Jim's imaginative superimposition of a "better" present on the flawed past (as in a screen memory); as such, it provides a stylistic counterpoint to Marlow's assemblage of the "facts" of the Patna affair. Will Ladislaw's qualities of transparency and comparative lightness as a character express his origin as Dorothea's, and perhaps Eliot's, own fantasy of reparative desire. Lastly, Brontë's investment in the socially viable second generation is counterbalanced by her persistent attention to the enduring ghosts of the first. In the working-out of the moral and aesthetic problems of regret and reparation, these authors call attention to the complexly layered acts of the imagination that constitute the artistic process of fiction motivated by the wish to undo or compensate for traumatic regret.

Each type of regret seen in literature has an analogue in the psychoanalytic setting: Martial regret is about trauma and injury to others and self, marital regret is about bad object choices and second chances, and mortal regret is about loss and the reassembly of the lost loved one in a different form. Painful regret—in traumatic injuries, object relation-ships, and irreversible loss—is often the impetus of patients seeking treatment. The formal aspects of the analytic situation are analogous to and favorable to initiating the process of working through. For example, the episodic feature of the sessions and the constancy of the setting establish the sturdy parameters of time and space. The structure of the frame, like in a text or a poem, establishes the physical proper-ties of the analysis. The analytic container offers what Winnicott calls a "holding" environment (1960) that encourages reverie and initiates the process of repetition as it appears in the reproduction of fantasy and in the transference–countertransference matrix. Impasses are often places where the elaboration of regret has reached a standstill and traumatic repetition has instead taken hold in the transference. Clinically, the patient who regrets may be stuck in an obsessive circularity of thought that does not lead to the kind of repetitions that are transformed in the process of mourning (working through), and that hopefully lead to the reparation and restoration of objects in their internal world.

Repetition, mourning, and reparation

Regret is expressed by agents we recognize as characters in a story. This kind of agent is felt by himself and others to bear a special moral rela-tionship to the past action. In such a case, the focus of regret is one's own agency in connection to the regrettable event, and in facing the truth that one might have acted otherwise. In Coleridge's *The Rime of the Ancient Mariner*, the first time the narrator uses the first person sin-gular is when he confesses, "I shot the ALBATROSS." The agent accepts responsibility, even in cases where there is a series of painful events to which he is subjected and which seem to lie outside his control. In Freud's (1914g) "Remembering, repeating and working-through," the traumatic neurosis emerges when a memory is *not* remembered but instead acted-out in a repetition compulsion. In cases of regret, the regretted event is vividly remembered *and* also repeated. Thus, regret is not limited to cases of voluntary action (as in an accident). This type of traumatic regret must be made conscious and worked-through in order for reparation to occur.

The emphasis on regret as a psychological concept is about the mobilization of this affect as a means towards change in the analysis. De M'Uzan (2013) takes up the economic point of view as used in Freud's metapsychology in order to account for the role of energy in the psyche-soma. De M'Uzan, referring to acts of binding and unbinding, observes the "quantity of excitation as it is—or fails to be—recruited in the service of mental elaboration" (cited in Scarfone, 2013, p. xiii). Similarly, what I call surge of affect, although originally an aesthetic construct, can be linked to "the economic scandal" or "influx of excitation" that de M'Uzan argues must occur in an analytic setting in order to produce change (1983, p. 55). The spare setting and containing function of the analytic space set the conditions whereby the surge of fantasies and conjectures of regret can be produced and worked-through by the analytic couple.

The symbolic conglomerates produced by regret take forms that express aspects of the content such that there is inner and outer coherence within the artifact itself and, moreover, bear the peculiar stamp of its producer. That is, it is not sufficient to generate symbols towards any kind of transformation, but these transformations must build through associative links towards a meaningful structure, one that resonates with its author. Successful narratives bear an idiosyncratic style, full of liveliness and spontaneity, that express what Winnicott (1960) might call the "true self" of the author, and not the "false self" imposter. The manic production of a succession of symbolic transformations, absent in this formal coherence, is a defense against loss and not a generative process or a meaning-making activity.

In an analytic setting, the production of symbolic activity is bound in the liminal aspect of the transference and countertransference relationship, and contained within the analytic field. According to de M'Uzan, analysts should be flexible enough to allow for "novel, even provisional arrangements" to occur to them in the analytic session (cited in Scarfone, 2013, p. xv). Allowing that kind of availability to unconscious processes creates a new entity in the treatment, what de M'Uzan (1983) calls a "chimera" (p. 56) and Ogden (1994) calls the "analytic third." I argue that the creation of doubles, subplots, peripheral and related characters that share a resemblance and other symbolic links in regret narratives can be seen as employing this same dynamic process, one that takes place within a particular kind of structure or container.

Repetition

In regret, the role of the past is both firmly established and temporarily suspended. Like screen memories, regret narratives are built in the process of repeating and remembering, like a layering of transparencies.

Such narratives proceed linearly and cumulatively, with a rhythmic movement between a fixed and traumatic memory, often characterized by a "flashbulb" or "flashback" quality, and a dynamic of *proleptic* thinking (the "if only" conjecture) that projects narrative possibilities into the future, and, in the clinical setting, into the analyst and the analytic field. Using the structure of Freud's *Nachträglichkeit* (1895), translated as "afterwardness," and involving the author's (or analyst's) reverie, the narrative is changed over time through a series of repetitions that redistribute features and register these movements in time. If this type of elaboration is achieved in the analytic process, using a sequence of repetitions in the many forms I describe, the agent (or analysand) can move farther and farther away from the fixed traumatic scene towards a new possibility that is reparative. Similarly, de M'Uzan (1969) argues that the act of remembering is a process of repetition in which the "'past' is elaborated in narrative form" (p. 12).

The repetition of regret resembles a dream but is *not* a dream in the classic sense. Instead, regret zooms in on a nodal scene of regret that is pivotal and that is replayed in the mind. In these cases, regret is conscious and the regrettable act is not repressed. Instead, the conjectures produced by regret are a conscious act and, formally speaking, the agent is set the task of reusing and reconfiguring elements that are features of the original scene. However, the agent experiencing a surge of affect also produces unprocessed "bits" that demand reassembly. Thus, the working-through process of regret takes place consciously and unconsciously, with some of the rawer aspects hovering at the periphery of the mind (or in the preconscious). In regret narratives, even slight alterations begin the process of establishing time and thus initiate working through. Moreover, as time accrues, the nodal scene of regret begins to have less importance than its subsequent elaborations. We can see this structural feature and rhythmic aspect in the specifics of time and space in the frame of analysis.

In a clinical setting, forms shape the free associations of patients. They bind libidinal energy and over time generate a developing plot. Analysands are often not aware of these formal features, but they make manifest the internal world they inhabit. The regretted scene, conjured up by the analysand in a kind hallucinatory wish fulfillment, alters itself as it repeats. Repetitions engender conjectures that multiply options and engender other characters. In some cases, peripheral characters or doubles enter into the narrative so that the analysand can make use of these objects to repair injury and achieve reparation. Analysts can also be the agents who introduce such transformative or prosthetic objects into the plot of a session and over the course of a treatment. By redistributing agency across a cast of characters, the analytic couple can produce many drafts of a single catastrophic event, altering outcomes by degrees and practice, until the shape of the plot, and the agent's role in it, becomes clear.

Mourning

Mourning is used as a means of working through regret. As I have previously argued (Geerken, 2004), regret reverses the Freudian trajectory of mourning in which the mourner divests himself, "bit by bit," of every "one of the memories and expectations" related to the lost loved one (1917e, p. 39). Instead, the mourner collects and reassembles these "bits and pieces" in order to repair her regret. In the Kleinian world, this dynamic signifies a shift from the paranoid-schizoid position into the depressive position, in which "anxieties spring from ambivalence" (Segal, 1964, p. 69). This ambivalence is captured in the backwards and forwards trajectory of regret, a mental activity in which both a grief and a wish are expressed. Regret is a longing that relies on symbol formation for its fullest expression. The mourning particular to regret is an active and creative process. Joan Didion (2005), in her memoir, *The Year of Magical Thinking*, writes about the sudden illness and lapse into a coma of her daughter, and days later, the death of her husband from a massive coronary. She writes: "Until now I had only been able to grieve, not mourn. Grief was passive. Grief happened. Mourning, the act of dealing with grief, required attention" (p. 143).

In regret, the wish to die or of being dead is expressive of regret to its furthest extreme. The agent longs to return to a prior state in a desire to undo the regretted act. Corpsing represents the symbolic state of dying, in which the agent remains, paradoxically, sentient enough to imagine and describe this state. For example, Christina Rossetti (1647) describes a gradual state of depersonalization in which not only the material body but the entire physical world, is placed under erasure. So, in "Cobwebs," all that remains after a series of negations is "one even plain" through which the "the sluggish air … broodeth." Poems such as Dickinson's "I Felt a Funeral, in my Brain" (#280) and Rossetti's "After Death" attempt to describe the sensations of death in material terms. The agent still sees, hears, and smells even as she occupies the "death-apartment." These paradoxical states are ones in which depersonalization and erasure are expressed such that the absent object becomes uncannily present (in a creative use of Freud's "return of the repressed," 1919h). Similarly, de M'Uzan (1976a) emphasizes that both analyst and analysand must experience a certain amount of depersonalization in the analysis for change to occur. Thus the "work of dying," rather than diminishing ties or symbols, produces a surge of libido, which frequently occurs when death is near (de M'Uzan, 1976b). The metaphor or enactment of "dying" in a clinical setting is an expression of a zero sum state which is the precursor to an acknowledgment of agency, a recognition of injury, and a helpless feeling about being unable to repair the wrong. The experience of depersonalization is often followed by a surge of affect that causes turmoil in the analysis, but if worked-through can lead to reparation.

Reparation

Regret can be distinguished from the fixation of melancholy by its emphasis on restoration. The omnipotent fantasy underlying these reparative acts is that a perfect assemblage of parts will repair the injury or resurrect the dead. Melanie Klein (1929) considered the wish to restore and recreate the lost loved object as the basis of all creativity. As I have previously argued, my model of reparation is based on the character of Agave in Euripides' *The Bacchae*. In a Bacchanalian frenzy, Agave (unknowingly) tore her son's body into pieces after he was caught spying on her. Realizing with horror what she had done, Agave desperately attempted to gather together and reassemble his body parts. *The Bacchae* ends with Agave's attempt to piece Pentheus' parts together: "Come, dear father, let us place that head/of that ill-fated boy where it belongs,/and let us fit, as exactly as we can,/the whole body together, shapely and straight" (p. 62). I call this act of putting together the pieces of a loved object "Agavic." In this act, the anxiety centers on an obsessional need to reassemble the pieces perfectly. Since no object exists in an ideal state, this attempt will produce many alternate versions of the thing itself. Thus, the lost object is rendered many times. If the obsessional impulse can be harnessed in the process of working through, these repetitions can resurrect a new form out of the original fragments.

Poetry, too, arrives in bits and pieces. In particular, Dickinson's characteristic use of dashes and staccato rhythm makes her poems a self-conscious rendering of the attempt at repair. Of poetry in general, one might ask the heartbreaking question asked by Agave about her dismembered son: "Are all its members pieced together well?" (Dickinson, 1960, p. 62). Reparation may include a fantasy of bodily reparation. In Sylvia Plath's (1960) "Colossus," the speaker laments the disarticulated memory of her dead father: "I shall never get you put together entirely,/ Pieced, glued and properly jointed." In Mary Shelley's *Frankenstein*, Dr. Frankenstein—motivated by the death of his mother—fabricates a monster out of a collection of disinterred body parts. In these works centered on loss, the act of bodily reparation is paralleled on a formal level by the many layers of narration that envelop the central act of revivification. The work of mourning literally becomes one of restoration.

Form

There are many forms particular to certain mediums that express and contain regret. I argue that attention to these forms (as well as to metaphor and metonymy) is important in clinical work because analysts can use them to facilitate a process that is stuck or already underway. According to Lévi-Strauss (1978), narratives can function as a "mini-myth" or an "explanatory cell." Although the elements of the story remain constant, the sequence of feeling and outcomes change over time, so that "when one element is transformed, then the other elements [are] arranged accordingly" (p. 39). The formal aspects of regret and reparation are often foregrounded in film and poetry and can be recognized as well in clinical work.

Run, Lola, Run

In films such as *Groundhog Day* (1993) and *Run Lola Run* (1998), regret is expressed by the medium itself. Although these films represent a protagonist who regrets his or her actions, it is the film that obsessively revisits an embedded or entrenched scene (as in a time loop). This is done without the conscious knowledge of the protagonist, so that the formal aspect does the bulk of the reparative work. For example, in *Run Lola Run*, three versions of the same scene are replayed, featuring a heroine, Lola, who must obtain a large sum of money in twenty minutes to save her boyfriend's (Manni's) life. In the first version, Manni commits robbery in a casino, and his girlfriend, Lola, is killed. In the second version, Lola commits the robbery, and her boyfriend, Manni, is killed.

In the third version, Lola gambles in the casino, winning against the odds, thus saving Manni's life and reuniting the lovers. The film is divided into three "runs" by Lola, in which each starts from the same situation, but develops differently and has a different outcome. Each run also has brief "flashforward" sequences that show how the lives of the people that Lola bumps into are changed after the encounter. In this film, the basic elements of plot are rearranged to reach a reparative end. The film conveys regret in flashbacks and flashforwards that alter the sequence over time even as the characters within the frame are seen to be changing the outcome through love.

Sestina

The sestina is a complex poetic form that achieves its often spectacular effects through intricate repetition. As such, it is a good example of the formal and affective aspects of the working through of regret. The sestina is an interwoven structure of six stanzas, wherein the six end words repeat themselves in a designated rotating order. The sestina ends with a three-line "envoi" that incorporates all the line-ending words, some hidden inside the lines.[1] The envoi, sometimes known as the *tornada*, must also include the remaining three end-words in the course of the three lines so that all six recurring words appear in the final three lines. In place of a rhyme scheme, the sestina relies on end-word repetition to effect a sort of rhyme.

For example, Elizabeth Bishop's (1955) poem "Sestina" describes the haunting interactions between a grandmother and her granddaughter on a gloomy autumn evening. The title identifies the poetic form that Bishop chose and is indicative of the way in which the story of the poem is inseparable from its form. Despite its formal constraints, the poem does not come across as mechanical, but instead expresses the raw intensity of an underlying sorrow that is both hidden and revealed as it transforms itself through a repetitive series of displacements. Bishop's six end-words create the intimate setting of the poem: A) house, B) grandmother, C) child, D) stove, E) almanac, F) tears. These words circulate through the stanzas to express the grief shared by the grandmother and child, but it is not alluded to directly. The poet is constrained and emboldened here by expressing affect not through the addition of new elements, but through the successive rearrangements of a fixed series.

In Bishop's poem, for example, the "tears" fall down the lines (as down a face) through a series of displacements that transform them over time into a reparative fantasy. In the first stanza, grandmother hides her tears; they reappear in the next stanza in the child's mind as the "rain that beats on the house." As the child stares, these drops appear on the teakettle as "the small hard tears" that "dance like mad on the hot black stove." Suddenly, the grandmother's teacup "fills with dark brown tears."

The child, who turns to fantasy, animates her objects: the Marvel stove says "It was to be," and the almanac adds, "I know what I know." In an aesthetic impulse that mirrors the poet's own act of formal severity, the child draws a "rigid house" to which she adds a "man with buttons like tears." Here, a new character, a man with tears, suddenly appears in front of the child's imaginary house. We realize that the mother is missing. She is not in the child's drawing or in the grandmother's house, or with the man. The poem both avoids and discloses this secret. As the grandmother "busies herself," the child hallucinates: she "secretly" opens the almanac and the little moons fall down its pages like tears. They fall down into the flower bed the child has "carefully placed" in front of the house. Like the poem, the almanac marks time and predicts the weather.

The first line of the envoi: "Time to plant tears, says the almanac" can be understood as referring to the literal "planting" of the tears inside the poem and to the way that the tears (like rain) can be used to grow flowers. Like Bishop, the child transforms her longing into a reparative fantasy through the creative use of "transitional" objects. In the final envoi of Bishop's poem, the child reassembles the available objects to create a new scene: "The grandmother sings to the marvelous stove" and the "child draws another inscrutable house." Through the repetitive drawings of the "inscrutable house," the child discloses the mystery of her missing mother. The child's "inscrutable house" is contained within Bishop's own "inscrutable" poem. According to biographers, "Sestina" refers to the time in Bishop's childhood when she lived in Nova Scotia, after her mother had been committed to an asylum.

Clinical vignettes

I will give two clinical vignettes that show regret as an overarching structure that alters as it repeats, and a more detailed example, in which

I zoom in on a scene that is in the process of being worked-through. In each case, an analysand attempts to repair a loss as expressed in regret and, also, as enacted in bodily gestures.

Mr. O

Mr. O came to me for an analysis because of his sexual affairs (which he regretted) and because of panic attacks that affected his academic performance. Early on, during our first separation, and while his wife was also away, Mr. O left a PTA meeting with the intention of getting a "lap dance" at a strip club. However, before he got there, he was stopped by the police and charged with reckless driving. He felt that the judge had clipped his wings. This regrettable scene was replayed over and over in varying ways in the analysis and especially through a strong erotic transference that masked a terrible separation anxiety. This was expressed first in his excited trips to the bathroom during sessions (a kind of "lap dance"), in the way he would flood the sessions, and through a dynamic in which I would "tighten and loosen" my responses (the way, as it turned out, his mother "loosened" and his father "tightened" his leg brace to correct a hip dysplasia as a baby). Mr. O consciously and unconsciously had set a template for a family romance in which his father (policeman and judge) interfered in his access to his mother and he remained stuck and submissive in this position. This had been repeated over and over in his affairs, and then with me in the transference, while his wife and I alternated parts, and often played the roles of policeman and judge. This configuration became complicated once his father fell ill and died just as he had successfully achieved his graduate degree. By understanding the formal features of this dilemma, we were able, over time, to change its elements so that Mr. O was able to leave his mother's lap, mourn his father, take on the role of husband and father, thus allowing his wife to play her part as mother and lover.

Ms. A

In another example, a young woman who had been rejected by her mother had come to me with a manic delusion that she was pregnant and she had, in fact, attempted to cause a miscarriage. Although the fact of her pregnancy was disproved by her gynecologist, she regretted taking this action (which unconsciously resembled her mother's rejection) even in her imagination. My patient arrived one day to say that she had gotten her "dream" job at an abortion clinic. Paradoxically, since she had been about to move away, this meant she could continue the analysis (which was always under threat of being "aborted"). This patient reported, over time, that she often "curled up in the fetal position" at her job, in between sessions. She did not seem to understand the irony of this (a fetus in an abortion clinic) until I observed it. In response, she turned very passive and refused to do any work. I linked this to her becoming a baby and wanting to be held. In time, she had a dream of a kangaroo with a pouch holding a baby. I linked this to her capacity to hold and contain herself as a baby the way her mother never did. She had another dream much later in which she did, in fact, have a baby. My countertransference, which had always been a wish to get rid of this patient, became, in the end, an affectionate one. She eventually moved away and got a more satisfying job in which she did not directly assist in abortions, but instead had a managerial position in an organization that protected women's rights to have access to such clinics.

Ms. B

At the beginning of the analysis, a young female patient, Ms. B, feeling helpless and regretful about not being able to initiate sessions, produced a fantasy of "curling up and dying" on the couch. In a subsequent session, this patient, regretting her inability to initiate contact and risk friendship with another young woman, remarked, "I want to roll over and die." I spontaneously replied, "Maybe you should *roll the dice* ..." Not skipping a beat, the patient countered, "No, I'm never lucky that way, I'd rather roll over and die." In this exchange, I responded to B's expression of regret with a homologous repetition (a kind of rhyme), but one that introduced the idea of taking a gamble, trying her luck. In B's response, she acknowledged the concept of luck (a feature of regret, as in being unlucky, something she complained about incessantly), while at the same time repeating her initial wish, to "roll over and die" (and *not* "roll the dice"). In so doing, she established her agency ("I would rather not..."), albeit in the negative, through her preference for resistance (a form of repetition in the transference). Nonetheless, this repetition represented a slight change in her initial expression and introduced a new idea into the field. Taking a risk, in this case, took into account both the negative and positive valences of initiating or failing to initiate an action: It could either produce *or* repair a regret (or both).

I noted to myself that the expression "*roll over* and die," was a developmental improvement on her earlier wish to "*curl up* and die" (she had, in fact, rolled over on her side). Her desire to initiate contact was reproduced in the transference and represented the fulfillment of a wish (thus producing "a dream"). I observed that she had, in this instance, *tried her luck* by striking up a conversation with me. This repaired to a small degree B's regret over participating in sessions and initiated a mutual process of elaboration: she was learning to *play with me*. Having been homeschooled all her life, B had fiercely resisted her mother's (intrusive and loving) efforts to teach her, and had instead chosen a life that was full of regrets over that unconscious injury to herself and her mother, and which had as a result left her developmentally stuck and consciously miserable. Beginning the analysis *corpsing*, she eventually softened by curling up on my couch, eventually using that state to represent not a corpse, but a baby (lying in a fetal position). Shifting from "curling" into "rolling" represented a movement forwards into being an agent responsible for her own choices: She could now choose to go either way, *roll over and die*, or *roll the dice*, by which I meant go on living. This kind of exchange became characteristic of our work and took on a playful form that became tolerable and, eventually, even pleasurable for her. This small "poem" was a small part of a much larger process that built on countless such repetitions (for example, when *hook*worms turned into *heart*worms), which required that I pay close attention to the form of rapport emerging in the analysis.

Conclusion

Regret is backward-looking. Emily Dickinson first describes remorse as "Memory—awake—/Her parties all astir—/A Presence of Departed Acts—/At window—and at Door" [#744]. This paradox—the Dickinsonian presence in absence—articulates the paradox of regret, in which the will is both asserted and denied. The agent, reliving the moment, wishes it had been otherwise, but is unable to alter what has already passed: The intentional act has been launched into the world (out the window and the door) and cannot now be recalled. Nonetheless, it *is* recalled (remembered) again and again; its constituent "parties" are astir at the agent's call, and may be mobilized for future action. Thus, regret is also forward-looking; it engenders a new set of possibilities (what *could* have happened; if *only* …) that is projected into the future. Even as the agent dissects the scene of regret, he is improvising alternatives that revise or avoid the regretted outcome. This imaginative act has its counterpart in the material world. In response to regret, the agent is driven to rectify or repair the regrettable situation. Together, the retrospective and the reparative drives produce the kinetic energy of regret, what I call a *surge of affect*. This surge of affect is released by the agent, and is accompanied by an aesthetic surge at the level of the text. The text is suddenly full of the agent's unrealized choices and reparative desires, and these features must be organized into a coherent story. Thus, regret is highly creative even as it works in the face of loss; the scene of regret becomes a blueprint for the future.

In analysis, the working through of regret is the result of understanding and accepting one's role in the regrettable situation (agent-regret), the harvesting of the unconscious and conscious symbols generated by the affect of regret (surge of affect), and, ultimately, the harnessing of this psychic, libidinal, and aesthetic energy towards reparation. The person feeling regret seeks to avoid a repetition of the identical. The agent generates many symbolic variants to ward off the pain, moving back and forth in time and space, in the interest of mastering the anxiety produced by the situation. The surge of affect is simultaneously an upswell of symbolic energy, and a temporary undoing (a kind of regression), that, when successfully harnessed in mourning, allows for a reworking of the basic elements of the traumatic scene. Using the economic point of view as proposed by de M'Uzan, there is an eruption in the analysis of libidinal energy that provokes turmoil and that is followed by the rearrangement or redistribution of these libidinal cathexes. The working through of regret generates many variations of theme and situation to arrive at a developmental and creative resolution of a painful psychological dilemma. In literature, this is paralleled by the emergence of a character within a world populated by other characters, the development of a regrettable situation that swells into affective feeling and symbolic excess, and the reworking of this situation towards a satisfactory resolution of the plot. Regret is also expressed in poetry, in its ludic significance and in the formal arrangement of its parts, and in the visual realm, through film. Each genre of regret plays its part in psychoanalytic treatment.

Acknowledgments

The author wishes to thank Wendy Katz and Klaus Wiedermann for their helpful comments on earlier drafts of this essay.

Notes

1. The form is as follows, where each numeral indicates the stanza position and the letters represent end-words:

   1. ABCDEF
   2. FAEBDC
   3. CFDABE
   4. ECBFAD
   5. DEACFB
   6. BDFECA
   7. (envoi) ECA or ACE

CHAPTER FIVE

Of regret and Plato's ghost

Nilofer Kaul

In a conversation with the psychoanalyst Arabella Kurtz, Coetzee speaks of the impossibility of writing a story which ends,

> "And his secret was forgotten and he lived happily ever after" …
> you cannot have such a story, at least not in its straightforward
> unironic version. In other words, not only the moral-religious tra-
> dition, but … perhaps even the very form of the story, refuse to
> concede that the past can be buried … there is a sense in which the
> great plot-shapes submit to, or evoke the notion of justice. That is
> to say, the story that can be told—the story of the man who tries
> but fails to bury the past—tells us something about cosmic justice;
> whereas the story that cannot be told—the story of the man who
> buries the past and lives happily ever after—cannot be told because
> it lacks justness. (Coetzee & Kurtz, 2015, pp. 32–33)

It is not so much that the past must be unearthed; in fact it often is not.
But more profoundly perhaps, moral-ethical questions and in particular
remorse, seem to be embedded in the very form of a story. It is the
psychic encounter with the transgression that then generates the story
and regret is one possible response to remorse.

The opacity of the word "regret" distinguishes it from its cousins: remorse, compunction, sorrow. Etymologically, the route can be traced to the Middle English *regretten*, the Anglo-French *regreter*, from *re-* + *-greter* (perhaps of Germanic origin; akin to Old Norse *grāta* to weep) and "to bewail the dead" (*Webster's New World Dictionary*, 1987, p. 1196). There are different possible ways of using it. It is used to prefix sorrow, repentance, distress. It is also used formally to speak of "failure to comply" (*Oxford English Reference Dictionary*, 1995, p. 1215). Sometimes, however, regret conveys not one's own loss but also an assurance of sincerity in contexts that appear ambivalent or culpable—"I regret having to lay you off" sounds valid while "I regret having cancer" is not. In the latter case, there is no doubt over either the enormity or the significance of the news. In this last sense, the antithesis to "regret" with its clipped restraint is "excessive." In the latter use it implies moderation, a tempered emotion, not a coming undone. This use would find no place in melodrama or in tragedy. It seems to stop short of deep emotion, tragedy, waste. There seems to be, in its sonorous, consonant-ridden sound, an attempt at containing the profusion of "too-muchness." So it seems the word has traveled a long way from bewailing to a formal expression of something unfortunate. The uses of the word tell a story about how the intensity, or the "temperature and distance" has fluctuated (Meltzer, 1976). Its etymological lineage also embodies how far the word has traveled from its origins: as if it had shed its weight. Is that really so? Is it possible for us to read a story here? Do we see this as a historical-cultural journey? Or as an intrapsychic one?

In this chapter, I will look at the varied uses of the word psychoanalytically by examining some literary instances of regret. I will search some narratives, long and short, to see the occurrence of the word. Nostalgia captures a large chunk of this territory. A short story by Willa Cather is a good instance of what Akhtar (1996) calls "if only ...." I will then discuss briefly a couple of stories by Alice Munro where the "hyperbolic" tone is replaced by a somewhat matter-of-fact one. The syntax of regret is interrupted by retrospective learning and to borrow from Yeats (1936), "what then" comes to replace "if only." In the second Munro story in the following section, regret flares up in the arrangement of lines. While Munro rejects sentimentality in different ways, the cadences, the form, the tense, and the non sequitur arrangement of her prose emotionally realigns the pain, which is not in the content, but in the dislocated rhythms of her writing. The final section looks at

Disgrace by Coetzee (1999) where "regret" smacks of ritual rather than reparation; here we see the word as a hollowed-out shell. But the book is also about a journey into the internal world. Cape Town, where he lives, represents surface (narcissism) while in Eastern Cape, where his daughter Lucy lives, he forages and finds that underlying the narcissism is pain, sadness, and loss.

From "if only" to "what then"

Fantasies by their nature, Akhtar (1996) observes, deny reality, often following either an "if only" or "someday ..." structure.

> "If only" looks back at the past, while "someday ..." may have an untenable optimism about the future. It is, however, unmistakable that the nostalgic individual ... is not only looking for the lost object but for an idealized object, and even more importantly, for the time before the object was lost. This covert element of search in the nostalgic hand-wringing is a clue to the psychodynamic kinship between the "if only" and "someday ..." fantasies. (p. 735)

What is common to these two sets of fantasies is that they seek to evade the inevitability of turns already taken. Willa Cather's (1911) relatively obscure and arguably queer story, "The Joy of Nelly Deane" illuminates the way these ubiquitous fantasies structure narrative forms. This story lays out the terrain of "if only" and this is compared later with a story by Alice Munro that follows an antithetical syntax of "what then" which I suggest as a counterpoint to "if only" from the opposite end of the spectrum. In the case of Munro's story, I read it as the former. It is told by a woman who loved the eponymous heroine, Nelly, who is married off to a miser and dies during childbirth. The narrator who has moved away from the hometown (Riverbend) hears of this years later:

> It was ten years before I again visited Riverbend. I had been in Rome for a long time, and had fallen into bitter homesickness ... Ah, that was what I wanted, to see Nelly's children! The wish came aching from my heart along with bitter homesick tears; along with a quick, torturing recollection ... chattering girl beside me ... It felt even then, when we sat together, it was all arranged, written out like a story, that at this moment I should be sitting among the crumbling

bricks and drying grass and she should be lying in the place I knew
so well, on that green hill far away. (p. 216)

The "homesickness" (nostalgia comes from the Greek *nostos*—to return
home, and *algia*—pain) has turned "bitter," as the narrator has tried
to escape while she "roams" (Rome) away from her "natural" course
(Riverbend, a metaphor for queerness?). When she finds out the circumstances of Nelly's death—the mishandling by the obstinate husband
who calls in the wrong doctor—she cries out: "Oh, Mrs. Dow, then it
needn't have been?" To which Mrs. Dow responds: "We mustn't look at
it that way, dear ... we mustn't let ourselves" (p. 218).

The unmistakable subtext suggests that the narrator fled from desires
that seemed to "bend" away from the course. This is also the moment
she regrets her anger and disappointment. The "if only" syntax works
as a smokescreen which conceals psychic truths that are embedded.
Nelly, as the forbidden object of desire, is the denied truth of the story,
where this very denial becomes the font for the story. Nostalgia for
lost time becomes a displaced affective ruse for the "love that dare
not speak its name." Regret here becomes an attempt to contain the
unutterable tenor of the real loss; ruling out any possibility of mourning.
The mean-spirited husband becomes the fall guy upon whom blame
must be projected rather than shameful love acknowledged. Nostalgia
with its bittersweet yearning leans towards melancholia which the voice
of Mrs. Dow prohibits. She encourages the contact between Nelly's
baby and the narrator, which is seen as reparative but is also secretly
a compensation.

The poignancy here is in the unnameable nature of the loss: When
the desire/object is unnameable, how can the loss be mourned? Regret
screens the truth, but reveals the loss. We can see melodrama with
its excessive sentiment and its persecutory structure of villains and
scoundrels and the sacred figure of Nelly as helpless victim. This clearly
obfuscates the true nub of suffering. Perhaps the appeal of melodrama
itself can be understood here as allowing some release of pain, but
somehow deflected, diverted, and located away from the wound. It
fosters melancholia by avoiding mourning. Pain intercedes on behalf
of the psyche and avoids the naming of the lost object. The syntax of
"if only" is haunted by what Adam Phillips (2012) calls the spectre of
"unlived lives"—all those multitudinous possible routes we could have
taken. "Our lives become an elegy," he writes, "to needs unmet and

desires sacrificed, to possibilities refused, to roads not taken ... the myth of potential makes mourning and complaining feel like the realest things we ever do; and makes of our frustration a secret life of grudges" (p. xiii). The quantum of regret by the narrator in Nelly Deane's story is unrestrained. But the story is an elaborate alibi for the real loss. The melodramatic plot and excessiveness of regret indicate the heaviness of what is silenced: Queer love is like the corpse in the attic of this story and the regret "if only" an attempt to contain this ineffable secret.

By way of contrast, I will look at a passage from Alice Munro's story, "What is Remembered" (2001), which marks a break from exaggerated sentiment. The reason I draw upon Munro's chiseled writing is to see how emotionality is embedded in the form, in the margins of the story, in the use of tense, in the pileup of inconsequential details that suggest the weight of emotion through form rather than words. I will look at the opening passage of the story to highlight the creation of an idiom of pain:

> In a hotel room in Vancouver, Meriel as a young woman is putting on her short white summer gloves. She wears a beige linen dress and a flimsy white scarf over her hair. Dark hair, at that time. She smiles because she has remembered something that Queen Sirikit of Thailand said, or was quoted as saying, in a magazine. A quote within a quote—something Queen Sirikit said that Balmain said.
>
> "Balmain taught me everything. He said, 'Always wear white gloves. It's best.'"
>
> It's best. Why is she smiling at that? It seems so soft a whisper of advice, such absurd and final wisdom. Her gloved hands are formal, but tender-looking as a kitten's paws. Pierre asks why she's smiling and she says, "Nothing," then tells him.
>
> He says, "Who is Balmain?"
>
> They were getting ready to go to a funeral. (p. 219)

I quote this at some length so we can pay close attention to some of its formal features which recur in her writing. The title of the story has already informed us about the idiosyncrasy of memory. We know this time is long gone, because Meriel is a young woman at the time. But written in the present continuous, it juxtaposes the present we inhabit in clock time (external reality) alongside psychic time (internal reality). The use of the present continuous for a long ago time corresponds to the presence of the past in the present. This is reiterated in the third line again. "Dark hair, at that time." Here the tense is unspecified. "Dark hair" is unspecific, but "at that time" wedges in time long gone by. The narrator's voice reports Meriel remembering something said by Queen Sirikit, who remembers Balmain. This visual frame of narrator looking back at Meriel who's looking back at Queen Sirikit who's looking back at Balmain is framed like a quote within a quote within a quote. It brings to mind Balter's (2006) ideas on "nested ideation": "Studies of nested ideation in dreams and in art both explore and elaborate two kinds of denial through representations of nonreality ('It is only a dream!' and 'It is only a work of art!'). Therefore, this is a very circumscribed investigation" (p. 440).

These nested frames here look back yearningly at a past looking back at another past. Different eras of time are evoked and multiple temporalities reveal psychic time as intricately inlaid textures within textures. We lose a sense of "now," and as time is denied, so is the painful reality! The "soft whisper of advice" brings in the tenderness of a bygone time and "absurd and final wisdom" gently undercuts the poignancy with irony. Pierre's matter-of-fact question which cuts into the dreamy reminiscence, the non sequitur quality of memory are voices lost but whose traces remain. From here, the tense shifts to a simple past, "They were getting ready to go to a funeral ...": Suddenly the ephemeral quality of memory is intercut with the straightforward third person, simple past. But the mood has been set, the frame and theme established. Meriel reminisces about an adventure she had with a guest who drops her after the funeral. This liaison is like a secret patch of memory which she embroiders, stitching, unstitching, but always holding it as a parallel life which runs alongside her real life. In her secret life, she unpacks and edits it:

> Take me, was what she had said. Take me somewhere else, not Let's go somewhere else. That is important to her. The risk, the transfer of power ... in all her reliving of this moment—of the erotic slide ... He took her to the apartment ... She would have preferred another scene, and that was the one she substituted in her memory ... for years to come. She would keep picking up things she'd missed, and these would still jolt her ... (pp. 235–236)
>
> The fact that he was dead did not seem to have much effect on her daydreams—if that was what you call them. The ones in which she imagined chance meetings or even desperately arranged reunions, had never a foothold in reality ... (p. 236)

When she was on her way home that night it started to rain, not very hard ... So she stayed looking at the froth stirred up in the wake of the boat, and the thought occurred to her that in a certain kind of story—not the kind anybody wrote anymore—the thing for her to do would be to throw herself into the water ... Was she tempted? She was probably just imagining herself being tempted ... (p. 241)

Writing about the non-lexical aspects of analytic communication, Meltzer (1976) notes the musicality "tone, rhythm, key, volume, timbre" (p. 25) as enabling a tuning in with unconscious communication. Transposing this onto a written text, we might see, for instance, the shifting tense from one passage to another is like the choir of instruments that allow the music to follow the shifting moods: excited, overwhelmed, lustful, remorseful, and finally ironic. The irony is important, lest the wistfulness, the evanescence, the nuances descend into romanticisation—which would be a travesty of the emotional experience. Perhaps what we denigrate as sentimentality is just such a false set of displaced affects which evades the core of the suffering and relocates it elsewhere; and romanticising would then be a symptom of this. This story is woven with the skeins of regret but it is not about wrong choices or mistakes. She regrets neither her unfaithfulness nor her marriage, but the inevitability and the irrevocability of choices which betoken ultimately the finitude of life. The act of looking back seems to have the sepia colors of nostalgia which it denies: It is so much water under the bridge now. However, it is the simultaneity of two vertices that give it poignancy: the present and presumably the future from where it is utterly insignificant and the past when it was portentous. This juxtaposition itself creates the lyric of regret.

The nostalgic regret in Cather's story for a dead beloved is more bearable than to mourn a life with her that could never have been. Her love was never reciprocated and was not even acknowledged. In Nelly Deane's story, the ostensible regret is that Nelly's death is avoidable, but this appears to cloak and obfuscate the truth. The narrative remains pregnant with the repressed wish that Nelly need not have married, and therefore could have remained the beloved of the narrator and alive. When this truth is obfuscated, pain is retained as a shadow of the real loss and takes on the syntax of regret, which we may refer to as "if only."

Munro's story in the same section, rejects "if only." Here regret is in the idiom and form, not in the content. The narrator may have remembered more accurately and if she had, she could have had another life, not better, just different. In the first story of Munro's, memories are woven into the present. The story muses on the nature of memory as fantasy as memories are tweaked and fiddled with constantly to compensate for the dreariness of quotidian life. Our memories as they dwell in fantasies sustain our lives, not escape them here. This notion of memory does not take on the dimension of regret. The malleability of memory is used to contain the discontentment. Paradoxically, even as the escapade remains the stuff of lifelong fantasy, it helps reinforce reality, rather than deny it. Had she remembered differently, she muses, her life may have been quite different, but she is quick to add, "not better," Nostalgic rhythms jostle against the questionable fantasy of regret. The story is located on the conversation between the paranoid-schizoid and depressive positions. The narcissistic fantasy embedded in "if only" gives way to a more depressive position, which one might term, following Yeats's (1936) poem, *What then?* If the paranoid-schizoid can be seen in Cather where there is an external agent of badness (husband), here the narrator strenuously steers the memory boat away from nostalgic "if only" ruminations towards a more depressive reminder that "even if things had worked the way she had desired, her life would have been only different and not better" (p. 242). There is only the internal machinery that has to be navigated and she does it by steering memories. She can hold in her mind different possibilities, but they do not carry with them unfulfilled promises.

Containing despair

> Personally of course I regret everything. / Not a word, not a deed, not a thought, not a need, / not a grief, not a joy, not a girl, not a boy, / not a doubt, not a trust, not a scorn, not a lust, / not a hope, not a fear, not a smile, not a tear, / not a name, not a face, no time, no place ... that I do not regret, exceedingly. / An ordure, from beginning to end. (Beckett, 1953, p. 37)

Unsurprisingly, these mordant lines from Beckett rip open the seams which encase the word "regret" and explode the walls of regret to reveal failed containment, taking us closer to the etymological origins of the word. The short story by Munro, "Gravel" (2011) deals with a terrible tragedy but the circuitousness of its narration resembles the path of sidestepped grief. This "pit" of grief has been filled with the gravel of life. But gravel can only try to fill, it cannot remove the pit. It is this throbbing presence of a wound that can never go which reverberates through the story. "At that time," the narrator tells us, "we were living beside a gravel pit" (p. 91). Once again, memory allows the muting of light and affect:

> My mother was the one who insisted on calling attention to it. "We live by the gravel pit out the service-station road," she'd tell people and laugh ... I barely remember that life. That is, I remember some parts of it clearly, but without the links you need to form a proper picture. (p. 91)

Some sense of impending disaster is ushered in by the choppiness of the narrative, its back and forth rhythm of tenses. The mother's memory feels remote with time; the tone also indicates an estrangement between the mother with her brittle laughter and the daughter/ narrator. She seems to be encircling an event that is not shared till much later, something which the gravel pit seems to represent. Slowly the pieces coalesce. The mother who was pregnant with her lover's child had walked away from her old life taking along her two daughters and dog. The narrator says,

> I do know, though I don't remember it, that my father wept and for a whole day followed my mother around the house, not letting her out of his sight and refusing to believe her ... and instead of telling him anything to make him feel better, she told him something that made him feel worse ... She told him the baby was Neal's ... My father gave up weeping. He had to get back to work. (p. 94)

The catastrophic beginning is captured in these brief lines, where mourning is amputated and regret is startlingly absent. That "He had to get back to work" forecloses (and therefore forbids?) mourning. The grief is in the foreclosed sentence. The rupturing of the family which has torn them apart is treated with breezy casualness if not insouciance: "... my father wept and for a whole day followed my mother ..." She stays distant from the moment, "does not remember, but has been told," to paraphrase. But the shadow of the catastrophe hangs over us from the beginning. And this despite the repeated disavowals:

> Sometimes I wondered about our other house. I didn't exactly miss it or want to live there again—I just wondered where it had gone. (p. 96)
>   What did he think of all this? Neal. His philosophy, as he put it later was to welcome whatever happened. Everything is a gift. We give and we take. (p. 94)

"What did the mother's lover have to say?" she muses. Here the word "later" is again ominous, reminding us of the treachery of the gravel pit. Caro, the elder of the two girls, drowns in a peculiar accident which remains unclear in the narrator's rendition. Out on a walk, that fateful day, Caro had instructed her sister to go back to the trailer van and tell the mother and her lover, Neal, that:

> … the dog had fallen into the water … Caro instructed me to do as I was told. Why? I may have just said that, or I may have just stood there not obeying … [but] When I dream of this, I am always running … All I have to do is watch and be happy—nothing required of me, after all. (p. 103)

She dips her toes into the moment when she says, she may have just stood there not obeying, but then the voice returns to the present:

> Josie is the only person who ever talks about Caro, and even she doesn't do it often. She does say that my father doesn't hold my mother responsible. My mother cannot be made to recall any of those times, and I don't bother her with them. I know that she has driven down the lane we lived on, and found it quite changed … I went down the lane myself but did not tell anyone. All the eviscerating that is done in families strikes me as a mistake. (p. 107)

Both mother and daughter drive down memory lane. But they go there separately, each wrapped in her peculiar anguish and shame. The darkness of an internal world can never be shared, lest the mutual rage explodes the shreds they have held onto. An emotional fork seems to shape the story—a voice that decries excessiveness, muffled grief, but which is quickly followed by the refusal:

> Accept everything and then tragedy disappears. Or tragedy light-ens … "I see what he [Neal] meant. It really is the right thing to do. But in my mind, Caro keeps running at the water and throwing herself in, as if in triumph, and I'm still caught, waiting for her to explain to me, waiting for the splash". (p. 109)

This recurrent dream betrays the presence of the past, which the words shrug off. She still awaits an explanation, the paralysis of that moment carries on. She's still awaiting understanding, because that involves letting go of Caro and her own omnipotence. Both mother and daughter drive around the lane separately, each one unable to relinquish the pain and the subsequent omnipotence latent in "if only …" This inability to relinquish the object, with all its concomitant pain and the crushing loss of omnipotence is shared by the narrator of this story as well as Cather's. But here we see painful reality as modified by the narration. The details of the past event are punctuated by age and distance, indicating the uncontainability of the loss; whereas in Cather's story it dwells in the hushed silences, reality is evaded. "Such a manoeuvre," Bion writes, "is intended not to affirm but to deny reality, not to represent an emo-tional experience but to misrepresent it to make it appear to be a fulfil-ment rather than a striving for fulfilment" (1962, p. 49). Cather's story misrepresents the emotional truth and the melancholic strand of regret which provides the background strumming, is woven out of just such a painful evasion of the truth; in "Gravel," the remorse is almost too great, it is in fact uncontainable. The mother and the daughter can drive back to the old lane, but never have it back. Nor avow the culpability. But this is not to obfuscate, because the magnitude of remorse demands private suffering, there is no reprieve, no shared suffering that alleviates the pain. The narrative attempts to contain this as do the different voices in the story. Not saying it directly is here not denial, but acknowledg-ment that to put it down in words is to try to seek comfort and to seek reprieve which would be wrong. The gravel pit which stands for the pit of despair and remorse is about the attempt to symbolise. But while it endeavors to contain, it is more like a burial ground that holds in the dead remains, rather than a container that metabolizes grief. "Gravel" can be read as a story about the limits of containment. It may be read to represent the twin aspects of the word "regret" which is the impulse to contain (evident in writing the story, finding a metaphor) but also the immutable aspect of the remorse which refuses containment and collapses into a pit. Nelly's death, unlike Caro's, is metonymic, it lends itself to the expression of loss, it is associated to her unnameable loss, but it is not the loss itself. She cannot mourn what she lost, because the object of love is yet to be recognized. Queer love is yet unnamed and Cather's stories are full of substitute deaths, driven by a need to hunt for a substitute tragedy, and all the time, striking some false notes (hyperbole) evident in melodrama.

From shame to remorse

David Lurie, a middle-aged professor of English in Cape Town, twice divorced, has only the occasional comfort of prostitutes, teaches romantic poetry to desultory students, and is trying to write an opera based on the lurid life of Byron. His ecstasies seem all out of place, his life irrelevant. Life itself is puttering out, when in walks this student who stirs him. He allows himself to be swept by Melanie Isaacs, with whom he has an affair after the briefest pursuit. For some moments, his moribund life is lifted out of its dreariness and there's a flicker of hope. It all ends badly. A complaint is filed against him by her, there is a scandal, and he becomes a pariah. When he consults his lawyer, the latter asks him, "Was it serious?" And he responds, "Would serious-ness have made it better or worse? After a certain age, all affairs are serious. Like heart attacks" (Coetzee, 1991, p. 42). His truth here is that for him it was a matter of life and death. His life is empty from the moment the novel opens and it is an irredeemable deadness, till the girl crosses his path.

His ex-wife, Rosalind, tells him off at dinner. He reflects later upon her brutal words and admits, "Perhaps it is the right of the young to be protected from the sight of their elders in the throes of passion. That is what whores are for, after all: to put up with the ecstasies of the unlovely" (p. 44). He feels this to be true. When called in by the committee after his resignation, he is charged, "Ms. Isaacs did not attend … or submit all the written work … for which you have given her credit." He responds, "I plead guilty to both charges." He confesses, but there is a bloodthirsty clamour for "abasement." He has a choice: He can express his regret and return to his job, or lose his job. The media turns up hungrily:

> "Do you regret what you did?"
> "No," he says. "I was enriched by the experience." He appears stony and one is tempted to add heroically so.
> "Manas," he says to a well-meaning colleague, "we went through the repentance business yesterday. I told you what I thought. I won't do it ... I pleaded guilty, secular plea. That plea should suffice. Repentance is neither here nor there. Repentance belongs to another world, to another universe of discourse." (p. 58)

Lurie here waves off guilt and remorse as out of place in a secular world. He is being tried and the register ought to be secular, legal. He does not submit to the clamor for public avowals. Does he sincerely feel remorse? He says he doesn't, not on the charges he's facing. He does not consider it in the metallic light of "abuse." Honesty must be brutal and towards that all sentiments must be cast aside that soften the edges of truth, and political correctness which is the contemporary version of sanctimony must be dispensed with. "He has never been afraid to follow a thought down its winding track, and he is not afraid now" (p. 76).

Lurie feels antiquated. He is writing on Byron's period in Italy, where he went to escape a scandal; where he also had his last big affair. This dovetails Lurie's own life. It seems as if his refusal to express regret is not so much a lack of reparative guilt, as it is a defiance of a sanctimonious culture that seeks ritual expressions of guilt. Whatever he is, he remains authentic to his feelings, to his emotional truth. But it is a partial truth, we learn along with him. For him to regret possibly his last great affair feels false and the emptiness of his life resonates powerfully with the reader. The closest to family he can claim is his daughter Lucy, who lives a peasant life on a smallholding. She has clearly turned her back on her parental legacy of bourgeois white intelligentsia. These two solitary figures cohabit for much of the novel. She asks him why he's so unbending, he could have offered to have done counselling, after all, it's an admission to being imperfect. He says he's too old-fashioned for public apology, that he would rather be shot. What he does not say is that reparation must emerge from guilt—or more accurately remorse, not shame and disgrace.

"No appeal. I am not complaining. One can't plead guilty to charges
of turpitude and expect a flood of sympathy in return. Not after a
certain age. After a certain age one is simply no longer appealing,
and that's that. One just has to buckle down and live out the rest of
one's life. Serve one's time." (p. 67)

His "disgrace" comes from the world that valorizes superficial gestures
and rituals; it is a culture of shame, located very far from the world of
remorse. During the trial he says:

"Our paths crossed. Words passed between us … Suffice it to say
that Eros entered. After that I was not the same … It is not a defence.
You want a confession, I give you confession. As for the impulse it
was far from ungovernable. I have denied similar impulses many
times in the past, I am ashamed to say." (p. 52)

He is "ashamed." That is also why the register of remorse is out of
place. His fatal flaw is narcissism in that there is no otherness; which
has an obvious resonance as a white man in South Africa. The breach
of code does not require remorse, but symbolic contrition, ritual abjec-
tion. He refuses hypocrisy which substitutes for contrition in a post-
remorse culture.

Living with Lucy is in fact his encounter with otherness. It is where
he sees her living so far from his academic life in which he finds mean-
inglessness and boredom; here in the wild regions, he sees hate in
visceral ways; Lucy is raped. They survive it. Towards the end he has
been able to make connections with the odd circle. He helps bury cast-
away dogs:

The dogs are brought to the clinic because they are unwanted:
because we are too menny … He may not be their savior … he
has become a dog-man: a dog undertaker; a dog psychopomp; a
harijan … Curious that a man as selfish as he should be offering
himself to the service of dead dogs. There must be other, more
productive ways of giving himself … But there are other people
to do these things—the animal welfare thing, the social rehabili-
tation thing, even the Byron thing. He saves the honor of corpses
because there is no one else stupid enough to do it. That is what he
is becoming: stupid, daft, wrongheaded. (p. 146)

The punishment is complete in one sense of the term: From teaching poetry, he is now helping to lovingly kill unwanted dogs. The reparation is embedded in the actions, even as the ironic tone dismisses an old-fashioned language of reparation and remorse; what it is actually turning away from are the gestures that have come to replace this. In the world he inhabits, shame substitutes guilt, regret replaces remorse, counselling sessions act as confession boxes, and so on. Lurie has to encounter otherness; the painfulness of this encounter is the price he pays for his selfishness. This had to come from within him and hence he had to turn away from its cynical substitute. To express a formal regret there would have saved him from the utter alienation he actually undergoes, but it would never have allowed him to refind a meaningful contact with another, as he does with Lucy and her cohorts.

The first part of the novel set in Cape Town and a shallow academic world is not so much a cause of his moral turpitude, but a symptom of it. He has been unable to forge a real communication and contact with anybody. He has to make do with occasional bouts of empty sex. Going to Lucy's world with all its alienating otherness, its lack of sophistication, its bareness and frugality, he is forced to look within; and the brutal rape of Lucy, the attack on her dogs and belongings bring in him tenderness, fear, and concern. The relentlessly ironic stripping of meaning gives way to deeper, more painful underlying parts. He drives back to George and tracks down Melanie's father. Mr. Isaacs invites him home for dinner. The meal is awkward and full of prevarications. Then it is time to go and he says:

> "One word more, then I am finished. It could have turned out differently, I believe between the two of us, despite our ages. But there was something I failed to supply, something"—he hunts for the word—"lyrical. I lack the lyrical. I manage love too well. Even when I burn I don't sing, if you understand me. For which I am sorry. I am sorry for what I took your daughter through ... I apologize for the grief I caused you and Mrs. Isaacs. I ask for your pardon." (p. 171)

So, where at the beginning, he refuses to comply with expressing regret, by the end he feels contrition. Not for the situation, but for a failing in his character. His failure is in fact the blindness to the other. Irony represents here, as it sometimes does, the denial or even denudation of meaning. In fact it may not be too much of a stretch to argue that if regret as an affect attempts to contain intensity, irony as a mode attempts to contain through denial and disavowal. The story takes a deeply ethical turn towards reparation, and through that suffering, meaning emerges; meaning is not in writing Byron librettos but in being able to feel and "sing." The novel carries almost through it a tension between an ironic stance and an ethical one. And yet in a world where sincerity is always suspect, for the regret to be believable, there must be the prior establishment of Lurie's amoral irony.

When he comes to Lucy, he is totally bereft of honor and money. She suggests that he helps Bev Shaw who helps dogs die. He says he will help as long as he is not "expected to become a better person." But as if belying his cynicism, while talking to Lucy he also admits that every woman he has encountered has taught him something about himself. We can also see the formal and structural cleavage in the novel as two different worlds that Lurie inhabits. There are two different responses to a morally emptied universe, the collusion by his colleagues or a cynical, grandiose amorality. But when he journeys away from this world to his daughter's, the story takes an ethical turn. Pitted against the elements, stripped of the grandiose cover of brilliant wit, he is reduced to ordinariness, and confronted by the starkness of his narcissism.

Disgrace captures the journey of the word. It travels from a narcissistic plane where it is a byword for hypocrisy: Where there is an absence of remorse or concern, regret is an empty shell. But eventually the protagonist in exile learns to bear remorse, and mourns, and the original meaning of the word is restored. The loneliness is relentless but he finds shreds of meaning in helping dying dogs to die: there is an identification with the lowliest and most unwanted. When he is able to bear his pain, he also restores the original meaning of the word. This is also conveyed tonally by the whittling down of his relentlessly ironic voice. He learns to bear the suffering which was buried under his narcissistic relation to the world.

Coetzee believes that this painful encounter seems to be demanded by the very form of the story. Is it even possible for there to be a story that does not carry within it a lattice of morality, however hidden? In the story of Lurie is also the story of the word's journey from an empty shell back to its original meaning of bewailing and pain. This journey of Lurie's from the narcissistic city into a remorse-bearing wilderness feels analogous to the psychoanalytic quest. The breakdown of all internal objects brings a catastrophe which is at the center of the novel, but the journey does not end with the catastrophe; by contrast in Munro's second story, the messiness remains unresolved as the dream keeps recurring and the catastrophe occupies both center stage and the immutability of grief. Here the suturing of the wound is not a possibility.

To end with a discussion on *Disgrace* is to return to Coetzee's point about the inextricability of morality and narrative. If this novel is read politically, which it seems to invite, it seems to suggest that the white man's "turning a blind eye" from the truth, creating a libretto to turn a deaf ear to the atrocities must lead to a moral bankruptcy (Steiner, 1985). In that sense, David Lurie is a fiercely honest admission to such moral failure. His inability to feel for the other is admirable because he exposes the smugness with which "regret" is bandied about. In order to restore emotionality, there has to be the recognition of otherness and the journey to this deeply painful truth is what "regret" was meant to be. To him and his ilk, this turning away comes at the cost of complete alienation from the self. The savage violence brings on a catastrophe that allows for the working-through at the end.

We might find here a primitive notion of equalizing, injustice for injustice (an eye for an eye, a tooth for a tooth), which seems to structure the book and illuminate Coetzee's point about the inextricable tie of narrative with morality. There are also echoes here of the Truth and Reconciliation Commission. Interestingly we can read this story both intrapsychically and politically, and depending on which vertex we read it from, the journey can be read as internal as well as allegorical. Tempting as it might be to read it only as a political allegory or a cultural commentary, however, takes away from the poignancy of the internal journey which is at the heart of the subjectivity of both narrative and psychoanalysis. It would also denude the peculiarity of Lurie's choices and his own distance from the cynical world he is a part of. The return of the repressed is not just a function of the harsh superego, but what we seem to need to create in order to keep our disorderly selves in check. Narrative, it seems, is shaped by the Scylla of transgression and the Charybdis of reparation.

Conclusion

"Nothing will come of nothing, speak again ...". In this line from Shakespeare's *King Lear* (1606, p. 104), which, in many ways, is the quintessential play about regret, King Lear asks Cordelia famously to revise her words, or regret the consequences. Blow after cruel blow, it is he who must learn to regret the consequences: "I have no way and therefore want no eyes, I stumbled when I saw" (p. 206). Lear mourns that he could not see the truth when he had eyes, and therefore Oedipus-like, he deserves blindness.

Like all affects, regret too can be misleading. There is a kind of swimming against the current of psychoanalysis when we try to define an affect, because what we see is never what we get; in fact we have to remind ourselves to keep peeling the layers of the onion. Nevertheless, as the rug of meaning threatens to get pulled away from under us, we still try to stand on a vestibule and map affects. Freud obviously paves the way for such a language of suspicion. Walking down through a "smiling countryside" (Freud, 1916a, p. 305) one summer evening, with Lou-Andreas Salome and the poet Rilke, he found himself surprised by the refusal on the part of his companions to take pleasure in the countryside. The knowledge of its transience appears to mar the moment for them, he notes with surprise. He finds two responses to transience: one of anguish, the other of rebellion. Neither can accept the transience, Freud (1916a) writes, because:

> ... what spoilt their enjoyment of beauty must have been a revolt in their minds against mourning. The idea that all this beauty was transient was giving these two sensitive minds a foretaste of mourning over its decease; and, since the mind instinctively recoils from anything that is painful, they felt their enjoyment of beauty interfered with by thoughts of its transience. (p. 306)

When the mind recoils thus from pain, it also abjures the pleasure and the transient nature of all beauty, and nostalgic regret forms a melancholic substitute for mourning.

Having looked passingly at a few stories, what we might cull from here is that there is a lability in the word which can be seen by comparing its etymological origin to its more common usage. The word allows a gathering in of the emotion it refers to, representing an attempt at containment while its more prevalent usage betrays the terror of its intense potential. Harking back to Beckett's tragicomic lines from *Watt*, it might be possible to conjecture from this that culture frowns upon what is excessive, ushered it seems by the fears of catastrophic breakdown. We can also see the terror of excessiveness embodied in the consecration of work of which the Protestant work ethic is just one instance; while the underside reveals a demonization of dysfunctionality as pathology.

What it does sanction often is a displacement of this excessiveness onto false theatres which spawn melodrama, sentimentality, and exaggerated affect pinned onto mismatched contexts. The shrinking of the emotion linked to the word "regret" tells a story that embodies the psychic terror of catastrophic collapse which is then marshalled into a collusive culture of avoidance. So instead of asking the question which we are often carrying in our heads constantly—is it the psychic or the cultural or is it the inside or the outside—here, for a moment we can tarry and say, in the journey of this word and its "penumbra of associations," lies a pause where the outside, the cultural, the collective, come together with the psychic, the solitary terrors. Eventually, what is at the heart of the matter is the terror of being overwhelmed by our helplessness. "It is a mark of our own resistance to our helplessness," Phillips (2010) writes, "that we deem the ineluctable to be catastrophic; as though anything we don't make for ourselves is bad for us" (p. 148).

CHAPTER SIX

Regret on the screen and regret as a screen

Apurva Shah

At the very end of Ritesh Batra's movie, *The Lunchbox* (2013), the protagonist, Saajan, overcomes his inhibitions and self-doubts and interrupts the beginning of his retirement to go look for Ila, the woman he has come to love through notes exchanged in the lunchbox she has been sending him, instead of her husband, for months due to a rare routing mistake by a tiffin courier system in Mumbai. Meanwhile Ila, whose secure, if humdrum, life has been turned topsy-turvy by her father's death and the subsequent realization of how unhappy her mother was in their marriage and by the discovery of her own husband's infidelity, has been inspired by her correspondence with Saajan to move to Bhutan with her daughter to try to find genuine happiness. In an ending reminiscent of those of O. Henry, the two are about to miss each other, *again*.[1] Since the scene leaves us hanging, we fear that Saajan will suffer from deep and everlasting regret, a fear so great that most people prefer to believe that they *will* meet, sometime, somewhere, somehow.

There is something about the very experience of regret that many people find disturbing and disrupting. It triggers a profound sadness—the deepest, if the poet John Greenleaf Whittier is to be believed, for his poem "Maud Muller" (1856) contains the famous verse: "For of all sad words of tongue or pen/The saddest are these: 'It might have been!'"[2]

In general, there is a pervasively negative attitude around regret in our society. Most believe one should lead one's life in ways that one should never have to regret anything. And if one does have regrets, it is considered to be useless or worse—it is seen as a sign of pathology, weakness and/or futility. Psychotherapists have various suggestions on how to let go of regrets or overcome them. There are alternative views that have emerged more recently. Landman (1993) writes about the constructive functions of regret, which she considers has the potential to lead to action and transformation. Kavaler-Adler (2013) coins the term "psychic regret," which is critical to bringing to consciousness the guilt surrounding one's aggression to and loss of the primal object, and the developmental mourning that has to take place in order to create authentic psychic change and self-integration.

Perhaps the most poetic and passionate perspective on regret and related phenomena is the one by Adam Phillips (2012). He talks about the universality of regret (and resentment) along with frustration of our desires, and what it creates—an "unlived life," the life we wish we had, that we imagine we could have had, perhaps should have had. While acknowledging that this can lead to an ongoing sense of loss and anger, he feels it can also lure us into the future. Given the Darwinian revolution and the reevaluation of our species as "nothing special," the promise of fulfilling our potential inherent in regret, even if never actualized outside of the imagined but unlived life, sustains us and makes our lived life more bearable and pleasurable.

This chapter first defines and describes regret, differentiates it from remorse, and then discusses some of the possibilities inherent in the experience of regret—its potential to create change and influence the future, positively or negatively—what it *can* do, and often, *does* do. After an overview of the concept and a brief review of the literature, two movies, *The Remains of the Day* and *On the Waterfront* will be discussed in depth to present the case.

A brief literature review

There has been a fair amount of research done on regret in academic and cognitive psychology, especially as it pertains to economic decisions, at least since the early 1980s. A negative affect or event, or a choice in front of us, may trigger counterfactual thinking, in which one imagines alternative realities, contrary to what actually happened or the choices one has, and this generates both negative affects, mainly regret, and positive inferential reasoning, which will lead to an impetus to do better in the future (Kahneman & Tversky, 1982a, 1982b; Landman, 1993; Roese, 1997; Schwartz, 2004, and others).

Regret does not have a strict psychoanalytic definition as it has been, by and large, neglected as a distinct concept. When it does occur, it is, like in our daily usage,[3] not sharply differentiated from remorse. Freud himself never mentions the word "regret" in a technical sense. It is found more than 200 times in his writings, mostly in his letters.[4] He defines remorse, in *Civilization and Its Discontents* (1930a):

> When one has a sense of guilt after having committed a misdeed, and because of it, the feeling should more properly be called remorse. It relates only to a deed that has been done, and, of course, it presupposes that a *conscience*—the readiness to feel guilty—was already in existence before the deed took place. (p. 131, italics in the original)

Freud goes on to say that remorse predated the conscience and feelings of guilt, and arose out of the ambivalent feelings, the love, of the primal horde toward their father after they killed him (p. 132). Melanie Klein (1935) expands on and modifies Freud's concept of remorse and it is central to her theory of the depressive position. But she also rarely mentions regret, with one notable exception. She writes:

> Even if development is satisfactory and leads to enjoyment from various sources, some feeling of mourning for irretrievably lost pleasures and unfulfilled possibilities can still be found in the deeper layers of the mind. While regret that childhood and youth will never return is often consciously experienced by people near to middle age, in psycho-analysis we find that even infancy and its pleasures are still unconsciously longed for. (1960, p. 268)

In Kavaler-Adler's otherwise excellent book on regret (2013), the word "remorse" does not appear in the index at all, even though her concept of "psychic regret" is better understood as a form of remorse (see below).

Salman Akhtar (2009) goes to some length to rectify the neglect of the term regret within psychoanalysis. He compares and contrasts regret and remorse, calling them "twin sisters." He first points out the similarities—that they are both about one's acts (of commission or omission) in the past which lead to a wistful rumination to undo the past, thus being a part of the "if only ..." fantasy (more on that below). He adds that they can both serve defensive functions. To this, one could add that both are, properly speaking, conscious phenomena. According to Akhtar, the most important difference between the two is that regret is about how one's actions have affected oneself, and hence is narcissistic, while remorse is about how they have affected others, and hence is object-related and also, much more closely related to guilt.[5] By a logical extension, remorse is always tied to morals and values, while regret may be amoral. It is also worth noting that regret is both a noun and a verb, while remorse is only the former.

In everyday use, the word "regret" is used much more broadly than what Akhtar defines above. For example, people routinely regret, but never express remorse over, events not due to their own (in)action and hence entirely outside of their control. Winston Churchill famously expressed regret that the human race ever learnt to fly.[6] Regret can also be collective—as is apparent in the recent headlines stating that Britain will "regret" the Brexit vote—while remorse is almost always an individual emotion. Occasionally someone will express how the other person is, or must be, feeling regret. Mark Twain, the witty misanthrope that he was, was certain that God had a "regret or two" after creating man (ibid., p. 33). Such liberties are rarely taken for the more private emotion of remorse, at least without direct interaction. It is also possible to *know* that one is going to regret something in the future, even if one doesn't *feel* it (anticipatory regret), and yet, this feeling is not strong enough to prevent the act. This happens to me every time I cheat on my diet and eat an unhealthy dessert! A corresponding concept of "anticipatory remorse" is illogical, presumably because the greater intensity of remorse and its more intimate connection with guilt will ensure that it has an inhibitory effect.

Finally, and perhaps most important, regret is often felt and expressed even when referring to how one's (in)action hurt someone else. This occurs under at least five distinct circumstances: 1) when the person who committed the act is incapable of feeling guilty or has not reached that level of insight or is simply unwilling to express any remorse; 2) socially, when one sends one's "regrets" to an invitation or to an occasion one is expected to be at but cannot attend, to mitigate the hurt of one's rejection of the host/hostess or co-attendees; 3) when it was a genuine accident that led to the hurt, a hurt that was unexpected, even if avoidable, at least retrospectively; 4) when the person acted out of good intentions and faith and the hurt was totally expected, even inevitable (say doctors who diligently carry out heroic but experimental treatments in terminally ill patients), and 5) when the person knew it was wrong but had no other viable option (e.g., the movie, Sophie's Choice[7]). In all but the first case, regret is arguably the more appropriate emotion to feel and to express, as remorse implies guilt and an intent to hurt.

As these examples illustrate, linguistically, regret has a much broader definition than remorse. To complicate matters further, Miller (2003) makes a persuasive argument that remorse can be faked fairly easily and one can never really be certain if the person apologizing is truly remorseful. Following Landman (1993), remorse is a much more specific term than regret—one which is usually felt more intensely, is only felt for oneself and for one's intended (in)action (whether the intention was conscious or unconscious) that has already caused hurt to someone else, and when the (in)action was against one's morals or values and thus leads to feelings of contrition and guilt. To put it another way, remorse can be considered a specific type of regret. There remains an overlap, both clinical and experiential, and regret often precedes or leads to remorse. Persistent regret can also serve a defensive function, not allowing the more painful emotions of remorse and guilt to emerge.

Another area worthy of consideration is the link between regret and omnipotence. This connection is evident in the case of "obsessive regret" (Landman, 1993, p. 15) of a mother who has lost her child to an accident. Here, regret acts as a defense against the lack of omnipotence and helplessness. Or, in our puzzled reaction to the passage from Genesis 6:6, "The Lord regretted that He had made man on the earth, and He was grieved in His heart." If God is omnipotent, why would He do something He would come to regret later?[8] In other instances, the relationship between the regret and omnipotence, if present, is more obscure. Could it be that when we send our regrets to an RSVP, we are really bemoaning the fact that we cannot attend every single invitation? Or when we regret the consequences of an act of nature, we wish that we could have prevented it from ever happening? Or somehow averted that accident, even if we did everything right? Perhaps linguistic and social conventions persist as psychic traces in cases of secondary ego autonomy.

Akhtar (2009) links regret to the "if only ..." fantasy, a fantasy that he describes (1996) as:

> ... at its core, a product of incomplete mourning over the loss of the all-good mother of symbiosis. It expresses a position whereby the idealized primary object is neither given up through the work of grieving nor assimilated into the ego through identification. Instead, the object is retained in psychic limbo. (pp. 736–737)

He goes on to link the fantasy with the (idealized) memory of our first two years of life, in which "omnipotent" people took complete care of us and we were secure, even if it meant a lack of individuality.

No regrets?

There is a general feeling in our society that we should ideally lead a life without regrets. Celine Dion (2003) urges us not to find a reason to ever say "Coulda Woulda Shoulda." Katherine Mansfield (cited in Solomon, 2007) believed that regret is an "appalling waste of time" (p. 7), and that no one should ever look back. And such attitudes are not restricted to the contemporary society. A Chinese proverb goes "To regret the past is to forfeit the future." And so on and so forth.

While it is tempting to imagine a life with no regrets, the fear of having regrets, and the defensive need to not feel regret can be as destructive, if not more so, than regret. Schwartz (2004) talks about "regret aversion"—how the prospect of regret is an important determinant of many decisions, not always in a more logical or beneficial direction. A newly coined colloquialism, applicable to millennials, is FoMO, or "fear of missing out"; it refers to the blend of anxiety, inadequacy, and irritation that can flare up while skimming social media. The notion is akin to the well-known concept of "keeping up with the Joneses," but on steroids,[9] as a combination of greater economic freedom and information about available choices has significantly increased the chance of painful comparisons and "post-decision regrets" (Schwartz, 2004). Professor Dan Ariely (cited in Bar, 2015) talks about FoMO as basically being a function of regret. Specifically, he relates it to counterfactual thinking and anticipatory regret, both of which are significantly more likely to occur because of the explosion of social media. The fear of regret and its dynamics as described also indicates the connection between regret and feelings of omnipotence (e.g., "I should be able to read every article and joke and look at every photo on Facebook") and jealousy (e.g., "I need to go to the vacation spot that my friend posted on Instagram").

Two significant movies

Regret is the theme of many novels, plays, movies, and other narrative forms. The choice of the following two movies is ultimately a personal one. They illustrate two vastly different outcomes of intense regret. Their contrast might help one understand the divergence of views about regret.

The Remains of the Day

Arguably the best of the Ivory-Merchant-Jhabvala collaborations, this 1993 period piece is based on a 1989 Kazuo Ishiguro novel by the same name. It garnered eight Academy Award nominations, although it failed to win any, losing in most categories to Steven Spielberg's *Schindler's List*. The movie begins with the voice-over of Sarah "Sally" Benn, née Kenton, as she writes to James Stevens, the near-perfect butler of Darlington Hall, after a gap of some seven years. We learn, through the letter and its visualization, that Lord Darlington has died recently and had been labeled, perhaps unfairly, as a traitor during World War II and that an American millionaire, the ex-Congressman Jack Lewis (appropriately enough played by Christopher Reeve, the *Superman*), rescues Darlington Hall, and Stevens's job, by buying the property. Kenton informs Stevens that she has left her husband, perhaps for good, and her life seems empty. This letter sets the plot into motion as Stevens gets permission to take a vacation to the West Coast, ostensibly to solve the domestic help problem at Darlington Hall by asking Kenton to return to the job of the housekeeper that she held so very capably for a few years in the 1930s. Lewis generously insists that he take the Daimler, a majestic car that belonged to Lord Darlington.

The rest of the film is told from Stevens's perspective (the novel is written in the first person) and moves between the "present time," c. 1959, and, via flashbacks, the mid- to late 1930s. This is important as the unfolding of the story, and the stories within the story, reflect the subjectivity of the protagonist, Stevens, and his psychological journey. All the four flashbacks are presumably Stevens's, although there are many segments which he could not have witnessed. One has to assume that those pieces are (re)constructions created out of a combination of his conversations with Kenton and his fantasies. Thus, following Spence (1980), the flashbacks are best treated as one would a patient's memories, as narrative truth, rather than a historical one.

The movie narrates two journeys and two stories: the external, framing one—Stevens's road trip to Clevedon and his reunion with Kenton, and an internal one told mainly through flashbacks—his recollections, regrets, remorse, and finally, reparation. These two journeys crisscross at crucial points. The intersections serve to split the memories into three parts, each part dealing with one major loss, and subsequent deepening regret/remorse.

As Stevens starts his journey, he remembers the first day he met and interviewed Kenton for the job of the housekeeper, left vacant by the betrothal of her predecessor to the under-butler. Even though she has excellent references and work ethic, Stevens harbors misgivings about her youth (and, left unsaid, beauty), believing that she too may fall in love with one of the other staff. The defensive structure of this anxiety becomes clear later on in the movie at the hire of another pretty, young woman, Lizzie, as a housemaid, who does fall in love with a footman. Kenton, on her part, tries to ingratiate herself, only to be rebuffed as Stevens does not want to be "distracted."

Stevens next hires his father, William Stevens (referred to as Stevens Sr. in the movie and here), also a butler for decades who now wants a lighter job, to fill the other vacancy of the under-butler, thus setting into motion the oedipal dynamics of the movie. Stevens reprimands Kenton for addressing his father by his first name, William. Kenton reminds him that this is protocol, and Stevens has no good answer for this, but insists on it. Later on we find out that Stevens's mother was "carrying on," which is why his father left her; and that Stevens is fiercely protective of his father. This would help explain Stevens's barely repressed anger toward Kenton initially. Stevens Sr., going against the very protocol that he holds so dear, steals his son's thunder at the servants' dining table, first by finishing his speech about the most important trait for a butler (being dignified under all circumstances) and then by relating a very funny anecdote around a tiger. As Long (1997) writes, the tiger hiding under the dining table and killed with supreme aplomb by the English butler in India represents the passion, the libido, that both Stevens and his father have had to "kill" as part of their pursuit of perfect poise within their chosen profession.

Kenton reacts to the reprimand by becoming feisty and finding fault with Stevens Sr. at every opportunity, of which there are several, as he is clearly having memory lapses and difficulty coping physically with the tasks assigned to him. The inevitable crisis occurs when he takes a fall on the uneven flagstones while serving tea. Afraid of such an event being repeated at an upcoming informal but important[10] international conference on how best to respond to Germany's increasing aggression, he is demoted to a footman by Lord Darlington. Meanwhile, Kenton's attitude, as Stevens remembers, undergoes a sea change with his father's illness. Now she becomes very attentive toward Stevens Sr., and much less feisty with Stevens. This suggests that Stevens has stopped ideal-izing his father and, consequently, is able to have a more harmonious relationship with Kenton.

The conference goes mostly as planned and everyone in attendance, with the notable exception of US Congressman Jack Lewis, endorses Germany's right to breach the Treaty of Versailles and increase her army. Meanwhile, Stevens Sr. has a stroke on the first day of the conference and dies on the last. Stevens is too busy with the arrangements of the conference to attend to him, leaving it mostly to Kenton. The narra-tive makes it clear that Stevens is mourning the loss of his father, and regretting that he did not tend to him during his terminal illness or fin-ish the conversation his father wanted to have with him hours before his death, or take the chance to assure him that he had been a good father. The regret and mourning is shading into remorse and guilt about withholding his love and his repressed anger, represented by the acts of omission mentioned.

At this point, as if unable to carry on the onus of remembering any fur-ther, the film emerges into the outer, framing story, and Stevens stops at the Collingbourne post office to pick up Kenton's letter confirming their rendezvous. Inside the store, he denies knowing Lord Darlington, thus exhibiting (and experiencing?) shame about his ex-employer for the first time. Stevens's remembering Lord Darlington's sympathy for the Germans, although portrayed as reasonable, along with the death of his father, represent the process of de-idealization of Lord Darlington.

We, as the audience, now realize that this is no ordinary journey but a therapeutic one for Stevens. Kenton's letter, which he reads in the car, helps begin his second "analytic session."

Lord Darlington accepts two Jewish refugee women from Germany into his service. However, we are made to believe that he did so more to practice his German than his humanity. Kenton takes them under her wing and becomes highly protective of them. Meanwhile, there is another, smaller, meeting of people influential in foreign relationships. This time the focus is on a Sir Geoffrey (who is a vegan in a not-so-subtle reference to Hitler's dietary preferences), who tries to explain away anti-Semitism and other forms of discrimination and labels concentration camps as a type of prison, a necessary evil for the running of a lawful society, perhaps "overdue." Sir Geoffrey's butler, Thomas Benn, happens to be an old acquaintance and ex-colleague of Kenton's, and soon becomes her suitor. Stevens briefly befriends him and expounds his philosophy of being true to his employer, and believing his employer to be morally impeccable. Benn questions his own employer's morals, and rightly so. Thus Stevens, in his retelling, concedes the moral high ground to Benn, justifying Kenton's ultimate choice. Stevens himself then questions *his* own employer's morals, as the very next scene shows Lord Darlington reading a particularly repulsive and anti-Semitic paragraph from Chamberlain's then-influential work, *The Foundations of the Nineteenth Century* (1911). Influenced by this, he orders the two Jewish housemaids fired. This upsets Kenton to the point of her threatening resignation. Stevens initially appears to be siding with Lord Darlington, or at least, defending his views. However, in a later scene, he surprises Kenton (and us) by admitting that he too was upset at his employer's views and decision.

This sequence appears to end somewhat abruptly with the hiring of Lizzie Hull to replace the Jewish housemaids, as Stevens literally runs out of gas. Stevens goes to a pub in Moscombe where he pretends to be a "gentleman" and talks about how he "consorted" with Winston Churchill and Anthony Eden. Basically, he pretends to be Lord Darlington, trying to walk in his shoes,[11] while at the same time he denies knowing him. This creates an intriguing dynamic—he essentially denies knowing himself. Here is a man searching for an identity, for some clue of his own desires and feelings. He really does not know his own self, outside of his role as a butler. Even as a gentleman who knew all these dignitaries, we find him struggling to say anything substantial. This is truly his first vacation and a-vocation. As if to underline the contrast, he gets an earful from a Harry Smith, clearly not a "gentleman," about the hard-fought right of every Englishman to have and voice his own opinion.

Later, Stevens learns about the death of his landlord's son in the battle at Dunkirk. These exchanges allow him to finish the second leg of his internal journey, and the final memory of this sequence surfaces. He is summoned by Lord Darlington to try to answer some questions by one of his friends, Spencer. Stevens is game, but it soon becomes clear, to him and to us, that Spencer is playing a sadistic game. He asks for Stevens's opinions on arcane matters of international politics and finance. When Stevens professes his inability to "assist" him, Spencer turns triumphantly to the little group, having proved his point about the shortcomings of democracy. Stevens then has finally allowed himself to realize the full extent of his employer's fascination with fascism and culpability for not trying harder to contain Hitler. Thus, he experiences the loss of Lord Darlington again, this time as an ego ideal/father figure. But more poignantly, he realizes that, in serving such a flawed master[12] so faithfully and for so long, he lost not only his own voice, but also his birthright to make his own mistakes. As Zeul (2001) points out, the movie is making a connection between Stevens's longing for a blissful state of merger with Lord Darlington, wherein he loses his individuality *and* his morality, and what happened in Nazi Germany leading up to the Holocaust.

Back on the road trip, Stevens takes a ride from a Dr. Carlisle, who easily sees through his pretense and guesses that he is a manservant. Stevens again denies knowing Lord Darlington, but soon recants his story and admits that he was his butler for years. He does continue to defend him, and claims that Lord Darlington was remorseful about his actions and felt that he had been duped. He again defers on giving his personal opinion but admits that he has made his own mistake, one which he hopes to correct soon. These interludes between his flashbacks serve as mile markers, a way to assess the progress of his therapeutic journey. From anger at his ex-master's perfidy to an acceptance of his humanity, from shame at the very mention of his name to a feeling of remorse, from a near-total self-denial and effacement to a recognition of his own desire, his own mistake, and the need to try to remedy the same, he has indeed traveled many a mental mile.

The final leg begins with Lord Darlington expressing contrition for firing the Jewish housemaids. His ardor is gone, his spirit broken. Even when there is a secret rendezvous at his home between the prime minister of the UK, the German ambassador, and others, the focus is on the German contingent coveting the art pieces, marking them for the future, and Lord Darlington is very much in the background, mostly silent. Stevens is past needing him as an idealized object and his focus has shifted. This indicates that he has forgiven Lord Darlington for his naïveté, even as his well-intentioned actions contributed to disasters. As Long (1997) points out, even the name Darlington suggests a "sweet innocent." This forgiveness is important for Stevens, as it allows him to move forward psychologically.

Meanwhile Lizzie, the new housemaid, falls in love with the head footman, Charlie, and both of them resign and plan to get married, against the advice of Stevens and Kenton. This parallels a growing intimacy and familiarity between Stevens and Kenton. But that spell is broken cruelly when one night Kenton visits Stevens in his pantry and playfully, flirtatiously invades his personal space and pries the book he is reading from his grasp. Given the level of his discomfort, Kenton is expecting a racy, scandalous book and is surprised and disappointed that it is only a "sentimental old love story".[13] For the paragon of restraint, this forced exposure of his schmaltzy underbelly, hinted at earlier in his selection of music ("Roll Along Prairie Moon"[14] while socializing with Benn), is devastating. In addition, Kenton's physical proximity and her seductiveness triggers his intense anxiety around his sexuality, already witnessed previously in his acute distress while talking about the "birds and bees" to Lord Darlington's godson, at his request. So he withdraws back into his shell and drives Kenton out of his sanctum and later puts a halt to their cozy evening chats-cum-planning sessions. Kenton in turn reacts by accepting the proposal of her by-then suitor, Benn. But not before giving Stevens one last chance to propose, an opportunity that he is unable, perhaps at that time incapable, of grabbing. The flashback ends with Kenton's face fading, his last, and most profound, regret, the one that he is trying to roll back.

Stevens arrives in Clevedon only to discover that Kenton plans to reunite with her husband, after receiving the news that they will soon be grandparents. She states that she has often had regrets[15] and a lingering handshake while saying goodbye reveals the depth of their mutual feelings. Stevens appears to revert to character—he reassures her that everyone has regrets, announces that he is looking forward to returning to work and bids her a final farewell. Back in Darlington Hall, he busies himself with his duties, including the hiring of a housekeeper. In the final scene of the movie, Stevens helps Lewis free a pigeon trapped inside one of the rooms.

The ending has generally been seen as tragic, a devastating defeat for Stevens's daring venture (Long, 1997; Stein, 2003; Zeul, 2001). There can be an alternative reading. The ending of this movie is similar to the ending of another film about two parallel journeys, an internal voyage and a rail trip—Satayajit Ray's *Nayak* (1966). In both movies, the protagonist is in the same physical space at the beginning and end of the movie, but in an entirely different psychological space (Shah, 2015). In *The Remains of the Day*, by the end of the movie, Stevens has mourned for his father's death, overcome his need to idealize him and Lord Darlington, forgiven Lord Darlington for his fascist views and Nazi sympathies, found his voice, and recognized his desire for Kenton. If in the end, he does not pursue his desire further, it is by his choice, not out of his inhibitions. He recognizes that it is better for her to be with her husband, daughter, and grandchild, that while they both love each other and it was a mistake not to have gotten together earlier, to do so now would be an even bigger mistake and that his place was with Lewis.[16] So he returns, not to Darlington Hall, but to Lewis, not to another stint of self-denial and subservience, but to a job with much more room for his own subjectivity, something that Lewis has been shown to be more than willing to provide.[17] The pigeon, freed by Lewis with Stevens's help, then represents servitude and subjugation. He still has the same job, and maybe the same regrets regarding Kenton, but with a very different perspective. As Freud (1895d) says, a lot can be gained when one "changes hysterical [neurotic] misery into common unhappiness" (p. 305).

On the Waterfront

Considered by many to be one of the greatest American movies ever,[18] Elia Kazan's 1954 black and white, relatively low-budget movie about crime and corruption in the unions which ruled the docks in and around New York City was nominated for thirteen Oscars and won nine, in 1955, including for Best Picture and Best Director. It was written by Budd Schulberg, who went on to write a novel, *Waterfront* (1955), and a play (with Stan Silverman), *On the Waterfront* (2001) on the same theme.

The movie begins when Terry Malloy, a somewhat slow-witted ex-boxer and a longshoreman, calls on Joey Doyle, ostensibly to return his lost pigeon. But this was just a ploy to get Joey up to the roof where he is pushed to his death by the goons of the corrupt and criminal waterfront union led by Johnny Friendly, to prevent him from testifying against the union. Terry appears to be genuinely surprised at this, naïvely believing that "they were only going to lean on him a little." This reaction by Terry, while locating him in a moral grey zone, clues us to the level of denial in his psyche. As Lee (2003) mentions, Terry knows about Johnny's ruthlessness and that Joey was not the first (nor will he be the last) to meet this fate. The rest of the movie is about his letting go of this denial, accepting the brutal realities and his reactions to them. The driving force for this psychological development is regret, which leads to repentance, reparation, and, arguably, some remorse and revenge.

From the very beginning then, we find the protagonist in a somewhat pensive mood, having regrets about his part in the murder. Johnny tries to cheer him up by giving him $50 and ensuring that he gets the cushiest job every morning at the shape-up on the docks. Terry accepts these as payoff for betraying his fellow pigeon-keeper, albeit churlishly. He is reminded of his indebtedness to Johnny by his brother Charley "the Gent", who is one of the leaders of the union, the "brains" of the team.

The very next morning he takes a small step toward reparation as he manages to grab an all-important tab, necessary to get work for the day, in a melee at the shape-up. When Edie Doyle, Joey's younger sister who is home from St. Ann College in Tarrytown,[19] wrestles him for that tab, he initially enjoys it. But as soon as the friend for whom he had procured it (for he himself already had one) informs him of her identity, he gives it to her; she in turn gives it to her father, Pop Doyle. The atonement only goes so far though, as he willingly follows the common code of all dockhands: "D and D," to be deaf and dumb, and not squeal like a rat or sing like a canary. When agents from the Waterfront Crime Commission (WCC) start asking questions, he, along with Pop Doyle and everyone else, remain sullenly silent.

Edie is very upset at Joey's death and is determined to get to the bottom of it. She shames the local priest, Father Barry, into taking a more active role and reach out to his parish beyond the confines of the church. Father Barry, witness to the shenanigans of the union but not privy to the details, offers the church as a sanctum for like-minded people to gather and plan how to fight them. Friendly gets to hear about the planned meeting and delegates Terry to infiltrate it. He does, but only a few people attend and no one dares to speak up. As a backup, Johnny sends a group of thugs to disrupt the meeting and then beat up the attendees. One of those beat up most badly is Kayo Dugan, earlier the recipient of Joey's windbreaker—the "reformer's mantle" (Lee, 2003, p. 65)—and shown to be a bit of a rebel. Father Barry comes to his rescue and encourages him to speak up. In turn, he promises to fully support Kayo, to go with him "down the line." Importantly, this conversation happens in an isolated area, out of anyone's earshot.

Meanwhile Terry rescues Edie from the thugs[20] by escaping down the fire escape. They then take a stroll in the park and along the waterfront before Terry sees her home. In the park, the local "bum," Mutt, implies that Terry knows something about Joey's death. Terry first shoos him away and then buys him off, the way he himself has been bought off. Mutt nevertheless gets a parting shot in, calling Terry a "bum." Terry's reaction to this epithet, which is thrown at him a few more times, is intense and immediate, but incomprehensible until later. In the much acclaimed scene that follows, Terry tries on the glove that Edie drops, symbolizing his intent to try and look at life from her perspective. They flirt and court each other, against her father's expressed wishes, and end up in a bar drinking beer. Terry opens up, to a point, and talks about his father being murdered and growing up in an orphanage and learning to fight for everything at a very early age. His philosophy is simple— "every man for himself" and "get them before they get you." Edie is half-appalled, half-fascinated, and appeals to his better side to help her in finding Joey's murderer. Terry comes close to admitting his complicity, but again Edie appears to be blind to this. They end up dancing, but are rudely interrupted just as they are about to kiss, first by Johnny's gofer, asking him to see him urgently, and then by the WCC agent, serving him with a subpoena. Terry tears up the summons, showing his intention to remain D and D, just as he had done earlier when he professed his inability to help Edie. Edie, frustrated by his stubbornness around this, calls him a "bum" and leaves in a huff.

Terry's actions in the movie, especially from this point on, have almost universally been interpreted as signs of his developing a conscience (Braudy, 2005; Lee, 2003; Rapf, 2003; others). His attraction to and tenderness toward Edie may be partly because of his guilt, but there are other more powerful motivating factors shown, though rarely commented on, for his increasing defiance of Johnny and his gang.

Immediately after Edie leaves him, we learn that Kayo has given a thirty-nine-page statement to the authorities about the union. Johnny, along with Charley and others, track Terry down and accuse him of neglecting to find out about this during the church meeting. He knows that this is unfair, and we know it. But that does not prevent Johnny from humiliating him by slapping him and then demoting him to working in the hold, the "sweat gang," and Charley from reprimanding him and blaming all of it on his infatuation with Edie. They leave after making none-too-veiled threats against Kayo.

The next day, while working in the hold with Kayo and others, Terry tries to warn him, half-heartedly. Kayo, busy pilfering Irish whiskey, rebuffs his attempt and is soon crushed under a cascade of whiskey boxes, a staged accident by the union hoods. Father Barry, true to his promise to Kayo, gives a fiery speech, part eulogy, part sermon, as he tries to inspire everyone to follow Kayo's example and speak up. While most listen in silence, the union thugs pelt him with bananas and a can. Terry punches one of the union leaders before he can throw another banana. This is noted by everyone, especially Charley, Johnny, and Edie. Edie's respect for Terry increases at his heroic gesture, and she resumes their affair and passes on Joey's windcheater to him. However, Terry is not yet ready to put it on. He does seek out Father Barry the next day and confesses his role in Joey's death, though he continues to claim that he thought they would "only lean on him a little." Father Barry urges him to follow his conscience and talk to the WCC. Terry's response is telling: "Conscience—that stuff can drive you nuts." He justifies his continued refusal to talk to the WCC by his indebtedness to Johnny, who took him to baseball games as a child, and was the one good thing that happened to him when he grew up in the orphanage. He does agree to tell all to Edie, but we do not get to hear what he says as it is drowned out by a loud and shrill horn from a passing ship—the shrillness of his conscience that he cannot handle. Neither can Edie handle what she surely knew by then, and runs home distraught.

Meanwhile one of the WCC investigators, Glover, tries a very different approach with Terry and talks about his all-too-short boxing career while Terry is pottering around in his pigeon coop. And we learn that Terry had thrown his last boxing match, at the (Madison Square) Garden, four years back, at the behest of his "pals" who had a bet riding on it. He becomes very animated and self-confident when he talks about his technique in the ring and the progress of the fight and we suddenly see a different Terry, one that had potential, that could have been, in his own words, "somebody." Glover has done his job, lit the match.

At the union office, Johnny is getting more and more anxious about Terry's loyalty and grills Charley about it. When Charley is unable to guarantee his silence, Johnny asks Charley to silence him, one way or another, and makes it clear that if he is not silenced, Charley will pay. Horrified, Charley initially refuses, but agrees later, hoping to convince Terry. They talk in a taxi cab, in what is the psychological core of the movie and its most memorable scene. Charley first tries to bribe Terry with a cushy job in a new pier, in exchange for his silence. When Terry shows ambivalence Charley becomes desperate and lets on that they have very limited time. Finally he alternately threatens and pleads with Terry while brandishing a gun. In sharp contrast to Charley's increasing panic, Terry remains calm and confident. He pushes the gun away and gently admonishes his brother. Charley, realizing that he can neither kill his brother, nor convince him, thus sealing his own fate, now starts reminiscing about Terry's years as a boxer and blames his lack of success on his ex-agent. Terry disagrees and reminds him that he had a golden chance, but threw the match at Charley's behest. He chides him for not looking out for him more and making him take "dives" for others to earn some money. When Charley reminds him that they also placed some bets on him he says, "You don't understand. I coulda had class. I coulda been a contender. I coulda been somebody, instead of a bum, which is what I am. Let's face it [pause] … It was you, Charley." At which point, Charley gives him the gun for his protection, drops him off, and drives away to his own death.

There is a Malloy in the movie who develops a conscience—Charley. Out of guilt for betraying Terry and selling him short on Johnny's orders, and out of love for his kid brother who he has always protected, Charley sacrifices himself to try to save Terry. Terry, on the other hand, remains extraordinarily naïve and self-centered. He gives no further thought to his brother, or perhaps, feels that Charley deserves his fate. Instead, the first full expression of his deep regret that had slowly been bubbling to the surface throughout the movie fuels his anger and need for vengeance. His first thought is Edie and when she refuses to allow him into her apartment, he practically rapes her by breaking down the door and kissing her forcibly against the wall. Edie gives in after some resistance. As Chown (2003) brings up so pointedly, how are we to understand this capitulation? Up until that point, Edie has been shown to be an assertive, self-confident woman with an independent mind, pushing Father Barry to do the right thing, lovingly but firmly going against her father's wishes and demanding "more, much much more" from Terry. She has been a driving force, propelling the plot forward, unusually so for a Hollywood movie of the 1950s. After Terry forces himself on her, it is as if she is castrated and loses all her drive. From then on all she does is to beg Terry to leave town to save his life, pleas which falls on deaf ears as Terry completely ignores her.

Terry, on the other hand, is doubly emboldened after this phallic transfer of power and ventures into the night when someone calls out his name, luring him with the plea that his brother needs him. Edie is instantly suspicious and follows him. They are almost run over by a truck and only manage to escape when Terry breaks open a glass door, symbolically getting blood on his hands. Certainly, he should have blood on his hands as he is already at least partially responsible for two deaths—Joey and Kayo. Soon enough he discovers the third—his brother, shot and hung with the longshoreman's hook. Terry swears violent vengeance and goes looking for Johnny in a blind rage. Father Barry intercedes in time and persuades him that it is better to avenge his brother's death by testifying at the hearings.

Terry does so extensively (most of it off-screen, both his confessions seemingly too shameful to be heard) which incriminates the union leadership. However, when he returns home to Edie, he is morose as he quickly finds out that he is shunned by everyone for ratting, for defying the D and D. Edie tries to persuade him to leave town, go inland, and start a farm. However, Terry has not achieved the psychological resolution he sought. He still has to prove that he is not a "bum" and that he can fight. Also, he does not like the pariah he has become for testifying, but does not want to regret his action, as he is afraid of going back to the dark place he was in. So he puts on Joey's windcheater (symbolizing that now is his real fight) and goes to the shape-up to wait for his name to be called. When everyone pointedly ignores him and even the bum Mutt is preferred over him, regret threatens to overwhelm him again. He reacts predictably with even more anger and vengeance and goes to the union office to loudly and proudly defend his decision to testify. By now, everyone is curious and keenly watching the spectacle. Terry and Johnny goad each other and Terry finally rushes Johnny. They start sparring in front of everyone, in a boxing match that was four years in the making for Terry. When it appears that Terry is getting the better of

Johnny, the other union bosses and goons join in and thrash Terry. They leave him battered and bruised, barely conscious, on the pier.

Father Barry and Edie somewhat belatedly come to his aid. Edie wants to call a doctor, but Father Barry has other ideas. He is aware that the group of longshoremen have turned against Johnny and are by now rooting for Terry to lead them into the dockyard, refusing to work unless he does so. So he seizes the opportunity, props up Terry, and urges him to walk to the gate. Father Barry again refuses to allow Edie, or anyone else, to help him. He even goes so far as to appeal to his need to avenge his betrayal, telling him that Johnny is betting against him being up to the task. In a melodramatic finish, by now far removed from the neo-realistic beginning, Terry barely manages to get up and walks, nay, lurches, to the gate of the dock. The camera lurches with him, even becoming blurry at times, leaving little room for any stance other than a total identification with the protagonist. As he enters the gate, and the rest follow, Father Barry and Edie hold hands and exchange a (conspiratorial?) smile. The final shot is that of the huge dock gates closing behind the workers, as Johnny curses them impotently and Father Barry and Edie look on happily.

Terry has salvaged his pride and dignity by proving to everyone that he *can* box and that he is not a bum and by avenging his betrayal(s). He has become a popular hero by taking on the union gangsters and surviving, barely. He has become the leader of the longshoremen, even if he himself has been manipulated by Father Barry and has no alternative to violence as a solution to all problems to offer. And he has become a "man" by forcing himself on Edie and putting her in her "proper place." What he has *not* become is someone who has a healthy superego—someone who can accept responsibility for his role in three deaths, someone who can feel remorse, atone for his sins, and forgive others for theirs, someone who can accept the masculine in the female and the feminine within him, someone who can look back at things that went wrong in his life, experience regret, and bear that pain, without it leading to a vicious cycle of anger, vengeance, and counter-retaliation.

Discussion

Regret, the "shoulda-woulda-coulda" (Safire, 1994) feeling, is very often a powerful and intensely painful experience. It is a central element in many a literary work, such as Charles Dickens's *Great Expectations* (1860),

Marcel Proust's *In Search of Lost Time* (1913–1927), Ian McEwan's *Atonement* (2001), and Kazuo Ishiguro's *The Remains of the Day* (1989). Poets have categorized it as *the* saddest of all human emotions. That missed opportunity, the road you did not take, and that drunken one-night stand can haunt one for a lifetime. In a way, regret is an emotion which reflects how unfair life is. We are always coming across forks in the road and have to decide which way to go even though we are rarely able to see where either one leads. Major mistakes can go unpunished or even unnoticed, while minor slipups can lead to life-altering changes. There is little doubt then that most, if not all of us have at least a few regrets in our life.

The question is—what is the purpose of regret? Does it even have one? Is there any need to regret? Or any benefit from it? Philosophers have debated the merits and demerits of regret for centuries. Most famously, Nietzsche (1844–1900) felt that to be great is to regret nothing, ever, while Kierkegaard (1813–1855) felt that regret was inevitable, no matter what you choose. In some ways this debate, whether it is better to not cry over spilt milk or accept that the grass is always greener on the other side, continues to this day. Current popular opinion has it that regret is useless or worse. The "motto of the millennials" as enunciated by the artist, A. D. Graham (2011) who goes by the name of Drake, appears to be "YOLO"—"You only live once," a *carpe diem* for the digital age. As opportunities and choices increase, so does the possibility of regret. For the more roads we did *not* take, the more ways we can imagine our life to have been different than what it is. The combination of increased freedoms and a philosophy of constantly looking forward has led to a fear of regret and a need to deny it. It is not all negative, though, as people do talk about the moral sensitivity implied in the feeling of regret and its role in making better choices in the future.

The place of regret in our psyche remains to be clarified. It is closely related to some of the other negative emotions, namely shame, guilt, repentance, and remorse, and is sometimes admixed with them. It is evident that regret often needs to be, and is, defended against, denied, and/or dismissed. But regret can also act as what Greenson (1958) calls a "screen defense," wherein a psychic phenomenon (memory, affect, perception, identification, etc.) is used to deny or contradict another psychic phenomenon of the *same* type. He further differentiates between two types of screen activities—"filter" screens, wherein painful things are filtered out and only relatively innocuous and harmless ones are allowed through, and "falsified" screens, in which misrepresentations and distortions are created. Regret is an example of the former when it is used as a filter against the more profound and painful affects of intense shame, remorse, and guilt. To be clear, when regret acts as a screen, the memory is not significantly distorted. Reider (1953) links various screen functions (defenses) with recollections and reconstructions in analysis. So one feels regret, instead of the more painful emotions, after and *in spite of* a reasonably accurate remembrance of the events in question. No doubt there could be subtle differences in the emphases and emotional tones of things remembered. However, the defensive nature of regret lies elsewhere—in the displacement of the locus of responsibility for the negative outcome. Also, regret, as a screen affect, can be remarkably stable for years. And yet, being naturally oriented toward the past, it does tend to provoke repeated reminiscences, which can, in turn, lead to the unraveling of its defensive structure and the emergence of underlying affects.

In the Ivory-Merchant movie, *The Remains of the Day*, James Stevens, the butler of Darlington Hall, motors down the memory lane, fueled by regret. As he reminisces about the "good old days," he acquires powerful new insights and perspectives, and is able to stop idealizing his ex-employer, Lord Darlington, and his father, and also mourn their deaths. Having let go of a need for an idealized object, he finds a voice to his own desire. Even as circumstances do not allow him to consummate the love he has harbored in his heart for twenty-odd years, he is able to find peace within himself and resume his duties with his current employer, in a relationship newly marked by emotional maturity and psychological equality.

The regret felt by the central character in Elia Kazan's film *On the Waterfront* leads to a very different conclusion. Terry Malloy, ex-boxer and a longshoreman, starts feeling the first pangs of regret after he lures his friend to his death. But his real transformation comes when he is treated unfairly, *once again*, opening up four-year-old wounds. His self-righteous anger leads to more moral actions, but not a greater sense of responsibility. When he finally confronts his older brother about what he regrets most deeply, having to throw a career-changing boxing match four years back at his behest, he seeks revenge. He testifies against the union, but he has to undo the past by a final fistfight, *mano a mano*, with the corrupt boss. He overcomes his regrets, and stops being a "bum," but at a high cost and without gaining insight into his own culpability.

It may be instructive to compare and contrast the different outcomes of the two movies. Both have the protagonists feeling deep regret over events from the past, which they finally confront and try to repair/undo to a certain extent. Stevens regrets his blind devotion to Lord Darlington, which precluded him from recognizing his fascist sympathies and prevented him from even recognizing his own desires. He takes responsibility for what he can change, his own internal state, and tries to repair the possible damage to his would-be lover. Terry, on the other hand, regrets having to throw a fight, but never assumes responsibility for his role in that and all his subsequent actions. Also, Stevens is able to bear the pain of regret, and the remorse it touches on, somewhat stoically, and continue with his daily routines. Terry, on the other hand, finds the emergence of remorse too much, his conscience too "shrill." He has to act and react, continuing the cycle of violence.

From this focused analysis it emerges that the relationship between regret and responsibility is complex, and central to the psychological outcome of the experience and expression of regret. Regret resides in the grey zone *vis-à-vis* responsibility. It is felt when one accepts partial responsibility, neither distancing oneself completely from the event in question, nor taking full blame or showing contrition. The closer one gets to accepting the degree of responsibility appropriate to the situation, the more positive is the outcome. It remains to be determined what the appropriate degree of responsibility is. Should Stevens take responsibility for Lord Darlington's policy of appeasement and its disastrous consequences? Should Terry feel responsible for the deaths of Joey, Kayo, and Charley?

As we ponder such questions, I would like to conclude this discourse with an observation and a speculation. Stevens is clearly disturbed by certain memories and the regret it generates, as shown in the movie by breaks in his flashbacks, lying about his association with Lord Darlington, etc. However, by and large, he does not *act* on them, beyond the minor deceptions. Terry seems to spring into action every time he gets reminded of the bum he is or of the missed opportunity with the boxing match. What we learn from these screen depictions of regret is that it is best to resist using regret as a screen. Perhaps the capacity to tolerate regret, without counteracting it, is one of the signs of emotional maturity.[21]

Notes

1. The DVD/Blu-ray ends about thirty seconds before the screened movie did, and hence, is more ambiguous about whether they will meet or not. But the point remains that they *could* easily miss each other yet again.
2. Bret Harte (1867) composed a parody of it called *Mrs. Judge Jenkins: The Only True Sequel to Maud Muller*, in which the two would-be lovers of the original poem, Maud Muller and Judge Jenkins, do go on to marry each other and find out that they are not compatible. It ends with the verse:

> If, of all words of tongue and pen,
> The saddest are, "It might have been,"
> More sad are these we daily see:
> "It is, but hadn't ought to be."

This can be interpreted to mean that errors of commission are regretted more than errors of omission. Schwartz (2004) has found that people regret errors of commission in the near past more, while errors of omission are regretted more as years go by. Perhaps errors of omission, like the one made by the lovers-to-be in "Maud Muller" and *The Remains of the Day*, are easier to bear because they create and sustain the "myth of the potential" (Phillips, 2012), while errors of commission kill that myth.

3. The Oxford English Dictionary defines regret as: Feel sad, repentant, or disappointed over (something that has happened or been done, especially a loss or missed opportunity).
4. As per a pep-web.org search, on July 1, 2016.
5. Language is always messy. So the common term, "buyer's remorse," has nothing to do with guilt or hurting anyone else. It is really a form of regret.
6. As quoted in Solomon (2007, p. 24).
7. In both William Styron's novel (1979) and the movie based upon it (1982) by that name, Sophie, a mother of two, was forced to decide which one

of her children would live and which one would die, in a Nazi concentration camp.

8. The best explanation I have read for this is that God's emotions cannot really be translated into human terms. Or, psychoanalytically, our infantile experience of omnipotence, and its loss, is so deeply unconscious and/or preverbal, that we cannot adequately articulate its relationship with regret.

9. Perhaps the ultimate example, and cautionary tale, of FoMO in popular culture is Hermione with her Time-Turner in the Harry Potter saga (Rowlings, 1999).

10. The movie offers us some subtle hints that Stevens's account of his master's importance in world affairs may be an exaggeration, a reflection of his need to merge with an idealized, omnipotent object. See also Zeul (2001).

11. The suit he wore then indeed belonged originally to Lord Darlington, as we find out in a deleted scene. It was customary for butlers to receive their employers' old and surplus clothes.

12. In portraying the policy of appeasement as completely misguided, the movie is remaining true to its historical setting of the late 1950s. And this essay is remaining true to the movie. In actuality, since the 1960s, there is a much more nuanced view of the need for appeasement (See Dutton, 2016).

13. The book in question is Joan Butler's *Unnatural Hazards* (1950), a romantic comedy in the style of P. G. Wodehouse.

14. Composed by Ted Fio Rito, Albert Von Tilzer, and Harry McPherson.

15. Ishiguro's novel (1989) clarifies that Kenton often dreams about life with Stevens (pp. 238–239). The Blu-ray contains a deleted scene which also makes this sentiment more explicit.

16. As audience, we may be left regretting that the two of them did not get together earlier. Which may be why the movie is almost universally assessed to have a negative ending. However, the movie makes it clear that Stevens has gotten past his regrets.

17. In the novel, both Lewis's desire for a more egalitarian relationship and Stevens's change of heart around the same wish is coded in Stevens's readiness to learn how to "banter" with his employer.

18. It is number 17 on the American Film Institute's 100 best movies (2007 updated edition).

19. Tarrytown is one of several tongue-in-cheek names included in the movie. The name of the main agent of WCC is "Glover," while the name

of the union delegate is Mladen Sekulovich, the real name of the actor Karl Malden who plays Father Barry. Also, "Big Mac," who calls out the names at the shape-up, one morning calls out "Westerfield," the real name of the actor playing that character. In a movie shot mostly in the neo-realist style and on-site, this is possibly to clue the audience about the artifice involved (see Braudy, 2005, and the IMDB website).

20. Does she really need rescuing? He claims that they would not harm Pop Doyle because of his age. If true, how likely are they to hurt a woman?

21. This may not be specific for regret and be true of all negative reactions.

PART III

CLINICAL REALMS

CHAPTER SEVEN

Regret, nostalgia, and masochism*

Salman Akhtar

C ertain affects have the peculiar quality of linking the temporal characteristics of the system *Cs* and the system *Ucs* (Freud, 1915e). They pointedly exist in the present but are content-wise totally involved with the past. Remorse is one such emotion and regret the other. The former, though often conflated with guilt (Klein, 1935, 1940), has received considerable attention from psychoanalysts. The latter has not. The index to the Standard Edition of Freud's complete works contains no entry on "regret." The five major dictionaries of psychoanalysis (Eidelberg, 1968; Laplanche & Pontalis, 1973; Moore & Fine, 1968, 1990; Rycroft, 1968) also do not mention "regret". The PEP Web, the electronic compendium of psychoanalytic literature spanning 116 years and containing nearly 90,000 entries, lists one single paper (Kavaler-Adler, 2004) with the word "regret" in its title. It is therefore clear that despite its being ubiquitous and troubling, regret as an emotion has received almost no attention within our literature.

---

*This chapter first appeared under the title "Regret" in the author's book, *A Web of Sorrow: Mistrust, Jealousy, Lovelessness, Shamelessness, Regret, Hopelessness* (2017, Karnac, pp. 93–108). It is reprinted here with the author's and publisher's permission.

My contribution here is aimed to fill this gap. I will begin my consideration of "regret" with delineating its phenomenological characteristics and differentiating it from the related affect of remorse. I will then trace the origins of regret and attempt to demonstrate the intricate scenarios of ontogenesis and "actual" missteps of adult life that undergird it. Following this, I will make a brief sociocultural foray and then address the clinical implications of the proposals made so far. I will conclude by summarizing and synthesizing the diverse material in this contribution and by noting areas that merit further investigation.

Etymology, definition, and phenomenology

The current English word "regret" is derived from the addition of prefix "re" to the Old German or Old Norse word *greter*, which meant "to weep." Regret thus originally meant "to weep again." This etymological nuance is, however, restricted to the hyphenated form (i.e., "re-gret") of the word which has largely become extinct in contemporary English though still mentioned in certain dictionaries. There the definitions of "re-gret" and "regret" appear different. "Re-gret" is defined as "(i) a: to mourn the loss or death of, b: to miss very much; (ii) to be very sorry for," and "regret" as "(i) sorrow aroused by circumstances beyond one's control or power to repair, (ii) a: an expression of distressing emotions (as sorrow or disappointment); b: a note politely declining an invitation" (*Merriam-Webster Collegiate Dictionary*, 1993, p. 985). Of note here is that the temporal implication of the old "re-gret" is obfuscated, if not entirely lost, by "regret" which entered the English language in the late sixteenth century. Compare this to the stunning poem "Regret" by Charlotte Brontë (1816–1855) and the moorings of the emotions in events past shall become unmistakably evident. I will cite the entire poem later in this essay and restrict myself here to declaring that this poem is a treasure trove of insights about the emotion of regret. It subsumes the role of intentionality and agency, loss, wistfulness, nostalgia, and desperate wish to undo what one has done—all under the throbbing rubric of regret.

This leads me to the psychoanalytic perspective on regret. Kavaler-Adler (2004), the only author to have written a psychoanalytic paper on regret, states that "[R]emorse and regret interweave intra-psychically" (p. 40). In my *Comprehensive Dictionary of Psychoanalysis* (Akhtar, 2009), I elucidated the overlaps and distinctions between the two emotions in the following manner.

"Regret" shares many features with its twin sister, "remorse" (see separate entry). Both are about the past. Both are about one's own actions. Both can involve acts of commission or omission. Both lead to a wistful rumination to somehow erase or undo the events of the past. Both can, therefore, underlie the "if only" fantasies. This fantasy assumes that, in the absence of this or that "calamity," everything would have turned out alright. Both "regret" and "remorse" can impoverish the ego and contribute to anhedonia, depression, and suicidal tendencies. Finally, both "regret" and "remorse" can serve screen functions and both can be put to secondary (e.g., sado-masochistic) uses. However, there is one very important difference between the two emotions: "remorse" involves feelings about how one's actions have affected others, while "regret" involves feelings about how one's actions affected oneself. In other words, "remorse" is more object related, "regret" more narcissistic. (2009, p. 244)

Elaborating on these concise remarks, I now suggest that regret is a complex, dysphoric state that can be situation-based and fleeting or characterologically anchored and sustained. It can be about actions that had an unfortunate outcome or it can be about acts not undertaken and opportunities missed. Here, I disagree with the philosopher, Irving Thalberg (1963), who suggests that personal responsibility is a defining feature of remorse while only a characteristic feature of regret. In his view, regret can arise about events that one had little control over (e.g., the passing of summer). My counterpoint is that even such events are "personalized" in the unconscious of the regretful individual; he might think: "Ah! The summer passed and I did nothing to enjoy it." This causes him distress. In fact, there is some evidence that the distress arising from acts of omission is often greater than that from acts of commission (Kahneman & Tversky, 1982).

Chronic regret also includes intricate disturbances of ego and superego functioning. The impaired ego functions are evident via loss of flexibility in considering matters of the inner world and external reality and disturbances in the subjective experience of time which seems to have stopped, and masochistic submission to a life in bondage. Cognition is flooded with "contrafactual thought, or imagining states contrary to the fact: especially what might have been" (Landman, 1993, p. 37). The superego disturbances include hyper-criticism of past actions (or inactions) and their (real or imaginary) consequences and lack of self-forgiveness, a mockingly triumphant attitude towards the hapless sectors of the ego, and a clever jettisoning of current pleasures at the altar of ever-unachievable peace in life at present. Linking the ego and superego reactions is the wish to undo the past decisions that have turned out to be self-damaging. Lady Macbeth's handwashing is a well-known example of an act intended to magically expunge something that was done in the past.

At times, a well systematized "if only ..." fantasy comes to dominate the mind. Elsewhere, I have elaborated upon the psychic constellation of this fantasy in the following words:

> Individuals with the "if only ..." fantasy lack interest in the future and constantly wring their hands over something that happened in the past. They insist that if only it had not taken place, everything would have turned out (or would have been) all right. Life before that event is glossed over or retrospectively idealized. When a childhood event, for example, parental divorce, gets involved in the "if only ..." fantasy, an elaborate "personal myth" (Kris, 1956) tends to develop that, with its seductive logic, might even go unquestioned during analytic treatment (e.g., my case of Mr. A. in Kramer & Akhtar, 1988). The "screen" nature of such "if only ..." formulations, however, is clearer when the trauma, relentlessly harped on, is from the recent past. Individuals who remain tormented year after year by the memories of a failed romance from college days, a psychotherapist who moved out of town, or an extramarital lover who withdrew his or her affection often give histories of having been painfully "dropped" from maternal attention during early childhood. (Akhtar, 1999b, p. 222).

Those afflicted with chronic regret claim to be suffering from the narcissistic depletion consequent upon "bad" decisions of their past. An impulsive marriage, a reckless resignation from a job, an abrupt emigration, a hasty purchase of a house, and a thoughtless abortion are the sort of themes that preoccupy them. To be sure, any and all such events can lead to adverse consequences and to a retrospective wish to undo the decision, which is a central feature of regret. However, matters are not as simple as they appear. Careful scrutiny invariably reveals that not all their current suffering is due to the alleged "wrong turn" taken years ago. Even more important, the regretful individual remains focused upon the consequences of his earlier decisions and shows little curiosity about the potential origins of that decision. In other words, the fact that something already problematic in his psyche might have propelled that "bad" decision is completely ignored.

Developmental origins and later elaborations

Exploration of the development background of such individuals often reveals earlier wounds that have resulted in a generalized or focal self-care deficiency and/or to unconscious masochism. Their inability to be vigilant and self-protective while making important decisions had arisen from early maternal neglect; they simply do not feel valuable and worthy of loving care, even by themselves. Their masochistic surrender to a rejecting mother (and perhaps also a similar father) had led to an inner imperative to dissipate themselves and act in irresponsible ways.

A concomitant to the resulting regret is inactivity and chronic waiting to be put together right all over again. Abraham (1924a) made the following astute comment pertaining to such dynamics:

> Some people are dominated by the belief that there will always be some kind person—a representative of the mother of course—to care for them and to give them everything they need. This optimistic belief condemns them to inactivity. (p. 399)

The optimism that Abraham refers to exists on a covert basis in the regretful person. In a disguised and chronologically inverted manner, such hopefulness pops up in the form of nostalgia. The wish to capture an idealized past and an admixture of pain and joy characterizes this emotional state. Pain is evoked by awareness of separation from the now idealized object and joy by a fantasied reunion with it through reminiscences. "It is the subtlety, iridescence, and ambivalence of these feelings that gives nostalgia its inimitable coloration" (Werman, 1977, p. 393). While often attributed to a loss during adult life, this characteristically "bitter-sweet pleasure" (Kleiner, 1970, p. 11) has its origin in the incomplete mourning of a traumatic disruption of the early mother-child relationship. Sterba (1940) was the first to correlate homesickness with a longing for the maternal breast. Fenichel (1945) also explained nostalgia as a wish to return to the preoedipal mother. Fodor (1950) went so far as to correlate nostalgic yearning with a deep-seated longing for the undisturbed prenatal state. However, these references to prenatal bliss, maternal breast, and preoedipal mother are better regarded as largely metaphorical. Much takes place between a premature traumatic rupture of the infantile bliss and its alleged counterpart in adulthood. Hartmann's (1955) warning regarding the "genetic fallacy" must be heeded here. Recall of such early events is questionable, fantasies involving them are retrospective creations, and the idealization is intended to keep aggressively tinged self- and object representations in abeyance. It is, however, unmistakable that the nostalgic individual is looking for a completely untroubled state. Such a person is looking not only for the lost object but for an idealized object and, even more important, for the time before the object was lost.

The accompanying "if only …" fantasy is a product of incomplete mourning over the loss of the all-good mother of symbiosis. It expresses a position whereby the idealized primary object is neither given up through the work of grieving nor assimilated into the ego through identification. Instead, the object is retained in psychic limbo by a stubborn nostalgic relationship which is:

> … characteristically indeterminate in its representations, and by its imaginary nature the subject is able to maintain separateness from the object. This leads to an indefinite and indefinable quest—and if an object should appear that seems to correspond to the nostalgic desire, it is promptly rejected, it becomes demythologized; it is not what it promised to be: the subject's projection of what it should be. The subject can thus only enjoy the search and never the possession. (Werman, 1977, p. 391)

At the same time, the displaced derivatives of this "loss" are harped on ad infinitum. Splitting mechanisms also play a significant role here since the aggressively tinged representations of the lost object are totally repudiated and/or displaced onto other objects.

The nostalgic yearning for the past often coexists with the "someday …" fantasy which propels excessive hope on an overt basis, and a relentless search for ideal conditions. Individuals with the "if only … fantasy live in the past and those with the "someday …" fantasy live in the future; both are alienated from the present. A temporal fracture of this kind is central to the experience of regret. Even the regret of the elderly that they did not devote enough time to their families when their children were young is often a shield against the horror of realizing that they ended up becoming like their own busy and neglectful parents. The "old" past gets buried in the poisoned garden of the "new" past and the self is cleaved in time.[1]

Sociocultural vicissitudes

The emotion of regret with its characteristics of hand-wringing and masochistic self-laceration is a captivating theme for fiction and poetry. Proust's (1871–1922) *Remembrance of Things Past*, written between 1912 and 1921, might have a greater dose of mourning and nostalgia but does contain a dollop of regret as well. Four prominent illustrations of regret in modern fiction are the following:

Ernest Hemingway's short story, The Snows of Kilimanjaro (1936), which has a protagonist who has lived a life of sloth and procrastination whose full-of-promise past has ended up in a harrowing present of despair. Erosion of values pervades the tale: loose sex, lost love, revenge, war, and heavy drinking.

Joseph Heller's (1966) novel, Something Happened, which is a meandering saga of a middle-aged mid-level executive who feels directionless, bored, and morose, but inwardly clings to the "hope" represented by the innocent and unconsummated passion he felt for a girl when he was a teenager, a girl who committed suicide long ago.

Louis Begley's (1993) novel, The Man Who Was Late, which describes the life of a middle-aged investment banker who masks his existential angst by an opulent lifestyle but lets his undue vigilance and lack of faith in human bonds torpedo his last chance for fulfilling love. His preexisting sense of isolation is compounded by the ensuing regret and leads to his suicide.

Julian Barnes's (2013) novella, The Sense of an Ending, which is a meditation on memory, aging, and how perverse permutations of human choices can cause enormous damage and inconsolable remorse and regret.

To be sure, more examples can be given from the world of fiction.[2] A far greater impression, however, is made by the poetry pertaining to the emotion of regret. I have earlier in this discussion referred to Charlotte Brontë's (1846) poem, "Regret." Here I quote it in its entirety.

Long ago I wished to leave
"The house where I was born;"
Long ago I used to grieve,
My home seemed so forlorn.
In other years, its silent rooms
Were filled with haunting fears;
Now, their very memory comes
O'er charged with tender tears.
Life and marriage I have known,
Things once deemed so bright;
Now, how utterly is flown
Every ray of light!
Mid the unknown sea of life
I no blest isle have found;
At last, through all its wild wave's strife,
My bark is homeward bound.
Farewell, dark and rolling deep!
Farewell, foreign shore!
Open, in unclouded sweep,
Thou glorious realm before!
Yet, though I had safely pass'd
That weary, vexed main,
One loved voice, through surge and blast,
Could call me back again
Though the soul's bright morning rose
O'er Paradise for me,
William! even from Heaven's repose
I'd turn, invoked by thee!
Storm nor surge should e'er arrest
My soul, exulting then:
All my heaven was once thy breast,
Would it were mine again!

The opening two lines of the poem tell it all. The first line, "Long ago I wished to leave," lays down the anachronistic foundation of things to come; it all began elsewhere, in some other time, the poet declares. The second line, "The house where I was born," is rendered within double quotation marks as if to remind the reader that he may or may not have been born in that particular house or to nudge the poet into an impish complicity with a "personal myth" (Kris, 1956). Starting from these lines, the poem goes on to idealization, search, failure to find a haven, and ultimately a "psychic retreat" (Steiner, 1993) of confession and nostalgia: "All my heaven was once thy breast, would it were mine again." That Brontë titled a poem of futile choices, loss, wistful longing, and retrospective idealization "Regret" (without ever using the word itself in the body of the poem) testifies not only to her artistic savvy but to her deep psychological grasp of the experience of regret. While this poem is exemplary, good poems on regret must exist in other languages. I, for one, am aware of the striking poem, *Humesha der kar deta hoon maiN*, by Munir Niazi (1986) in Urdu, which bemoans the author's tendency to be late for all important occasions and how this causes him great pain.

An interesting point to note about the poems by Brontë and Niazi is that the affect of regret is intermingled with a bit of remorse in them. This is because both poets take their own self as an object and thus can "empathize" with its distress. The ensuing regret thus gets imbued with tenderness. This is what I call "warm regret".[3] In contrast to this is the "cold regret" where the self is not taken as an object and the concern remains purely narcissistic. The poem, "The Miser," by the Nobel Prize winning Indian poet, Rabindranath Tagore (1861–1941), is a depiction of the latter variety of regret.

> I had gone a begging from door to door in the village path,
> When thy golden chariot appeared in the distance
> Like a gorgeous dream and I wonder
> Who was the king of all kings!
>
> My hopes rose high and me thought
> My evil days were at an end,
> And I stood waiting for alms to be given unasked
> And for wealth scattered on all sides in the dust.
>
> The chariot stopped where I stood.
> Thy glance fell on me and thou camest down with a smile.
> I felt that the luck of my life had come at last.
> Then of a sudden thou didst hold thy right hand
> And say "What hast thou to give me?"
>
> Ah, what a kingly jest was it
> To open thy palm to a beggar to beg!
> I was confused and stood undecided,

And then from my wallet I slowly took out the least
Little grain of corn and gave it to thee.

But how great my surprise when at the day's end
I emptied my bag on the floor
To find a least little gram of gold among the poor heap.
I bitterly wept and wished that
I HAVE THE HEART TO GIVE THEE MY ALL. (1910, p. 58,
upper case used in the original)

Literature is not the only cultural vehicle for the expression of regret, however. Politics and social etiquette are other realms which involve both expression and denials of regret. In the political arena, remorse and regret often underlie strategic decisions and shifts in governmental policies. Responding to remorse, a nation can acknowledge its misdeeds and attempt to offer reparations; the affirmative action policies in the United States towards its racial minorities, the German reparations to Holocaust survivors, and the work of Bishop Desmond Tutu's Truth and Reconciliation Commission in South Africa are some illustrations of the beneficial political praxis catalysed by national remorse. Concern for the injustice done to others undergirds such operations. Regret is, however, a different thing altogether. Here a nation or a community feels that it has missed out on the opportunity to be supremely powerful, even omnipotent, and thus resorts to large-group nostalgia and fundamentalist attempts to revivify the preexisting (real or imagined) grandeur. Ex-Nazis reincarnating as the German skinheads, white supremacists in United States, Serbian nationalists of the 1990s, and the current radical Muslims (especially of the ISIS stripe) represent the political praxis of regret. Remorse seeks to repair a damaged object while regret attempts to restore narcissistic integrity.

A less virulent entry of regret into political arena is evident in its replacing the offer of apology. Politician after politician expresses "regret" at their misdeeds instead of apologizing. President Ronald Reagan stated the following as an "apology" for his selling arms to kidnappers linked to Iran who would release US hostages in return and would divert some funds to right-wing groups in Nicaragua the Reagan administration backed: "A few months ago, I told the American people I did not trade arms for hostages. My heart and my best intentions still tell me that's true, but the facts and the evidence tell me it's not …. It was a mistake" (cited in Battistella, 2014, p. 107). And, President Bill Clinton deftly transformed remorse into regret in the acknowledgement of his sexual liaison with the then nineteen-year-old Monica Lewinsky. He said "I know that my public comments and my silence about this matter gave a false impression. I misled people, including even my wife. I deeply regret that" (cited in James, 2013). The use of the word "regret" in the post-Donald Trump denunciation comment by US Supreme Court Justice Ruth Bader Ginsburg seems, on the other hand, well chosen and correct. She said, "On reflection, my recent remarks, i.e., response to press inquiries were ill-advised and I regret making them" (cited in Alvarez, 2016, p. 14). She was regretful but decidedly unapologetic.

The reluctance of political leaders to apologize is based upon both idealism and expedience. A leader is not supposed to be weak, after all; he must not admit to doing something hurtful to others though he might acknowledge having made a "mistake." Moreover, apologizing opens up the risk of the victim asking for reparations. Replacing apology by regret bypasses such "inconvenience." The ex-governor of Virginia, therefore, was willing to say that he "deeply regret(s) accepting illegal gifts and loans" (cited in Dockterman, 2014, p. 16) rather than that he was apologetic to his constituents. Similarly the wealthy investment banker, Tom Perkins said, "I regret the use of that word" when he retracted his comparison of popular attack on the richest one percent of Americans to being put in a "concentration camp" (cited in Takahashi, 2014). Statements of such sort are intended to wipe out a self-blemish; they do not reflect any concern for others.

Further dilution of "regret" is found in social discourse where one is almost relieved to "regret" not attending a cousin's brother-in-law's daughter's engagement party or an out-of-town ninetieth birthday of an ex-boss that would warrant considerable expenditure and would most likely be a dreadfully dull event. "Regret" under such circumstances is welcomed by the one expressing it. Conversely, the real estate colloquialism "buyer's remorse" should actually be "buyer's regret" since it has little to do with hurting the seller or the agent. All in all, in the chamber of language, regret, remorse, guilt, shame, counter-phobic confession, and expedient mendacity frequently masquerade each other. Such "sliding of meanings" (Horowitz, 1975) is also witnessed in clinical work with narcissistic individuals.

Technical implications

The treatment of patients whose mental life is suffused with regret is, in essence, no different from that of patients with other types of problems. The "trio of guideposts" (Pine, 1997), that is, neutrality, abstinence, and anonymity on the analyst's part, and abiding to the "fundamental rule" (Freud, 1900a) of free association on the patient's part, form the structure of the treatment just as they do in other circumstances. At the same time, some specific guidelines can be offered in dealing with cases where regret is chronic and occupies considerable space within the clinical dyad.

First, the analyst must make gentle remarks that validate the patient's regretful stance. For example, if a middle-aged business executive laments his failure to attend his son's college graduation or his nephew's wedding owing to work-related commitments, the analyst must "agree" that such decisions were unfortunate and have resulted in wistful despair. Doing so does not fixate the patient in his *mea culpa* but paves the way for the exploration of why such "bad" decisions were taken in the first place. At the same time, the analyst must be willing to acknowledge that some losses will never be recouped and the passage of time does preclude the possibility of undoing the related damages to the patient's self.

Second, the analyst must help the patient bring forth the changes in his ego ideal that have taken place over the course of time. Clearly, when he took this or that "bad" decision, he was aspiring to be someone other than what he is aspiring to be now. Regret represents not having lived up to one's wished-for self-image and this image during the wistful hand wringing is different from when the decision was taken to do (or not do) what is now regretted. What led to the change? Encouraging the patient to reflect upon this question can yield therapeutically useful information.

Third, the analyst and the patient must be able to observe and discern the "screen" functions of the overt sources of regret. That crying over the impetuousness of adult life helps disavow the impulsivity born out of childhood hunger has to be brought out in the open. For instance, the man who did not attend his son's graduation must come to see that his neglect is a replication of his father's abdication of his paternal responsibilities which, in turn, had acquired an even greater significance for him because of his mother not loving him enough. In other words, the multi-layered roots of contemporary concerns must be unmasked and made subject to mourning. In the course of such unearthing, one might come across "screen memories" (Freud, 1899a) which, to wit, pertain to regret and yet are themselves containers of even earlier dysphoria. No better illustration of this can be given than is embodied in the following reminiscence of the protagonist in J. M. Coetzee's (1998) novel, *Boyhood*.

> He is sitting beside his mother in a bus. It must be cold, for he is wearing red woollen leggings and a woollen cap with a bobble. The engine of the bus labours; they are ascending the wild and desolate Swartberg Pass.
>
> In his hand is a sweet-wrapper. He holds the wrapper out of the window, which is open a crack. It flaps and trembles in the wind.
>
> "Shall I let it go?" he asks his mother.
>
> She nods. He lets it go.
>
> The scrap of paper flies up into the sky. Below there is nothing but the grim abyss of the pass, ringed with cold mountain-peaks. Craning backwards, he catches a last glimpse of the paper, still flying bravely.
>
> "What will happen to it?" he asks his mother, but she does not comprehend.
>
> He thinks all the time of the scrap of paper, alone in all that vastness, that he abandoned when he should not have abandoned it. One day he must go back to the Swartberg Pass and find it and rescue it. That is his duty: he may not die until he has done it. (pp. 30–31)

At first, this passage makes the reader feel that the boy is full of regret at letting the candy wrapper go. Upon giving the matter some thought, however, one notices the inattentiveness of the mother (e.g., her lack of curiosity about the boy's first question and her non-responsiveness to his second question) which might be the real cause of the boy's distress. The lost candy wrapper serves as a screen for the breach in his communication with his mother.

Fourth, the masochistic dimension of regret must be addressed. In commenting upon my paper on "if only ..." fantasies, Arnold Cooper noted.

> Those with ferocious superegos and masochistic inclinations are involved in endless self-condemnation: "If only I had said this, if only I had done that" etc. These fantasies have a way of paying

back one's conscience without really intending to do anything different in the future. They are mea culpas ...: "I have confessed to
being guilty. And now we can close the book of this episode." (cited
in Akhtar, 1999b, p. 222)

The unconscious masochistic pleasure and the concomitant induction
of helplessness in the analyst that is central to such developments in the
clinical process must be unmasked. The defensive aims of regret against
the emergence of remorse also need to be kept in mind: to carry on endlessly about how one has hurt oneself can preclude acknowledging that
one has hurt others as well due to this or that decision.

Fifth, it should be remembered that a patient's repeated incantations
of regret over a past inaction can serve as a defense against ongoing
procrastination and unwillingness to take on hard work.

Sixth, even during the time when such work is in progress, the analyst must remain respectful of the patient's psychic "soft spots" and be
prepared to oscillate between credulous listening with affirmative intervention (when thwarted growth needs and ego deficits seem to dictate
the transference demands) and sceptical listening with interpretive
intervention (when conflict-based transferences are in the forefront).

Finally, throughout this work, the analyst must remain highly
vigilant towards his own emotional experience. He must avoid a quick
unmasking of the patient's material due to his own restlessness and
exasperation. He must resist the "compulsion to interpret" (Epstein,
1979) and exercise patience both as an attitudinal element and as therapeutic intervention (Akhtar, 2015a). Neither cynicism nor masochistic
submission are permissible to the analyst though their allure is great
while working with such patients.

The guidelines outlined above should not be turned into a rigid
strategy. Maintaining a firm allegiance to the "principle of multiple
function" (Waelder, 1936) in accordance with the patient's material
would help the analyst develop an optimally responsive technique
which fluctuates between "evenly suspended attention" (Freud, 1912e)
and interventions based upon a therapeutic strategy.

Concluding remarks

In this contribution, I have elucidated the phenomenological components of regret and distinguished this particular emotion from the

related one of remorse. I have noted that regret is often accompanied by compromised ego functioning, a ferocious superego, masochism, and the "if only ..." fantasy. I have traced the origins of regret to early breaches in the mother-child relationship and underscored the "screen" functions of the contemporary trauma evoked as a cause of wistfulness by regretful individuals. After a brief foray into literary and sociopolitical realms, I have devoted a section of my discourse to the technical implications of the psychoanalytic understanding of regret.

Now, as I approach the end of this contribution, there are three other areas I wish to comment upon. The first pertains to "survivor's guilt," that is, the feeling of guilt at having been more fortunate than an impaired sibling or having survived while a loved one died in an accident, natural disaster, or a concentration camp (Niederland, 1968). Often the individual who died had been the recipient of guilt-expiating activity; there was unconscious hostility towards him, and his death precluded the possibility of diminishing this guilt by kindness and indulgence towards him (Sonnenberg, 1972). These formulations are impressive but conflate guilt (at the unconscious hostile intentions towards the deceased), remorse (at having "killed" the person via the omnipotence of primary process thinking), and regret (at having done or not done something to protect oneself from the consequences of one's hostility). This link between guilt, remorse, and regret has not been clarified in the existing literature on the topic.

The second area I wish to comment upon is the relationship between regret and suicide. Regret, in tandem with remorse or acting independently, can lead to self-flagellation and diminished self-esteem. When affixed upon actual "misdeeds" and poorly executed decisions of adult life, the emotion of regret can become the *leitmotif* of one's existence. Klein's (1935) suggestion that some suicides represent an individual's effort to rid his love objects of some aspect of himself (e.g., greedy, inconsolable) provides a link between remorse, regret, and suicide. More forceful than this is Winnicott's (1960b) declaration that, at times, suicide is "the destruction of total self in avoidance of annihilation of the true self" (p. 143). This statement suggests that suicide can be a way to thwart a life that seems destined to be replete without authenticity, wistfulness, sorrow, and regret.

The third and last issue I want to touch upon pertains to the self-reform and redemption that can be mobilized by regret. The gnawing awareness of having taken a wrong turn in life or of having missed important opportunities can, sometimes, lead to contemplative self-scrutiny and character transformation. To be sure, some losses cannot be made up (e.g., becoming pregnant in old age) but can be reversed. A high school dropout can pass a GED test and resume education, an immigrant can go back to the country of his origin, an alcoholic who has ruined his physical and financial status can improve on both these fronts. Indeed, substance abuse treatment programs regard the feeling of regret as an ally in the process of recovery. Landman's (1993) assertion that "Regret stimulates thoughts and failings that form a bridge between a regretted past and a better, free future" (p. 23) comes to mind in this context. Kavaler-Adler's (2004) observation that "When regret is conscious it can be grieved on an affective level and learned from on a cognitive level" (p. 75) is also pertinent in this context. A parallel can be found in processes leading to a healthy outcome of remorse. Under fortunate circumstances, meaningful reparation can arise from remorse (Klein, 1935, 1940) and beneficial self-redemption can grow out of regret. No emotion is inherently "good" or "bad" and such qualifiers must be reserved for what one does with a particular emotion's pressure. This applies to all emotions. Regret is no exception.

Notes

1. I have elsewhere (Akhtar, 1996) elucidated the link between nostalgia and optimism in greater detail. There I have demonstrated the essential similarity between the "if only ..." and "someday ..." fantasies.
2. For further references of this sort, and for the place of regret in the culture at large, see the magisterial work of Janet Landman, 1993.
3. Another good example of such "warm regret" is to be found in the 1957 Bollywood film song, "*Sub kuchh luta ke hosh mein aaye to kya kiya*," which means "After having squandered everything, what good is it that I am wise now!"

CHAPTER EIGHT

Developmental perspectives in the treatment of regret

Theodore Fallon

"No Regrets" was the signature song of Edith Piaf, whose life was portrayed in the 2007 movie, *La Vie en Rose*. The song croons that the good and the bad of the past hold no sway in the face of a new blossoming love. The song is all the more poignant sung by a woman who is portrayed as suffering throughout her life and even seems to be suffering as she is singing it. Such is regret early in life. On the other hand, in the song, "My Way," sung by Frank Sinatra among others, the lyrics come from someone at the end of life who says, "Regrets, I've had a few/But then again, too few to mention" (Anka, 1968). The singer takes pride and satisfaction from doing life "my way." Oddly enough, when the Muppet character, Gonzo, sings the same song, he leaves out the part about regrets, perhaps not to scare children with such a feeling.

In both songs, regret seems to be something to be avoided, and certainly to be kept away from children. It is, after all, a negative emotion. On the other hand, a recent TED talk by Kathryn Shulz (2012), a staff writer for *The New Yorker*, dealt with not regretting regrets. Numerous writers have pointed out that we probably do not want to be friends with someone who has no regrets. People who are not capable of regret may be on the spectrum with sociopaths. And at the same time we are told that regret can weigh us down, leaving us depressed and discouraged (Greenberg, 2012).

So, what is this feeling that we hold so ambivalently? Where does it fit in our external world? Perhaps, more important, where does it fit in our internal world? Is it a useful emotion that we can use to move ourselves forward in life and help others do the same? Or is it something that just weighs us down in life? As therapists, should we view regret as something to help our patients avoid, or can it be used to help someone move forward in their development?

Toward a definition of regret

Let us begin by considering what regret is. Most of us have had a feeling of regret, which usually can be easily recalled and deeply felt in that moment of recall. When we see it in others, most of us readily empathize, feeling a deep pang within us. Miles Little (2008), writing about regret, noted:

> Regret is a negative emotion ... Like all words in common use, it has gained a penumbra of meanings. At one extreme, it conveys a ritualized sense of being apologetic for something untoward, as in "any inconvenience is sincerely regretted." We may also say that we regret someone else's death or misfortune, when we mean to express sympathy, sorrow or grief. To say we regret someone's choice of a course of action may also register resentment, anger or sometimes resignation at the deleterious effects of the action ... Regret is a word that is both vague and ambiguous. It is vague in the technical sense because it occurs in degrees, from strong to weak, and it is difficult to say precisely how much negative emotion constitutes regret. It is ambiguous because, as we have seen, it has several possible meanings. Comments like these can be made about many of the words we use each day to express complex concepts: trust, love, admiration, alienation, needs—all suffer from the same apparent shortcomings. Yet we use them all the time, and manage to exchange meaning through their currency. (pp. 50–51)

C. L. Stevenson (1944), a philosopher of ethics, wrote, in the middle of the twentieth century:

> Such is the typical situation with vague terms. When subject to definition or analysis, their meaning is seldom treated as a *fait accompli* (as might be the case when a scientific term is analyzed

for the benefit of a beginner); rather the meaning is in the course of becoming what the analyst makes of it. And the analyst has a choice in deciding what it shall become, no matter how anxious he is to abide by common usage. As Wittgenstein once remarked: "To remove vagueness is to outline the penumbra of a shadow. A sharp line is there after we draw it, not before." (pp. 86–87)

Yet, despite regret being a vague, ambiguous term, and one that we feel ambivalently toward, people have no difficulty identifying regrets. A survey of the general US population (Parker-Pope, 2011) reveals that about twenty percent have regrets about some romantic relationship. One in six people has regrets about some family interaction. Education and career are the next most common realms of regret followed by decisions that parents make regarding their children and decisions that people make regarding their own health.

Of course, who you are and where you are in life has an influence on what regrets you have and how you feel about regrets. Younger people tend to look at regret optimistically as something that will guide them to make better decisions in life, while older people tend to see regret as something sad, depressing, and associated with failure. College students and young graduates most often identify regrets in choosing education and careers. Women tend to have regrets in the context of relationships while men more often point to professional and career choices.

Individuals from cultures that have more circumscribed roles within the family and community, such as traditional Asian societies, tend to suffer less regret than individuals from cultures that offer more choice. For example, if marriage is arranged by parents and families, then the individuals being married have regret much less often than individuals who choose their own mates. It may also be that in our present day "Control-Z culture," in which we can undo any operation from word processing to video games, regret has become a more dominant experience.

Not only do most people easily understand and identify regret, many fields have used regret to explore, understand, and explain. Janet Landman, in her 1993 book, *Regret: The Persistence of the Possible*, considers the many fields that have examined and used regret: psychology, economics, philosophy, sociology, anthropology, law, medicine, and literature. For example, the field of economics uses regret in its decision theory (Loomes & Sugden, 1982), which quantifies and devises equations using regret to describe and predict why people might make some choices and refuse others. Another example is the use of the concept of regret to better define informed consent in medicine (Little, 2008).

In seeking the definition of regret, one finds a range. Consider the following: "To feel sad or sorry about (something that you did or did not do); to have regrets about (something)," and "Used formally and in writing to express sad feelings about something that is disappointing or unpleasant" (*Dictionary.com*, 2016). Another source reads "To feel sorry, disappointed, distressed, or remorseful about," and another "To remember with a feeling of loss or sorrow; mourn."

These definitions share a common theme of referring to a feeling in relation to some external circumstance. The common part of these definitions points to a negative reaction to a past event. Regret is usually considered a feeling after one acts in a manner to a particular context and then later wishes not to have done so, or fails to act when action would have been the better choice. Some descriptions of regret talk about the role of regret in recognizing missed opportunity in the past with the possibility of correcting the past decisions. Other descriptions consider the missed opportunities in the past with the possibility of not missing such opportunities in the future. These views and definitions have to do with external circumstances and the behaviors that accompany the circumstances.

However, if we look closely at the definitions of regret, there are significant differences. The differences in definitions point to differences in the internal processes and experiences. The various definitions include different words such as remorse, loss, sadness, guilt, shame, embarrassment, depression, and annoyance. These words call attention to internal processes rather than focusing on an external context and behavior. The different words suggest different internal experiences.

From another perspective, we can consider regret as a set of processes in reaction to a sense that we could have done better. Experiments in decision theory reveal that the closer we are to having taken the better course, the more we regret. For example, we are more likely to regret our actions if we miss the train by one minute than if we miss it by thirty minutes. We think about "what if": "what if" I spent a little less time in the shower; "what if" I had gone through that yellow traffic light (Gilbert, Morewedge, Risen, & Wilson, 2004).

Another way of considering the process of regret is to examine the experience over time. Upon having learned or realized that there might have been a better outcome, most people initially push away the realization—denial. Then there is bewilderment—how could I have done that? From here, there can be a self-punishment or a perseveration but ultimately if regret is to lead us in a more productive direction, we have to take personal accountability. We have to acknowledge our failure, accept the irrevocability of our past decision and of the person we were who made that decision, and incorporate this newfound wisdom into our new model of the world.

Regret can be a wonderful, although negative and painful emotion. On the one hand, we can use the regret to remind us that we are flawed and can do badly. On the other hand, however, if we recognize the universality of failures and are not so badly wounded by our failures as to lead us to hate ourselves, it can remind us that we can do better. Regrets are learning opportunities.

In addition, we can use regret to make better decisions in the present using anticipated regret. In thinking about making a decision, we can weigh and balance anticipated satisfaction and anticipated regret. In other words, it is a way of thinking about the positive and negative consequences of future actions—a way of calculating risk and danger, leading us to "good" decisions (Little, 2008). Let us consider some clinical material to illustrate.

Clinical vignette: 1

Mr. A, a man in his late thirties, grew up in a family, the eleventh of twelve children, feeling he was lost among the throng. He presented for therapy with one complaint (among others) that for as long as he could remember, from early childhood onward, he had never been excited to get out of bed and face the day. "Why bother?" he said in passing. Although he reported that he had worked very hard sacrificing much in his life to become a very successful artisan (both financially and in reputation), and had felt good about his creations, he had not been able to produce in the last five years. He now reported that he had met with his aging mother who was beginning to show signs of dementia.

He met her in the home of his estranged sister as his mother was preparing to leave the area and go to live with another sibling several thousand miles away. There were no plans for the mother to return to this area and he had never visited his mother when she lived with this distant sibling before. Mr. A reported that he did not feel comfortable talking with his mother in a more intimate way, not wanting to reveal himself, lest his estranged sister overhear something he might say. He then added, "When my mother dies, I know I will regret not having talked to her more intimately."

We can poignantly feel Mr. A's regret, and the confusion and angst contained within. How do we understand Mr. A's regret in anticipation of the loss and mourning he will face in the future? He tells us he felt lost among the multitude of children when he was growing up. We might imagine that he felt neglected by his parents, as well as frustrated with his competitive feelings in relation to his older siblings. All of this might be connected to his comment, "Why bother?"

We might also imagine that his lifelong sacrifice to attain artistic and financial success might have been an attempt to undo his sense of smallness within the multitude of older siblings, while his recent difficulty creating in the past five years and his seeking help now at this point in his life might be the dawning of a recognition of the futility of his worldly success to address the anger, resentment, and sadness that he carried forward from his childhood. We can imagine that all of this turned on his painful anticipated sense of regret. Where was he to go with his regret? As observers of this process, is there anything we might be able to do to help Mr. A in the present and in anticipation of his regret?

Historical context

When pointing to regret, Sigmund Freud used the German word "*bedauern*," a neuter noun as well as a transitive verb. This word appears frequently in Freud's correspondences with others (mainly Fliess) and occasionally in his published works. He used the word to describe a process happening within himself (a verb, I regret). However, he never explored the meaning of regret (*bedauern*) or the implications it might carry in the psyche. It is curious that as insightful and penetrating as Freud was, he did not seek to understand his own reactions in this case, something that seemed to occur so frequently within himself. Perhaps even more curious, the psychoanalytic literature is mostly devoid of an examination of regret.

Akhtar (2002) considers a number of reasons why such words are rarely explored in the psychoanalytic literature. Of the possibilities that Akhtar proposes for this phenomenon, regret is perhaps somewhat of a hybrid concept spanning the social as well as psychological realm.

One might imagine (but would be wrong) that the relationalists or the interpersonalists might have grabbed hold of the concept of regret as it has strong implications and undercurrents in our relationships with others while at the same time connecting us to ourselves. At face value, regret does not seem particularly life enhancing, although I will argue below that it can be. I will also argue below that regret and its more potent sibling, "remorse," cuts into all of us deeply and perhaps analysts, like everyone else, do not want to feel the vulnerability that we inevitably do feel.

In comparison with the sparsity of the word regret, the psychoanalytic literature is replete with discussions of remorse. For example, Freud himself considered remorse in his writings. Here, Freud used the word *Reue*, a feminine noun and never a verb. For example, this word makes its appearance a number of times in both *Totem and Taboo* (1912–13) and *Civilization and Its Discontents* (1930a). Freud used the word as he objectively described a feeling that others experienced (a noun, they felt remorse) as they faced a terrible deed that they felt compelled to do, but then had a significant change of heart when they saw the consequences of their actions.

Melanie Klein (1935) carried this idea forward and created an extensive developmental concept from it. The words she used in her original paper written in German are *Schuldgefühlen und Gewissensbissen*, translated by Klein herself as "guilt and remorse." Collins German Dictionary (online, 2016) translates the plural noun as "pangs of conscience." In both of these papers, the first time she presented the word "remorse," it was by itself. In both papers, the remaining times it was used, it was accompanied by the word "guilt." It is interesting that Klein chose to use a different word than Freud. In pairing "remorse" with the word "guilt," she seemed to be emphasizing the internal angst.

Klein used *Gewissensbissen* (remorse) as the pivotal concept around which the paranoid position tilts to the depressive position. In Klein's description of the young developing child (she imagines this child to be around fifteen months of age), the child is portrayed as full of rage and desires to retaliate because she is not given everything she wishes for. Klein named the psychological position from which the child attacks, the paranoid position. As the child matures and recognizes the limitations of reality and her mother, she comes to realize that her attacks on her mother are unjustified, and mourns her earlier reactions and the hurt that she imagines she conferred on her mother. It is at this point the child feels *Schuldgefühlen und Gewissensbissen* (guilt and remorse). This leads the child to a mourning which Klein named the depressive position.

In considering the present day definitions and the historical context of regret, we might notice that the definitions and perspectives differ by the distance from the person experiencing the emotion and the intensity of the internal experience. For example, Freud seemed to lightly use the word "regret" (*Bedauern*) in corresponding with Fleiss but used "remorse" (*Reue*) when describing the feeling experienced after murdering one's father, for example. Klein (1937) further intensified the description of the internal experience using the words guilt and remorse (*Schuldgefühlen und Gewissensbissen*) perhaps to match Kierkegaard's (1843) "pain and suffering" and attributed these feelings to infants, people with manic/depressive states and those with schizoid/paranoid states, but certainly not herself.

Regret (*bedauern*) can be a verb or a noun (in both English and German). It can be a process that one experiences (internally) as well as something to be observed in others. The German words for remorse (both *Reue* and *Gewissensbissen*) on the other hand are only nouns, objects to be observed, rather than processes one might experience oneself. Perhaps we are seeing in the literature an objectification and a pushing away of the more uncomfortable if not painful parts of the experience, projecting them onto others.

Regret, remorse, and forgiveness

Another example of this distancing is the description of the "lack of remorse" for one of the most dreaded entities in the psychological field, sociopaths. However, we seldom consider that children under three years of age and many children in the autistic spectrum clearly demonstrate a more developmentally appropriate "lack of remorse." In fact, some two year olds and criminals share this "lack of remorse" and the main difference between them is the size and physical capability of the body to effect their feelings. On the other hand, we rarely see "lack of regret" in the literature.

Klein (1935, 1940) described movement from the paranoid to the depressive position as recurring throughout life, particularly in pathological states of manic depression (1940). More recently Kavaler-Adler (2004) presented a case of an adult whom she described initially as schizoid. Through a psychoanalytic process, she demonstrated a developmental process in which the patient came to recognize her "paranoid schizoid position" thereby effecting her maturation.

> Now that a mourning process had brought her into the depressive position with all the capacities to feel for the subjectivity of the other, and to feel her own agency as responsible for hurting the ones she loved, life became much more complex. Life also became more colorful, however as affects mixed all elements of pain, loss, longing, and anger, which was so easy to turn against oneself to avoid the feeling of grief. (p. 64)

Here we begin to see the interpersonal aspect of regret that makes regret the hybrid concept that Akhtar (2002) wrote about. In entering the realm of the interpersonal, we are considering the development of object relations. That is, the child has an internal model of how one interfaces with another human being and what purposes others serve for her.

Another perspective from which to approach the topic of regret is to consider its social complement, forgiveness. Take for example if someone commits a regrettable action against another, then asks forgiveness of the other. Akhtar (2002) reminds us that there are important internal processes that must occur in order to forgive. Schafer (2005) also considers this and goes even further to say that full forgiveness may not even be possible.

The social reciprocity between forgiveness and regret or remorse also reflects the internal processes within each of the participants. Just as Melanie Klein and Kavaler-Adler described, for both forgiveness and the resolution of regret and remorse, the participants must work through a series of processes. First there is a recognition of the hurt, then an acknowledgment of responsibility. This is followed by a mourning. Only after the mourning can there be a resolution. To put these processes in a broader context, consider maturation and development. To work through regret and forgiveness and come to a resolution, one arrives at a more mature understanding of oneself, others, and the world. In this context, forgiveness, remorse, and regret are part of a normative psychological development rather than as Klein considered, evidence of pathology. Let's consider another clinical example.

Clinical vignette: 2

A thirty-two-year-old man, Mr. B, presented with chronic anger, depression, and feeling like life was not worth living. As he explored these painful feelings, he came to understand the source of them to be his marital relationship with a woman whom he felt had insatiable wants. After a time, he came to regret his decision to marry his spouse and after considerable struggle, decided to leave the marriage. In the process of the divorce, his spouse continued to demand concessions from him (e.g., his entire income) that after some work, he came to recognize as unreasonable.

Sometime later in the therapy, Mr. B began another relationship. As the relationship became more intimate, he began to recognize that in this new relationship, as in the one that led to his marriage, he failed to express and delineate his own needs and desires both to himself as well as to his new mate. Gradually, he began to explore and understand the underlying processes that led him to ingratiate himself to his love interests.

After some time, he began to recognize that this was a process that occurred to some degree in all of his relationships. That is, he would ingratiate himself in all of his relationships. On one occasion, his boss even remarked that he would "twist himself into a pretzel in his efforts to work with others." As he explored this further, he recognized the origins of his self-effacement in his anxiety and anger toward one parent who was depressed and the other who suffered from a chronic post-traumatic stress response. In this context of his growing up, he felt both anxious for their distress and vulnerability, and anger at their unavailability. With this insight, Mr. B terminated his relationship with his present girlfriend. After some time, he was able to establish a more balanced relationship and felt much more satisfied with his life. At this point in his therapy, as he reflected on his regret at having married his wife, he realized that he had failed to take responsibility for his own well-being. He also came to wonder, if he had not had this extremely dissatisfying experience of his marriage, would he have ever learned that caring for oneself was not an option.

He came to see that as painful as his marriage and divorce had been, it was a necessary part of his growing up. Now, rather than regretting his marriage, he saw it as a significant and unavoidable developmental step, and recognized that although it was quite painful, it could have been worse. In this way, he resolved his regret.

Regret as a developmental concept in treatment

In the case of Mr. B, regret can be seen as pointing to an incomplete developmental process in which Mr. B was able to identify that a decision that he had made, getting married, was the "wrong" decision. And yet he initially did not clearly see how all of the pieces were connected and his role in the situation. When the full picture was better understood, regret became irrelevant. In the case of Mr. B, regret is what happened on the way to the more mature approach to life of caring for oneself.

Perhaps it is useful to consider Schafer's (1980) "action language" as a useful concept here. In the context of regret, the declaration of saying, "I should have done it differently," leaves out the part of the person that in fact made the "wrong" decision. Until a person integrates that part of himself into the rest, there will always be the possibility of the schism which falsely locates part of himself in the past ("that part of me that made that bad decision that I regret") with the all-knowing (in hindsight) part of himself that now says: "That was a bad decision."

If we carefully consider someone describing regret, it is important to listen to how the person considers his responsibilities, and the ways that he avoids the responsibility by disowning a part of himself. Consider how Mr. B failed to take responsibility for his own well-being. In his anger toward his parents' neglect of him when growing up, he had refused to take on the responsibility, failing to develop this aspect of himself sufficiently. Initially, he saw his failed marriage as making the wrong decision, rather than as a consequence of his failing to take charge of his own life.

However, if we are to make sense of regret, then it must address only what is possible. For example, it does not make sense to say "I regret that I can not fly (without a plane)," or "I regret that I can not be in two places at once." These are impossible wishes, although at times any of us can regress to a pretend world and imagine these as regrets. We must consider the reality not only in the external world with all of its possibilities and limitation. We must also consider our own internal world, where we are in the midst of our own development with all of our attendant strengths and limitations. Only then do we have a chance for regret to be something that happens on the way to maturing.

Now let us take a second look at Mr. A's regret. To begin with, he described an anticipatory regret, one that had not yet happened, and yet he was anticipating, even as the regret pointed to something to be avoided. If he knew it, then why would he not be able to avoid it? The case presented many possibilities as to why Mr. A would not be able to avoid the regret, but none of them were external contingencies. They were all internal contingencies. His anticipated regret was a clear signal of these potential internal vulnerabilities. When the therapist called Mr. A's attention to these vulnerabilities, Mr. A initially pushed them away. With continued support, however, he was able to tolerate the discomfort and then was able to devise a potential solution—call his mother regularly in an effort to experience as much of her as he could, now as an adult, before she faded into dementia. The idea then occurred to him that he might even get to know his mother, one adult to another.

These examples of Mr. A and Mr. B point to the usefulness of considering regret and its more potent sibling, remorse, as a normative developmental process that occurs throughout life, and how the concept of regret can be used in treatment. Regret and remorse are emotions that point to internal vulnerabilities which can be understood and worked through. The working through, although considered by some as the domain of therapy, can also be considered a process of normative development and maturation.

This perspective is particularly useful when we work with individuals considered to be in the autistic spectrum. By virtue of their being in the autistic spectrum, social and affective communication is compromised, which interferes with social development. Yet, with regret, this is where we can focus the work. It is not surprising, then, to recognize that classic psychoanalytic techniques with adults might not consider working with regret or even "lack of remorse." There is a setting, however, where one can directly experience development and devise psychotherapeutic techniques that can be used to work with regret. That setting is working with children. This setting can lead the way in finding techniques to work with developmental challenges.

It is precisely this social development that is at stake when we consider regret. Development can and does occur, in childhood as well as adulthood. Kavaler-Adler (2004) as well as others (Fallon, 2014; Singletary, 2015) have demonstrated the usefulness of conceptualizing and working in treatment with the development of basic social reciprocity, including regret, remorse, and the seeming lack thereof. As Metzl (2014) puts it in reviewing Kavaler-Adler (2013):

> [The] deeply human and existential anguish of regret is a process that must be traversed within the self, prior to communicating it to another. It is an internal emotional experience, felt in the stomach and in the gut as well as in the heart, and ... [includes] not only

the self but eventually the other. In a true moment of regret, the other whom one has offended is always the one with whom one is deeply empathic. ... [At] the moment of regret, the subjectivity of the other is heightened in one sense of consciousness as one feels the keen and acute affect of grief, longing, loss and love toward one whom one has offended and toward whom one now feels compassion, and at this moment of regret, total awareness is the only manner in which true behavior change can occur. ... [The] emotional release into grief, at the moment of regret, is the most critical sign of authenticity in reparation and regret through the path of emotionally laden grief, which can modify guilt and free the affect to experience yearning for reconnection. (p. 4)

Conclusion

Although regret is an uncomfortable feeling generated by a sense of failure, it is a normative process that can move us forward in development. As with all development, it is possible to get stuck, and weighed down, especially in the initial processing of regret, including being left in a state of denial, bewilderment, perseveration, and depression. However, at its best, the discomfort of regret moves us along in development to mourn failures and seek better decisions as we move on in life.

In the context of treatment, regret, looking at past failures, and anticipated regret, looking at potential future failures, signals an area of potential growth. In that moment of regret, however long that moment lasts, the self in not fully integrated, criticizing the past self for failures made, without taking into account the limitations of the past self. Hindsight is always 20/20. It is only when the person can take responsibility for the past self that she can see her way to a present and future where a better decision can be made the next time such a problem arises. As therapists, we can usher this process along, helping our patients and ourselves find new, more robust understandings of reality.

CHAPTER NINE

Clinical transformation of intolerable regret into tolerable regret*

Susan Kavaler-Adler

In classical psychoanalysis, we have been taught to not reassure patients. What does this mean? Why this caution? My understanding of this caution has been that the patient needs to struggle with his conflicts over his own impulses, to find his own resolutions by consciously confronting impulses that formerly were unconscious or out of control. The analysand needs to have this process without any interference in it. Whatever the patient's struggle, he needs room for it. The patient needs the psychic space, analytic space, and transitional space to struggle with his own dilemmas. To not offer reassurance is thought of as allowing such space. Refraining from offering reassurance also allows patients to experience that the analyst is not afraid of their experience. When a psychoanalyst does reassure a patient (and this happens probably more often than we admit), it is mostly our countertransference enactment of a rescue fantasy. Perhaps, getting the patient off the hook is a way of gratifying our own wish to restore our own inner harmony through a gesture that seems kind and compassionate at the time. Perhaps in this way we

---

*This chapter first appeared in *The Anatomy of Regret: From Death Instinct to Reparation and Symbolization through Vivid Case Studies* (Karnac Books, 2013, pp. 97–122) by Susan Kavaler-Adler. It is reprinted here with permission of the author and publisher.

attempt to create reparation for ourselves; reparation with our internal parent, through projecting that parental other onto the patient.

However, since the introduction of British object relations thinking, we have learned a few things about trauma and the early developmental arrests that can happen when trauma disrupts internalisations of "good enough" (Winnicott, 1974) object relations, developmental growth, and ongoing levels of psychic self-integration. When we look at an object relations psychoanalysis that aims to heal trauma, to give insight into trauma, and not to have trauma reduced to drive conflict, a whole new question confronts us about the difference between validation (validating psychic reality, but also real reality) and reassurance. If we, as psychoanalysts, mistake validation for reassurance, we might deprive the patient. So, validation needs to be defined in terms of trauma, which, by definition, relates to actual reality and not to psychic reality, although psychic reality and psychic fantasy always interact with the concrete realities that are related to trauma.

Validation of trauma is critical in the healing of the self after trauma. Validation is also important in affirming the dimensions of the trauma, as it repeats itself in compulsions and projective identifications in present life. The psychoanalyst needs to help the patient discover and validate her own trauma, and also needs to be an active source of validation at times. In addition, the psychoanalyst needs to help the patient find validation at its source—with the parents—whenever possible, or at least needs not to discourage the patient from seeking it with the original parents. However, at times, this can become a masochistic pursuit, which needs to be interpreted in terms of the parent who is incapable of tolerating the guilt and anguished sense of loss within the conscious experience of psychic regret.

When the parent is incapable of tolerating regret, and therefore, of communicating validation of early traumatic events in the family, the analyst naturally becomes a primary source for the patient's validation. The analyst must also help the patient salvage her sense of reality in the face of the parents' denial of the traumatic events that have had such an impact on the patient's psyche and on the patient's view of the world. The analyst needs to help the patient see the parents' incapacity to offer validation by helping her understand the psychic capacities needed to face the regret. This can help the patient differentiate, and separate, from the parent, rather than remaining stuck in endless rage and retaliation, or stuck in cycles of effort to extract the yearned-for validation from the parent, like Sisyphus endlessly pushing his boulder up the hill, only to have it roll down again.

My own definition of validation, as it contrasts with reassurance, is that validation is an active and explicit acknowledgment to a patient of traumatic experience. It involves being a witness when the patient discovers the trauma through memory, free association, the interpretation of reenactments inside and outside the treatment, etc. The patient must discover the trauma at an affective level, and have a gut feeling that the trauma occurred. However, this moment of affective realization can be forgotten all too quickly in the face of the psychic compulsions to protect the image of the parent. Therefore, the witnessing of the affective level disconnection becomes of critical concern, and it is the psychoanalyst who is there to be a witness in this way. To witness and verbally validate must be clearly distinguished from reassuring someone that she is good when she confronts hostile or sexual impulses in herself. To validate is not to reassure; it is to be a witness to what is holding, and to what has held, the patient back from living a new and healthy life in the present. The following case illustrates the critical role of validation in promoting psychic healing and psychic integration. In this particular case, the validation is of the parent's psychic arrest and of the parent's pathological intolerance of the conscious experience of guilt, intolerance of the psychic transformation of guilt into an affect-level experience of grief within regret.

Validation of a patient's intolerance of regret: the case of Amy

Amy, a Latin American woman in her late twenties, had discovered significant childhood trauma in seven years of psychoanalysis with me. She attended sessions two, three, and four times a week. She started treatment with no former psychotherapy experience. She made herself accessible to lying on the couch. The crucial trauma discovered in this manner was that of Amy having been molested by her middle-aged alcoholic father when she was between the ages of four and six. Amy recalled her molestation through dreams, through masochistic experiences of abuse with sadistic and seductive men, and through her sense of being "held" psychically on the couch, which allowed Amy to free associate. Amy recalled that her mother had been a key player in the malevolence of the experience by neglecting to help or acknowledge that her small daughter was being visited each night in the dark by a drunken father. The mother failed to help her daughter by confronting the father or by acknowledging the events.

Instead, the mother added emotional abuse to sexual abuse by screaming with rage at her daughter when she washed her off the next day, cleaning her of her own husband's ejaculatory fluids, which had been left as unwanted evidence overnight on her daughter's body. The day after each night's sexual intrusion, Amy's mother would assault little Amy with hostile epithets. She called her daughter a whore, a bitch, or scum. She blamed her daughter for being a little seducer, when she was obviously a small child and a helpless victim. The mother seems to have been in a jealous rage, discharging the entire accumulated wrath she stored up towards a rejecting and alcoholic, philandering husband (older than she) on her small daughter.

Consequently, the usual oedipal stage dynamic played out an unconscious fury in this family. Much later in analysis, when Amy had come to terms with some of what happened and had got past her rage at her father, she spoke of the longings she had for her father, beyond the trauma. She spoke of feeling abandoned when her father "went back to her," left her bedroom in the middle of the night and went back to her mother's room. And in most of Amy's romantic or dating relationships with men, she would end up feeling abandoned. There was one exception to this, in a long relationship that she was able to follow to its end, with her making the decision to part. But her tendency was to be drawn to men who would seduce and abandon.

The deeper abandonment, however, with its confounding with abuse, was to be found with her mother, the one who had actually been the better parent of her two. Her mother had left Amy in their country of origin to come and forge a path in America when Amy was eight. However, she allowed Amy psychic survival by sending her a letter in which she said she missed Amy. She enclosed a dollar with the letter each week. Left with a cold and rigid aunt, Amy clung to these letters of reassurance, waiting to be reunited with her mother. Not having had enough of her mother, and yet unavoidably being so deeply attached to her as her one and only real parent, Amy suffered from the anguish of seeking acknowledgment from this mother for the horrors of sexual abuse that had been inflicted upon her by her father.

Amy's psychic turning point in the monthly mourning therapy group

After the discovery of herself in seven years of psychotherapy and psychoanalysis, Amy joined a monthly therapy group, which I run for four hours (with a break) on a Saturday, for ten months a year. This group focuses on each individual's mourning process within the group process. For years now, Amy had separated from her mother in all practical ways, living her life in New York where she had been brought by her mother at the age of twelve while her mother lived in Miami, and working in her own chosen profession, which was not one suggested by her mother. Nevertheless, Amy's core emotional tie to her mother was still profound. To grieve her way out of this tie to a more individuated state, Amy would have to face a deep pain, a pain filled with the anguish and longing to reunite with her mother.

One Saturday during the group, Amy frantically related the account of her sexual abuse to all the others in the group. When she reached the part of her tale that concerned her mother's unwillingness to hear anything she would say about her past and the experience of her father's molestation, she shared an angry, yet pleading longing for her mother to remember what had happened and to acknowledge it. She did not accuse her mother as she spoke. She was not in her former rage about her mother's emotional abuse of her (the blaming, ridiculing, and humiliating of her when she had suffered the arousing intrusion and abandonment of her father).

In that moment, Amy let go of all the formulated accusations she might have directed like darts at her mother. She lay down her darts and arrows, and collapsed into the vulnerable longing of a child pleading for maternal love. The anguish of her cries was evident to all in the group as she disarmed herself and said, like a confused and bewildered child, "Why won't she admit it? Why won't she remember it? Why can't she just acknowledge it happened? Even her dreams are saying it to her, but my mother won't listen!" At the height of the pain of her longing, I said to Amy, as her former analyst and group leader, "Your mother is incapable of focusing on the truth. If she were to acknowledge it, she would feel like she is a devil. She would see herself as all bad, and as all destructive. She can never admit it, because she can't tolerate the guilt of regret without feeling annihilated by her own self-hate. She just isn't at a psychic level where she can bear it." At my words, a deep cry, a wail of pain, opened up from Amy's core being, where the internal infant self seemed to reside. A child's vulnerability had transformed into an infant's longing. Yet, she spoke words that revealed the meaning in her tortured cries: "I'll never get her back!"

Silence fell upon the group. The atmosphere opened to the poignant and universal longing that lay at the core of all our beings. "I'll never get her back," she cried again. There was a sense of feeling the internal psychic change in Amy happening right there in the moment. This pain of grief was the only road to true psychic separation for Amy, and in that moment, we all knew it. We all had our own core of pain to experience and transgress. Amy was suffering what is the essence of true grief. She had longed for reparation with her mother. Like all of us, she had fantasies of being close to her mother again. She had hoped that by speaking to her mother of her pain, of her knowledge of the past, of her little girl exploitation and trauma, her mother's caring would come out to meet her, bringing her together with her mother, as once she had felt as an infant. She had not blamed or accused her mother. She had let go of all of that to make her appeal. She tried over and over to find the right words. No words proved to be the right ones. There were no right words. There were only her words bouncing back at her. Her mother seemed to turn to stone.

As I spoke of her mother's incapacity to tolerate regret, which was related to her mother's more total incapacity to face what is, and what had been, as an overall mourning process, some realization was triggered in Amy that temporarily freed her, and transformed her entire being into a cry for love. This was a cry for love combined with an anguished realization of disappointment, a cry that would feel to the group membership like a wounded heart contracting into a final release of its agony: "I'll never get her back!"

In this therapeutic mourning group, I conduct a psychic visualization at the beginning of the group, a visualization in which breathing opens inner life. I ask all the members whether they can feel a connection to their heart. Some can and some cannot. But in moments of grief, like the one Amy manifested, the heart is felt by all. I did not have to explain more than I did. My confrontation about her mother's incapacity to feel regret was enough. I could explain it later. But now it was not necessary. The inner realization in Amy was complete. She was released as she let go and acknowledged for herself that she would never get her mother back. She gave herself her own validation, along with that which I and the group had given her. She could now witness her own fantasy of reparation and not be possessed by it. Her addicted need to cling to her mother was over. From now on she would deal as best as she could with her mother's demands on her to visit her or to call her, but she would no longer be as chained to her or to initiate contact with her mother and hope for love and understanding. She could increasingly—with relapses—let go of her mother, because there were others to go to now, now that she was internally free of the pathological tie that bound her. She could feel the love and understanding from the group and from me.

The mother who reaches a moment of tolerance for regret: the case of Lisa

Lisa had a different experience with her mother. It began with a psychic turning point that Lisa experienced in one particular session with me. This session was a moment of awakening for Lisa and for me, when our unconscious minds rose to the surface and met. Her courage to face her pain and my intuitive sense of her need at this time paved the way.

It was a late evening session in my uptown office in New York. It seemed dark that evening. The beginning of the session began like many others. Lisa seemed tortured in the silence, unable to speak, unable to begin. Something was building up inside her, and her surface facial expression showed her unspoken rage at me for not rescuing her from what was within her. Her body showed tremors of tension that cried out, reminding us both of the traumatized child within her that threatened to break into consciousness. The tremor spoke of the internal child, a child crying for attention in an emotional vacuum, with her mother withdrawn from her. Yet none of this was in Lisa's conscious awareness at the time; the child in the body was trapped by the mind that was forced to carry the memory, but which could not speak. I was only consciously aware of the tension, the waiting, wondering if she would find her way to words, wondering if she would find her way to feelings, wondering if it would be helpful for me to speak. Then, suddenly, Lisa darted out of the room, saying by her action that she could not take in any more. Lisa was angry again because I would get sleepy in the tense silence, where so much of her was pressuring from within a sealed-off emotional state, speaking only through the tension of its dissociation.

When she darted from the room and went out into the hall, I found myself leaving my office and going after her. I have developed an inner bond with her that compelled me, urged me to do it. With someone else, at another time, I might have sat there unmoved, feeling, "Enough already. Go! Leave me alone," as a countertransference response. But not in this case. I was outside my office, in the hall, standing by the banister of the stairs, while Lisa stood agonized and torn apart on the top of the stairs, leaning on, and beginning to bang against, the wall across from me. I watched while at first Lisa fought with herself, frantic with the pain and tension on indecision, seeking release, but terrified of losing control.

Turning a lifetime of rage inward against herself, Lisa began to bang against the unyielding cement wall, as all her life she had banged against the emotional wall put up by an unyielding mother, a mother who would not let her penetrate her or enter her to have her own crying need heard and met. As she seemed about to bang her head against the wall, the head that had the mental instruments of torture operating on her, derived from unprocessed memories which haunted her in the reliving of them, Lisa turned swiftly away instead. In a second she had pivoted away from self-attack and entered into self-surrender. She bent over like a swan, yielding to her pain. She surrendered to the child within her that had needed to cry for decades, decades that felt like centuries when we were waiting together in the silence.

Lisa's surrender was complete for the first time. She could no longer run away. She let go and began to sob and sob. Her body convulsed within its cathartic release, and I gently suggested that she come inside my office again. Having chosen to let go of her opposition, Lisa followed me, still at the beginning of the sobbing that would bring years of agonized longing to the surface. Her need to purge herself, and to wail, was already expressing its profundity through the body that had relented to let the sobs pass through her entire being. As she sat back in a chair in my office, further from me than before, near the wall, half turned away from me towards the door, and half towards me, I sat with a new sense of peace inside, feeling we had arrived, and were no longer waiting. My silence was now filled with the sense of a deep emotional core of holding in my body, as if I was holding her body in my lap as she cried.

Eventually, I said the words to her that came with the feeling. I said without thinking, "Mommy, hold me. Please hold me mommy". I spoke for the child within her. There was no effort. I knew she was inwardly responding. She did not have to speak to me. She continued to sob out her inner oceans of tears, tears from deep down, filled with sadness and longing, so different from earlier tears. I brought her the tissue box and handed her some tissues. Then I sat back down, tissue box in hand. We were deeply in communion now, and I was struck by how effortless it all was. The aggression that had caused so much resistance had temporarily left us, although it would certainly be experienced and understood at another time.

Describing the effortlessness of this session, as Lisa let go of her defensive controls and surrendered, brings back a memory of another time and place in my own life, when I discovered the abandon of total emotional and body surrender. I was at a therapy marathon in my early twenties. I had been crying for hours. It was in the middle of the night. Suddenly, a woman in the group expressed herself and opened up my entire being. I remember her exact words: "My mother came down hard on me, but my father always supported me." My chest and heart opened to the deepest wailing of grief, longing, and love. My tears poured out, but more viscerally prominent was the openness of my chest, so that I wailed like a baby, like a newborn infant just emerging from the womb. All my earlier crying had helped to open me up, but at that moment, when I heard the words from that woman that meant so much to me personally, I opened at a core level of body and being that cast my cries out at a volume and intensity that could touch all the other, sixteen or so, people in the room.

How effortless it all seemed now, as I could release all the longings for the father who had died when I was ten. He had died and left me with an extremely critical mother, the one who "came down hard" just like the woman said. The release of all my love and longing in a body surrender to all cries and sobs liberated me. This was the way into the present, into the Now, into an "eternal Now" that felt so peaceful, and which made me feel close to all around me as I could feel I was most truly myself. When a woman in the marathon group then spoke, saying directly and compassionately to me, "I feel your pain, Susan," I was able to turn to her and speak. In the midst of my release, I was totally in control, for the control was an authentic and centered control from within, not the defensive control of the mind that needs to be surrendered to in the Now. All was effortless, just as at that time with Lisa. And how these moments last. Even though mentally forgotten, these moments of complete contact and connection sustain us subliminally and come back. Once they happen, all has been changed; all has been changed for the good.

For Lisa, her transforming moment allowed her to reach forward into the core of the mother whom she had to confront in the present. She and her mother were to come face to face with love for each other, a love that they both had perhaps not known since Lisa's early infancy, prior to all the conflicts and traumas of the separation-individuation stages. It was through this encounter, the most tender of meetings, in a moment when her mother was tense with the conflict of whether to let go, that her mother's capacity for regret was momentarily—and perhaps eternally—realized. It was a moment that Amy, unlike Lisa, could never achieve with her mother. It is hard to say which mother (Amy's or Lisa's) was more damaged by her past. Yet one mother (Lisa's) opened to a capacity for regret, and another (Amy's) did not. Lisa's moment with her mother's transformation can be briefly related. It happened when Lisa's mother came to visit her and her siblings in New York, a unique event. Lisa's mother lived overseas in Eastern Europe. When she came to New York, it was a major event for Lisa, and her sisters and brothers who lived in the city. Lisa played a main part in preparing activities and visits within the family for her mother. She had no idea how her mother would respond. Lisa had frequently felt abandoned by her mother, not only in childhood, but also throughout her adulthood. Her mother had never called her—she always called her mother. She was also seeking something she could never find when she called. When she felt the icy chill of her mother's emotionally withdrawn state, and felt her mother's inability to listen, she either cried or raged from her intense disappointment.

Many times in her psychotherapy, Lisa related the devastated internal state within her that followed her attempts to reach her mother through phone calls. She also demonstrated her extreme sensitivity to not being listened to or to feeling as if she was not being listened to in her transferential reactions with me in sessions. Lisa demanded intent attention at all times, no matter how silent she was herself. This was quite understandable, given the extreme emotional detachment of her mother, which alternated with some capacity to listen and talk, as Lisa was able to open up more, and to reach out more to locate her mother when she called. Yet the overall impression of Lisa's mother was that of an extremely depressed woman in emotional withdrawal, conveying an emotional emptiness to her daughter. So the event that I am about to report seemed almost like a small miracle when it came about.

Maybe the mother's meetings with her children, without the presence of her emotionally abusive husband, had been wearing down her resistances, and the thought of going back to the emotionally starved family and nation she came from was probably beginning to haunt and threaten her. The combustion of these varying factors began heating up Lisa's mother's emotional terrain, finally bringing her to an emotional precipice where true grief was a possibility. Just as she was approaching the edge of the precipice, Lisa's mother hesitated, in conflict, tears behind the eyes, tears not yet cried. Her daughter saw her look. She recognised her own face in her mother's look, the one she had most strikingly on the evening of the session in which she surrendered to my emotional holding and to her own need for relief.

Seeing the entire body of her mother tense, with the internal censor humiliating her and holding her back from release, Lisa looked directly into her mother's eyes, and whispered, "It's OK, Mom. It's OK to cry!" Her mother yielded and let go of her censorship, and abandoned herself to her tears of grief and yearning. Filled with the emotions she had resisted for a lifetime, Lisa's mother spoke from the depths of her heart, and directly to Lisa: "I hope your life is better than mine!" Lisa's mother clearly articulated this poignant remark in a new psychic state, one born in the moment. Lisa had been with her in her place of hesitation and need. This one phrase said by Lisa's mother spoke volumes about the grief of her life and about the buried love that had dissolved in an intolerable regret, which in this moment had transformed to a tolerable heartfelt regret. Tears came to my eyes as Lisa told me of this poignant moment.

An intolerable regret becomes tolerable: the case of Lauren

Lauren came into the writing group with a letter she had written to the group members. It seemed appropriate that she should read it, because it was a writing group. The letter was lengthy. Someone in the group said it sounded suicidal, but it was meant to be an explanation for a comment that she had made that had hurt another group member. The letter seemed like a forced apology and an extensive explanation about what had caused her to react as she had. We all seemed to be witnessing a gross overreaction to the actual circumstance.

Lauren had told another woman in the group that she did not care what her feelings were, and did not care if she was changing and becoming more in touch with her feelings. Lauren said this with an edge of contempt in her voice, being, as she would later say, "cutting." She had been hurt by this other woman having called her a bully, and she was taking her pound of flesh in revenge. She had not killed anyone, but, being faced with the impact of her comment on the other woman, she unconsciously felt that she had indeed committed a murder. Not being conscious of this belief, she defended against conscious knowing by evading full ownership of her aggression.

Unable to tolerate the guilt of her regret at the time of her comment, Lauren did not face the woman in the group and did not apologize in the group. Instead, she wrote Adrien an email in which she apologized for the comment that hurt Adrien, but also externalized the blame on me, the group leader, rather than owning the regret. Something was still too intolerable to bear about owning her own guilt. Within the group, she read the letter she wrote, in which she spoke, with the lament of one wounded, of how miraculous it was that any of her own creativity even survived because of the annihilating emotional attacks of her father, as he particularly targeted her creative potential. Pressured by the unconscious force of a psychic fantasy, Lauren chose the role of a victim, defending herself and pleading her cause at her own self-created trial, rather than merely owning regret and moving on. A potential existential guilt about the matter of what indeed had happened, in reality and in her own psychic reality, became a neurotic guilt, and, therefore, too exaggerated to bear. It was now the guilt of psychic fantasy murder, a guilt harbored in her unconscious domain. Triggering a latent and age-old psychic fantasy, Lauren's guilt turned to persecutory proportions. She retaliated by blaming and attacking me, the group leader, and also the therapist of the woman in the group, Adrien, whom she felt attacked by in Adrien's comment about her acting like a bully. She decided to blame me because she also felt excluded from what she imagined to be a tête-à-tête about her going on in Adrien's therapy sessions. She was open about saying that she thought we talked about her together. In retaliation, she made sure to exclude me for the time being from her thoughts and from her conversations with others in the groups.

Lauren gradually opened up to discussing her father transference with Adrien within another group that I facilitated, a mourning group, of which they were both members. She allowed Adrien to open her own pain to her about Lauren's rejection of her. She allowed Adrien to speak of her secret wishes to be friends, and of her secret affection for Lauren, who Adrien said reminded her of "the best part of her mother." Still, she left me out, punishing me for seeing her transgression against Adrien, and for seeming to be on her side. I examined my own reactions, and saw that I felt favorable to Adrien when she had been rejected by Lauren with her comment about Adrien "chomping at the bit" and about Lauren not caring about her, just as Adrien had begun to open up more emotionally. I listened to Lauren as she became enraged at me in the mourning group, and said she did not trust me, and that maybe all I was interested in was the money.

Eventually, my patience seemed to pay off, and Lauren began to speak about having a negative transference to me in the mourning group and said that she wished to begin to talk about it. However, when she attempted to talk about it in the group, she could not go past a certain point. She acknowledged that she had been angry with me since the incident with Adrien in the writing group. She said that she knew her anger with me had become mixed in with anger she had for years with her mother and sister.

Yet when she attempted to go into her feelings, she felt blocked in a way that was totally unusual for her, because Lauren was someone who could go deep into her affect states, and she could be totally expressive about her anger, her rage, and the sadness of her grief. She had a sister who had tried to have an exclusive relationship with her mother, moving in with the mother, and excluding Lauren. Lauren was already conscious that her sister was trying to own her mother, since she had never had her mother to herself in her earliest years, as Lauren had, because Lauren was the oldest.

Lauren's anger with her sister for taking over her mother's life and excluding her certainly had played a big part in her anger with me for having therapy sessions with Adrien, therapy sessions which made her feel excluded when she was in conflict with Adrien and heard my empathy for Adrien in the group. Now, in the mourning group, she could not actively express her anger with me, other than at a time when she went into a rage at me, accusing me of many things which made her feel out of control. During the summer vacation from the group, Lauren called me for an individual consultation. She said that she thought she was inhibited in speaking about her anger with me and her negative transference because the other women in the group became her sister watching her and judging her.

I agreed to see Lauren for an individual consultation. She had been in groups with me for many years, and rarely saw me individually. She knew, however, that she could see me individually if she wished to. She began the session with memories of the downtown office that she revisited for the consultation, with memories of older writing groups she had been in with me, and of members whom she remembered from these groups. On a one to one basis she seemed fairly comfortable with me, despite her continuing apprehension about being with me in the mourning group. She told me that the group must conjure up transferential feelings towards her sister, which made her inhibited in revealing her feelings towards me in front of them. Lauren said that she had thought that her sister was trying to undo her own exclusive relationship with her mother, when she was alone with her mother up until the age of two, before her sister was born, and take revenge against her for it. I thought she might be right and told her so, impressed with her insights as usual.

The rapport between us over this kind of understanding allowed Lauren to go further, and to plunge into the heart of her anguish about herself and her own aggression. She said that her anger with me went back to the time of her conflict with Adrien in the writing group. She told me that she had felt that I was biased towards Adrien. She said that she had felt excluded. She also told me that she realized that she could be cutting and cold at times. I did not say anything, knowing that she had been afraid of some condemning judgments being made by me in the group, particularly after she accused me of things.

In the group, she had said that she expected me to hate her. When I had asked if she thought I hated her right there and then, she replied, "Well, you couldn't feel too kindly towards me." Having voiced this fear of my aggression coming at her in a retaliatory judgment, she had apparently felt more comfortable owning her negative transference in the group, and now she had felt comfortable enough to come and see me individually. I had not acted out the retaliation she feared. I had not judged her. I had not condemned her, even when she might have been projecting her own condemnation of me, which had once erupted in a rage towards me in the group.

As I now listened in the individual consultation, Lauren seemed to feel free to continue. She was testing out that she could define her own aggression, without fearing that I would be defining it for her, and thus, in her psychic fantasy, condemning her as bad. Lauren did say that she could be cutting at times, expressing a cruelty that she did not like in herself. As she spoke, I could feel the psychic weight of Lauren's burden as she felt regretful about attacking another (even when she justified her lashing out in retaliation against Adrien's remark, which was injuring and mutilating to her on a level of primal psychic unconscious fantasy).

As I felt the heaviness of her psychic weight, I said, "I have the sense of some sadistic murder in the background, as if you *really* believe that by making your insulting remark to Adrien you really committed a murder." Lauren immediately and poignantly responded, "MY mother always thought I committed a sadistic murder!"

Lauren released the weight of her psychic burden as she began to cry and to make the connections with her unconscious beliefs that she had not made before. As she could understand that her guilt had taken on the neurotic proportions of an age-old unconscious belief that she was a sadistic murderer, and as she saw this as her mother's projection of her own sadism, unable to bear the brunt of her own guilt and to consciously face it as a regret, Lauren felt free. She felt the pain and anguish of her own aggression, and the regret of the interpersonal losses that her aggression could create, but she could now clearly distinguish it from her fantasy that she was a murderer (Kavaler-Adler, 2006a, 2006b). She also could see how her mother's projections onto her (and her own identification with them) had their origins in aspects of her mother's disowned sadistic impulses. These disowned aspects of her mother included those when her mother had an exclusive relationship with one child, at the expense of the relationship with the other. With disowned parts of herself, the mother had also displayed passive aggressiveness, which sometimes provoked her husband's overt sadism. Yet, as Lauren spoke about her mother, she was also able to forgive her, because she could see her own sadistic impulses, defined in her cutting and cold manner when angry.

In this way, Lauren was facing her existential guilt in the form of a conscious regret. She was differentiating her existential guilt from unconscious neurotic guilt based on a psychic fantasy of being a sadistic murderer. As her own psychic burden was thus relieved, Lauren was able to forgive the mother who had unconsciously encouraged her to be overburdened with guilt so as to escape her own guilt. Lauren was immensely relieved by our discussion, and when she returned to the mourning group, she told the group about her session with me. It was interesting how she reported the session. She said that she had an "excellent" consultation with me, when she decided to discuss her negative transference with me. She said that even though it had actually been quite painful to confront her own murderous impulses, she had felt relieved. I found it quite illustrative of how Lauren had moved into the depressive position in facing her transference with me, and that she was able to view the session as confronting her own murderous impulses. Once she was relieved of seeing the psychic fantasy of being a sadistic murderer in a conscious form, whatever she felt before as intolerable guilt became a tolerable regret, in which murderous impulses could be accepted within herself. This process allowed her to integrate a whole part of herself that her mother still perpetually disowned, unfortunately having done so at Laura's expense. Owning her own regret now, Lauren made a point of saying in the group that our discussion about her mother's sadism had made her reflect on her mother's situation in her marriage and life, and had helped her to forgive her. She also said that she felt less forgiving of her sister, whose sadism she still felt being enacted on her, as she tried perpetually, in overt action, to possess their mother. Conscious regret had allowed Lauren to move into a sustained depressive position state of mind, in relation to her negative transference with me. Now, she was interested in how her own aggression projected within the negative transference onto me, rather than this aggression remaining an intolerable and overwhelming persecutory attacker from within. She still felt traumatized by her unconscious fantasy of being a murderer (and being stuck in the paranoid-schizoid position).

Lauren followed Klein's clinical phenomenology (separate from her metapsychology) by moving into self-integration, as her split-off and repressed aggression became integrated and her depressive position capacity became a more sustained psychic position. However, it is Winnicott (1960, 1965) who informs us of how important the therapist is as the protector of the holding environment. In not retaliating against Lauren, I was able to preserve the holding environment. According to Winnicott's (1969) idea of "survival of the object," I, as the therapist, could stand in for the early mother, having "survived" by not retaliating and by not abandoning Lauren when she had expressed her raw aggression towards me (enraged accusation). I also purposely did not interpret Lauren's aggression when she projected it onto me (when she was operating in a paranoid-schizoid state of mine), rather than operating in a depressive state of mind. To have done so would have felt like retaliation. Lauren was, therefore, able to move into the depressive position, where she could witness and reflect on her own aggression, and where she could own her own impulse to retaliate what she had expressed originally towards Adrien and then towards me (sister and mother). This kind of Winnicottian (1969) object survival is a key to psychic transformation in patients struggling with intolerable regret that is based on unconscious neurotic guilt, with its unconscious psychic fantasy base. Countertransference retaliation can sometimes prevent this psychic transformation that needs to take place. The transformation is from unconscious neurotic guilt to conscious existential guilt in the form of psychic and tolerable regret.

Following from Kleinian thought as well, we can see the developmental progression in Lauren from hostile and envious assaults to expressions of genuine gratitude. Expressions of gratitude renew an early potential for loving capacity within an authentic self-evolution, as this self-evolution takes place in terms of object relations development. In 1957, Klein published her paper on "Envy and gratitude", a paper which had already been presented at a conference in the 1930s (Grosskurth, 1986). In this paper, Klein articulates the dialectical relationship between hostile aggression in its object-targeted instinctual form of envy, and the development of the capacity for gratitude and for its expression.

When instinctual envy remains unconscious, it can be a constant source of destructiveness in the form of spoiling both external and internal object relationships. When unconscious, it is often heard in the adult form of devaluing criticisms that create psychic distance from others, and which, in their accumulation, create an overall cycle of spoiling and disconnection from internal loving capacities. When unconscious envy is thus enacted, it serves as a polarized psychic state in relation to a depressive position state of mind, a state of mind in which loving capacity can be enhanced and developed through the overt expression of gratitude. I would add that this expression of gratitude is, in itself, an expression of developmental achievement in terms of an achievement of separation-individuation and self-integration, which allows the other to be perceived as truly separate and to be perceived as a loving and "good enough" object to whom one can safely attach oneself, in terms of a "mature dependence" (Winnicott, 1971), without feeling threatened with retaliation or abandonment. In addition, the act of expressing gratitude directly to someone, and especially to a psychoanalyst, who also serves as a "good enough" real object for internalization and as a transferential mother figure, allows for the internalization of a "good" interpersonal transaction that can become part of a new and better psychic structure within the psyche and the internal world.

All this can be seen in the case of Lauren, as she evolved in her mode of communication within the monthly mourning group experience, with the help of the one individual consultation. In the same group meeting in which she reported being so relieved and helped by the individual consultation with me, in which she viewed the psychic fantasy of her sadism behind her angry comments in the group, Lauren evolved into a deeper affect experience of her gratitude. Towards the end of the group, she said, crying as she spoke, that I was "always here," and that I created an atmosphere of safety, in which she and all the others "could have our negative transferences."

The implication was that she, and the other members of the group, could all hate me if they needed to, and I would still be there, without retaliation or abandonment, thus loving them. In other words, they could hate me freely, and I would still love them, the essence of Winnicott's (1969) "object survival." By saying this so spontaneously, with such deep contact with her interior self core (Winnicott's 1960 "true self"), Lauren was taking another developmental step forward, and was looked at with admiration by other group members, who wished they could communicate from the depths of self-feeling as Lauren did.

Lauren could evoke the truest example of Klein's "envy and gratitude" dialectic, as she contacted primal love through the expression of gratitude, after having expressed the most hostile envy and rage towards me. Her self-reflective awareness of her mother transference with me was obvious as she spoke of my being there for her and for her transferential siblings (sisters). She contacted love through an awareness of loss and grief. This conscious regret allowed awareness of wishes for reparation. Lauren could then reach out through reparative gestures towards me as the other who represented the primal object, as well as all the displaced objects upon which she had transferred her ambivalence towards her mother.

A daughter's regret towards her father and her evolving capacity for spousal love: the case of Sharon

Although Sharon's story has been written about, Sharon is in continuing evolution. Having entered into four psychoanalytic psychotherapy sessions a week, she has been engaged in a continuing depressive position working-through process. Confronting psychic regret has played a major part in Sharon's analysis, resulting in critical self-integration. This self-integration has allowed Sharon to sustain a rather difficult marriage, and to enhance her capacities for mothering in relation to her two children. As she has owned her aggression through a process of facing regrets, her son (now thirteen) has become free to be himself and to connect to her second husband, gradually relinquishing a symbiotic and narcissistic mode of relating to his biological father.

Sharon's son has been freed by Sharon's self-integration process, because Sharon is no longer compelled to project out her disowned aggressive and inadequate parts (when she had formerly lacked self-agency) onto her son through projective identification, triggered by dissociative mechanisms. Her daughter (who is now six) has remained free to develop as a separate person, greatly supported by the love and admiration of her father, Sharon's second husband. Sharon had already been in psychotherapeutic treatment when her daughter was born, although it was a preliminary state of treatment, in which she had only attended sessions once a week. Sharon saw in her daughter a healthy vitality, self-assertion, and a capacity to play and to easily relate to others. She increased her psychotherapy sessions, which has become a more intensive psychoanalysis, to facilitate her daughter's growth as well as her own, and to deal with the difficulties in her second marriage. The following vignette on Sharon's treatment focuses on the poignant enlargement of her existential grief as it touches on her first consciousness of her former relationship with her now deceased father.

In one session, Sharon had felt the pain of regret over her characterological self-righteousness. She realized this self-righteousness was another aspect of the defensive contempt she had spoken of many times in analyzing her relationship with her husband, and with friends and acquaintances. We had spoken together of how she held on to her self-righteous attitudes, despite how destructive they were to her relationships, because it was a way of holding on to her mother. It was a way of identifying with her mother, and having her mother through this identification when she could not have her through direct affect contact and interpersonal communication and connection. Her mother's affect self was walled off behind narcissistic attitudes of martyrdom, contempt, and self-righteousness that hide intense shame and inadequacy, and a profound lack of self-agency. The mother could dissociate from her shame by inducing these feelings in Sharon and scapegoating Sharon. For Sharon, the only way out of feeling inadequate was to identify with her mother's false self: that is, with her defensive narcissistic attitudes. In this way, Sharon could put herself above others and above her own needs, needs that had lived only in an arrested child self, sealed off within her. Unconscious of it all, she had become an expert at condescension, even though appearing meek on the surface. She had become an expert in enacting Klein's manic defense, by which means she had warded off the grief of her own life losses and regrets. To consciously face her narcissistic defenses, as well as the schizoid ones of outward withdrawal and defensive self-sufficiency, Sharon had to take her attitudes one at a time.

After many psychic forays into Sharon's contempt, we came upon a related "animal," her self-righteousness. She realized that when she thought she was being open and confrontational with her husband, something she feared being, she would often provoke an angry tantrum in her husband. When we looked at Sharon's part in this—aside from her husband's defensive reaction to avoid seeing himself—we saw that she was actually speaking to her husband from a high-horse position of self-righteousness, which—without either of them being aware—provoked an immediate and reflexive tantrum rage in her husband. She was relieved that she played a part in these scenes, because her part she could change and control, once aware of it.

So, we spoke about how she believed that self-righteousness gave her a sense of having her mother's power, rather than just being a victim of this power, as when it was aimed at her in sarcastic and ridiculing comments throughout her childhood. Having come to view her mother's extreme degree of actual powerlessness in relation to her position in the world, Sharon was now inclined to recognize that "My mother's only achievement was her self-righteousness." Sharon told me that she was realizing that her mother desperately needed the false pride that she had perpetually portrayed in her self-righteousness, but that she, Sharon, no longer needed it. She knew she was sabotaging her life by inhabiting the self-righteous frame of mind, and also knew that she had created a life that was worth living, with her family, her new degrees of social life, her work as a professional, and her new success as a creative writer. She no longer wanted to isolate herself behind her own wall of a self-righteous attitude, but first she had to see how this attitude was operating.

As we spoke of her character defense, Sharon increasingly realized how she unconsciously transmitted to others the same attitude in her mother that had so injured her own sense of worth and self-agency, alienating the very ones she said she wanted to be close to, especially her husband and her son. But, from her internal child perspective, to be self-righteous was to be the powerful part of her mother, to share in the power that as a child she had felt monstrous and overwhelming, to be the sadist rather than the victim masochist. By letting go of her self-righteous attitude, of which she said, "It was all my mother had," she was saying "good-bye" to her mother. This had been the greater threat, to be all alone in the world, without a mother. No child could stand this, so being her mother's self-righteous narcissistic extension, as well as her scapegoated inadequate self, had been preferable. In saying "good-bye" to mom, Sharon was saying "hello" to new insights about the vulnerable position she had been in within her childhood family. That vulnerable position involved a relationship with her father that had long been buried in her unconscious, and had only recently opened up. As the mourning process related to her father opened up, it brought the pain of what would have been an intolerable regret, a pain which now—with each phase of recognition—was becoming a tolerable anguish.

It was at the end of this session on self-righteousness that Sharon began to sense that I was sleepy. She felt me fading away a bit. She asked me if I was there. I said I was sleepy, and would like to understand what it was about. Sharon said she thought I was bored with her, did not want her around, and asked if she should leave the session early. I asked her why she assumed I was bored with her or did not want her around, just because I had begun to feel sleepy. She said that it was obvious that if I was falling asleep, I was bored with her. I said it was not obvious, that this was only her interpretation of my motive for being sleepy. I said that there were many other interpretations that could be made. I also said that something out of her awareness might play a part in my being sleepy at that particular time, aside from how much sleep I got the night before, since I had not been sleepy before she came. I said that I often recognized these kinds of sleepy states that felt as if I was being pulled into some repressed area in a patient's unconscious mind, making me feel as if I was being affected by some unconscious pressure within the patient.

Sharon replied that it felt like a familiar place to her, to feel that I, like others, were really not there, as if she was not interesting enough to listen to. She said that it had always felt in her family as if there were nobody really there, nobody listening to her or present with her, nobody who thought she was important. She said that was how she felt with her father, especially after he was hospitalized for depression when she was eight, quit his job, and withdrew increasingly from the world. I wondered if I was not being pressured into playing a role in her unconscious, internal world drama, by being made to feel like the half-asleep father who was so detached that he could not respond to her. Sharon "woke up" as I woke up by saying this. Something seemed to dislodge itself from her unconscious at that moment. Sharon said that her unconscious might be making her feel as if she was with her father again. She had always felt rejected by him, because he was never "there," and that was how she was feeling with me, she said, as if my sleepiness meant I was rejecting her.

The following session began with a whimper, rather than a bang. Sharon said she had been feeling so much better lately—for the first time not having at least six things stored up in her mind that she was afraid to say to her new husband (the transferential mother monster). It was new to feel that she could express herself, and that she could feel pride and pleasure for the first time in completing a creative writing project. In fact, she said that she felt so much better that she felt as if she had nothing to say in the psychoanalytic session. I commented that when she had nothing to say, it was usually the beginning of something really important, because at that moment, she was free of her preprogrammed agendas that served a defensive purpose in the session because they were contrived from her head and did not allow her to be in the moment and have free thoughts and feelings (free association). She was always puzzled when I said this, but she saw that it generally turned out to be true that when she began by saying she had nothing to say, something new and important was about to emerge. Today would be no exception.

Sharon began to let her thoughts come up more freely then, and one of her first thoughts was that she could not remember what had happened in the last session. I suggested that she might not want to remember that her father had come up in the last session, after we talked about losing her mother if she were to give up her self-righteousness. She had clung to her self-righteous mother, through identification, because she was the only one there once her father started becoming ill with depression. I reminded her of how she had felt when I had become sleepy. She then remembered and said, "I guess I didn't want to remember!" She had felt left with a mentally and emotionally absent father.

Sharon began to speak about being left with her monster mother when she rejected her father because he had become such an inadequate parent. She iterated that he had been hospitalized when she was around eight years old. She said that this had followed her having lost her father by pulling away from him and rejecting him at an earlier time. Her imagining in the last session that I was the father rejecting her seemed to be a projection of her rejection of her father, at least as Sharon was seeing it now.

Sharon began to try reconstructing the memories of her early life during the session. She said that since our earlier discussions of her father had brought out the painful memory of how he had actually been there for her when she was little and had loved her, she was now wondering when she had lost him. I said that some girls are loved by their fathers until they become adolescents and start to develop adult female sexual characteristics that threaten their fathers. Sharon replied, quite emphatically, that this was not the case with her. She said that her father had withdrawn from her much earlier, before the time when he went to the hospital. Now she was speaking of him having rejected her, even though she had just referred to herself as a little girl rejecting him.

I asked her where her father was when she was three and her mother left her in the park alone with her brother, and then hit her for finding her way home again. She said that he must have been at work, but at that time she might have felt that he would have wanted to protect her. She had repressed memories of her early childhood for many years, but she had uncovered in earlier sessions that her father had been close to her when she was little. She sensed now that her father had been more comfortable loving her when she could be held and cuddled, and did not have to be spoken to like a more separate person. But then she had discovered him to be such a woefully "inadequate parent" that she had rejected him by mocking him, dismissing him, and by turning her self-righteousness and contempt as weapons upon him. Unfortunately, that had meant that she was left all alone with her terrifying mother, the queen of contempt and self-righteousness, who called Sharon stupid, implied she was bad, and assaulted her with sarcastic comments.

Sharon now said that it all became about "who was hurting and rejecting whom," back and forth between her and her father. She would coldly accuse her father of being inept, and he would reject her by being passive, silent, and withdrawn. "It got much worse after he was hospitalized and returned," she said. He just sat still and stared silently at her. She would become enraged, and would verbally attack him. Reflecting back on this time now, Sharon began to feel remorse. Her eyes filled with tears as she seemed to realize for the first time that "I never understood that he couldn't help it. I didn't know that he was cut off from himself and felt powerless to help himself. I was really cruel because I was so enraged that he was no longer there for me. I didn't realize that he couldn't help it. This is a really painful regret," she said, as she recalled her coldness towards her father.

I spoke to Sharon's vulnerability within the feeling of regret and the memories of her own coldness that were being stirred, creating both a mental sense of guilt and a bodily sense of grief and loss. I said that she was dealing with both a neurotic sense of guilt, and an existential guilt that had the grief of regret within it. I said that it was neurotic to blame herself now for something she was incapable of comprehending as a child or adolescent. I said that there was nobody there who could listen to her and help her to see her father as a vulnerable being that existed beyond his being for the purpose to reject her. She was all alone with an intolerable sense of rejection by her father, being scapegoated by her mother, and feeling abandoned by her brother, who left home quite early for college. Sharon said that this was true, but she did not think she had to choose to reject her father as she did. She was tearful as she said this. She regretted her cruelty towards her father, even though it was part of her youth, and not something she could reflect on from an adult position, as she could reflect now only after much therapy. I said that this was the existential guilt that she had actually rejected him and caused him much pain when he was already in a great deal of pain. It might be neurotic to exaggerate the guilt and to believe she could have acted and thought differently without any adult support or help, but, nevertheless, the existential effect of her rejection was still there, and she could feel it now as she had developed the capacity to love someone separate from herself. Sharon responded by saying that she hated discovering this truth of her regret, because it hurt so much.

In the following session, Sharon started by saying, "I'm impressed with my own abilities to dissociate. I don't remember what we talked about in the last session. I just know it was painful." Although she forgot what we had discussed, Sharon said that somehow she was feeling better. She said that she was feeling better with her husband, no longer obsessed with who was hurting whom, and who was doing what to whom. I said that even though she was not remembering specifically that we had talked about her father in the last session, she was associating to the session by demonstrating that she was no longer acting out with her husband the pattern with her father of always obsessively calculating in her mind who was hurting whom. It all came back to her then. She said that she realized that the session on her father had helped to free her. "It was a relief," she said, "but I don't want to go back there again today. Remembering how I rejected him, after he had been the one person who loved me early on, is too painful, although it is more tolerable than before."

CHAPTER TEN

Longing for a second chance

Richard Tuch

This chapter is about the workings of regret: that typically bothersome, gnawing feeling that develops when one looks back on a decision or action that had not panned out as well as one had hoped—in comparison to other conceivable options—and "kicks" oneself for having performed as one had. This may result in one's becoming hopelessly mired in regret that seems to be without remedy, particularly if the regrettable situation cannot be undone. Alternately, one may long for a second chance to rectify matters, seeking and achieving consolation in the silver lining of having learned one's lesson, which translates into efforts to anticipate future regret in the hope of avoiding it next time around. Such are the beneficial effects of regret.

Regret can have decidedly detrimental effects as well. Regret proves maladaptive when it becomes excessive and ceases to function as a signal affect that helps individuals avoid acting in ways that might prove regrettable in the future. Excessive regret triggers harsh self-reproach that begins to look masochistic or self-flagellating in nature. Other than guilt, shame, and remorse, no other self-recriminating emotions have the potential to trigger such a barrage of harsh, punitive, and unmerciful self-criticism. How long one persecutes oneself in this fashion has much to do with the size of the error (whether the consequences seem monumental), the degree to which the error makes one look ridiculous (evokes shame, mortification), the degree to which the consequences of one's behavior (decision or action) confronts one on a daily basis (becomes super salient), etc. Efforts to avoid future regret may also become excessive, negatively impinging on one's decision-making capacity.

Regret involves a complex of emotions and cognitions: disappointment, sadness, self-reproach, a lowering of self-esteem, heightened self-doubt, and a sense of lost opportunity that may need to be mourned. Regret is:

> ... associated with having a sinking feeling, thinking about what a mistake one had made and about a lost opportunity, feeling the tendency to kick oneself and to correct one's mistakes, actually doing something differently, and wanting to have a second chance and to improve one's performance. Hence, we conclude that the experience of regret involves a focus on *the self as a cause of the event*. (Zeelenberg, van Dijk, Manstead, & van der Pligt, 1998, p. 224, italics added)

Not all researchers agree that one only regrets outcomes that were of one's own making. Certain researchers (see Landman, 1993) believe that taking responsibility for a given outcome and the resulting self-reproach are defining features of "remorse" but not necessarily of regret. They would argue that one can be said to regret, for example, being laid off from work or being subjected to the abusive action of others, which makes little sense to other workers in the field (Gilovich & Medvec, 1994; Zeelenberg, van Dijk, & Manstead, 1998, 2000; Zeelenberg, van Dijk, Manstead, & van der Pligt, 2000) who restrict regret to outcomes one was chiefly responsible for bringing about. Remorse differs from regret in that the former has a moral dimension and entails deep anguish for having seriously wronged another whereas regret is less intense and akin to a lament that one had performed poorly.

The clinical manifestations of regret are many and varied. Regret can drive individuals to seek treatment when the pain of regret proves hard to bear and/or impossible to escape. Regret may lower one's self-esteem and self-confidence, unleash harsh and unmerciful self-rebukes, and seriously interfere with one's capacity to make decisions. One may be fully aware, dimly aware, or not at all aware of regret, which affects whether the individual will be able to work through regret by acknowl-edging the existence of the feeling, experiencing the full force of the feeling, accepting responsibility for one's actions, and mourning the loss of a better outcome that will never be.

Regret can be so painful and oppressive that it drives individuals to seek ways to lessen its effect. Examples of everyday adages that help individuals cope with regret include "a miss by an inch is good as a miss by a mile," which—while factually true—is not psychologically true. This saying in particular helps allay the feelings associated with near misses, which are known to produce intense feelings of regret for one's not having tried harder (Kahneman & Tversky, 1982a). Other adages also help alleviate regret—such as the saying that counsels "It's best not to cry over spilt milk," or Shakespeare's declaration, found in *Macbeth*: "What's done is done!" (*Macbeth*, Act III, Scene 2, pp. 8–12).

Regret is surprisingly commonplace, being the second most com-monly mentioned emotion (behind "love") found in everyday speech (Shimanoff, 1984). *Experienced regret* is predicated on a conviction that one had failed to either make the "right" decision or perform in a satisfactory fashion given the fact that better outcomes are now, in hindsight, easy to imagine or clearly evident.[1] People specifically regret having missed out on what, in retrospect, they've come to believe was an opportunity that would have made a world of difference in their lives if only they'd had the foresight or courage needed to take the leap.

Experienced regret in turn begets *anticipated regret* (Abraham & Sheeran, 2003; Bjälkebring, Svenson, & Slovic, 2016; Janis & Mann, 1977; Richard, van der Pligt, & de Vries, 1996; Sandberg & Conner, 2008; Simonson, 1992; Zeelenberg, 1999b), which leads to one's becom-ing vigilant about the prospect of future regret and dedicated to the task of making a better decision or performing more satisfactorily the next time around in the hope that one's behavior not prove regrettable yet again. In this way, anticipated regret exerts a beneficial effect on the decision-making process by "putting the decision brakes on long enough to identify and appraise each of the relevant alternative courses of action" (Landman, 1993, p. 22). Anticipated regret not only increases one's intention to do better, it has also been shown to generate measur-able behavioral improvement as well (Roese, 1994).

The title of this chapter is a bold statement that requires the author to deliver on the promise to cover what is known thus far about the subject of regret. The task of explicating the subject is largely facilitated by the work of cognitive scientists—chiefly those working in the related fields of "regret theory" (Bell, 1982; Loomes & Sugden, 1982) and "decision theory" (Landman, 1993; Machina, 1987; Savage, 1951; Tversky & Kahneman, 1981)—who have much to offer even though, as we shall see, certain of their conclusions gloss over everyday ways in which regret can manifest. Still, such research offers psychoanalytically informed therapists valuable information they can apply in their work with patients. Psychoanalysis is strengthened to the extent that it considers, weighs, and incorporates findings that derive from other ways of knowing. Compared to the sizable contributions of these cognitive scientists, relatively little has been written about regret from a psychoanalytic perspective.[2]

The cognitive approach to regret

Classic decision theory emphasizes the dual processes of *decision-making* and *imagining alternative decisions and outcomes* (referred to as "counterfactuals" because these alternatives run counter to what has actually occurred). Cognitive theorists specifically identify faulty decision making as the chief, if not sole, source of regret.[3] Poor decisions result either from failures of cognition or emotional contamination. A decider may have failed to properly investigate and think through his options. His decision may have been hastily made or ill-conceived. Expert advice may not have been sought, or if it was, may have been ignored (Sugden, 1985). The opinions of others may have weighed too heavily, making it hard for the individual to decide for himself which option looks most viable and promising. One may have placed too much stock in conventional wisdom, which describes how most would decide given the circumstances, rather than deciding for oneself. If circumstances would most likely lead the average individual to proceed in a given fashion, regret is less likely to develop if one follows suit. After all, who can be blamed for choosing a path that most others would travel if confronted with a comparable situation? On the other hand, if one goes out on a limb by taking the road less traveled, the payoff can be huge—bordering on heroic—just so long as things turn out well. But one runs the distinct risk of looking like a darn fool who ought to have known better if one bucks prevailing trends and things turn out poorly, leaving one to wonder, "What was I thinking?"

Beside cognitive factors, emotional factors may contribute to faulty decision making as well. Strong emotions can blind the decision-making process. So too can impulsivity, which may translate into a failure to perform with due diligence. Neurotic tendencies can also scuttle effective decision making. Self-defeating tendencies or conflicts over succeeding may have a hand in leading one to make poor decisions. A failure to give due consideration to a gut level feeling (e.g., deciding on the basis of what looks good "on paper" rather than attending to what it is one really wants to do) can also have detrimental effects on the quality of the decisions one makes.

Counterfactual thinking

Basic decision theory sees poor decisions leading to less than ideal outcomes that, in turn, trigger counterfactual thinking (Bell, 1982; Gilovich & Medvec, 1995a, 1995b; Kahneman & Miller, 1986; Kahneman & Tversky, 1982a, 1982b; Landman, 1993; Loomes & Sugden, 1982; Roese, 1997; Roese & Olson, 1995; Zeelenberg, van Dijk, Manstead, & van der Pligt, 1998), which has the individual wondering: "How else might this have turned out if only I had made a better decision?" To a degree unparalleled with most other emotions,[4] regret is triggered by a cognitive assessment of the consequences of one's actions (how satisfactory the "outcome" had or had not been) compared against an imaginative/ speculative construction of alternate actions and outcomes (Kahneman, 1995). Counterfactuals represent what might have been had one decided differently. Regret hinges on the road not taken, particularly paths one might have traveled that one believes in hindsight for whatever reason, rational or irrational, *would have* resulted (if the alternate outcome is known) or *might have* resulted (in the case of an imagined scenario) in a better outcome. According to decision theory,[5] in the absence of counterfactuals against which actual outcomes are unfavorably compared, there is little cause for one to feel regret.

While decision theory identifies the emergence of counterfactuals as the chief, if not sole source of regret, there are times when a decision works out quite well (which theoretically ought to quell tendencies to consider alternate outcomes) but, in spite of the fact, still generates a consideration of *even better* outcomes against which the more-than-satisfactory outcome is compared. Regret may also develop when one recognizes that one had been sloppy in the way in which one went about deciding, in which case what one regrets isn't the end result of a flawed decision but rather the decision-making process itself.

Characterological proclivities to experience regret

Characterological differences can predispose individuals to experience regret, to experience heightened levels of regret, to feel regret for a prolonged period of time, or to experience regret over errors that, in the scheme of things, had been relatively innocuous. Individuals differ in their tendencies to engage in counterfactual thinking. Individuals who are characterologically inclined to perpetually "second guess" themselves and endlessly ruminate about "what ifs" and "what might have beens" will be overly inclined to dream up counterfactuals that, in turn, constitute fertile ground for the generation of regret (Chin, 1993). Individuals with perfectionistic tendencies may regret a positive outcome that could have turned out *even better*, "if only ..." (Akhtar, 1996), in which case, pleasure is tempered by regret (Boninger, Gleicher, & Strathman, 1994; Gavanski & Wells, 1989; Gleicher et al., 1990; Kahneman & Miller, 1986; Landman, 1987; Sirois, Monforton, & Simpson, 2010). On the other hand, individuals who place faith in God or are fatalistic have little cause to dwell on such imaginings, which accordingly, makes them less inclined to feel regret. Believing that whatever has happened was "meant to be" because it was God's will or was fated tends to effectively shelter individuals from having to suffer pangs of regret (Kasimatis & Wells, 1995).

Regret can affect, and can be affected by, the state of an individual's narcissistic equilibrium. Individuals who suffer from low self-esteem have been hypothesized to be more prone to experience regret (Josephs, Larrick, Steele, & Misbett, 1992), more concerned with averting regret, and less inclined to take risks that expose them to acting in ways they will later regret (Landman, 1993). Such individuals can experience further diminution of their already diminished sense of self-worth when they conclude they had chosen poorly or failed to pursue a goal with sufficient vigor. Those who already suffer from low self-esteem may feel they can ill afford to risk the possibility of suffering any further diminution in the quality of their sense of self by virtue of their having made a bad decision (Josephs, Larrick, Steele, & Misbett, 1992; Steele, 1988; Zeelenberg, Beattie, van der Pligt, & de Vries, 1996).

"Anticipated regret" to the rescue

Coming to the realization that one had not chosen the path most likely to lead to the most optimal outcome leads one to regret the decision one *had* made. One way out of the maze to endless and harsh self-reproaches unleashed by the realization of such an error is to vow to learn from one's mistakes by examining where one went wrong. In this away, anticipating regret—imagining beforehand how a particular decision may play out going forward—lessens the chance of making yet another regrettable decision in the future.

"Anticipated regret" has been studied experimentally by asking subjects to imagine a hypothetical situation and to calculate the likelihood that the protagonist in the presented vignette will experience regret. This is exemplified by an experiment (Kahneman & Tversky, 1982a) in which subjects were asked to consider paired scenarios involving Mr. C (who arrives thirty minutes late for a plane that departs on time), and Mr. T (who arrives thirty minutes late to find his plane had taken off just five minutes earlier). The vast majority answered that they believed Mr. T would be more inclined to feel regretful even though both had missed their plane—in line with studies that suggest *near misses* and *known outcomes* both contribute to heightened levels of regret.

Another type of study involving anticipated regret attempts to experimentally stimulate individuals to imagine the regret they'd feel upon failing to live up to a goal they had set for themselves. Such studies demonstrate the extent to which anticipated regret powerfully influences how an experimental subject will subsequently act given his heightened awareness and concern that he will come to regret failing to achieve a self-determined goal. Inviting subjects to give due consideration to how they imagine they'd feel were they to fail to exercise (Abraham & Sheeran, 2003), as they'd promised themselves they'd do, or fail to practice safe sex, knowing the emotional consequences of failing to do so (Richard, van der Pligt, & de Vries, 1996) has a determining effect on whether individuals will end up dedicating energy to fulfilling these self-selected goals.

What makes counterfactuals salient?

The intensity of the regret that issues from comparing "what is" with "what might have been" depends, in part, "… on how easily one can imagine alternatives to an unpleasant reality. *The more readily counterfactuals come to mind, the greater the regret"* (Landman, 1993, p. 38, italics added). The intensity of regret is related to the ease with which one is able to imagine alternative outcomes (counterfactuals) that appear more favorable than what it was that had actually taken place (Kahneman & Miller, 1986). Some of the factors known to render counterfactuals salient—heightening the chance that alternate outcomes will spring to mind—include: 1) less satisfactory outcomes, 2) outcomes brought about by one's having acted uncharacteristically, 3) near misses, and 4) deciding to act versus instances when one considered acting but deciding against doing so.

Certain choices we make quickly fade from view while others capture our attention—notably those that resulted in a less desirable outcome, which tends to remain in the forefront of our minds perpetuating regret, sometimes for an extended period. According to decision theory, the chief factor that renders counterfactuals relevant and hence salient are less than satisfactory outcomes in comparison to better outcomes that might have been. Hence, dissatisfaction plays a central role in the genesis of regret.

A negative outcome that results after one had decided to act in an uncharacteristic fashion is another factor that makes counterfactual possibilities more salient in comparison to outcomes that follow on the heels of one's acting in a completely customary and routine fashion (Kahneman & Tversky, 1982a). For example, if an individual is in the habit of picking up hitchhikers and ends up being robbed by one, he will be less inclined to generate counterfactuals (e.g., imagining "if only I had decided differently …") and will be less inclined to act as he had since he was, after all, acting in accordance with his typical modus operandi. By comparison, an individual who makes an exception to his usual practice, picks up the hitchhiker who then proceeds to rob him (Kahneman & Tversky, 1982a, Landman, 1993) is much more likely to feel regret, illustrating a basic tenet: Exceptional behavior that ends in a poor outcome is much more likely to lead to regret (in the wake of generated counterfactuals) than ordinary behavior that ends badly (Kahneman & Miller, 1986, p. 145).

"Close calls" and "near misses" (Seelau, Seelau, Wells, & Windschitl, 1995)—instances when something *almost* happens—are particularly apt to render counterfactuals more salient, whether the outcome had been regrettable (e.g., barely missing out on a highly desirable outcome) or had been a huge relief (e.g., dodging a bullet). But near misses that entail a loss (a positive outcome that had nearly been within one's grasp) prove much more salient (and hence memorable) than close calls, when things turn out much better than they might otherwise have. This is consistent with the finding that negative outcomes are much more likely to stimulate counterfactual thinking than positive outcomes (Boninger, Gleicher, & Strathman, 1994; Gavanski & Wells, 1989; Gleicher et al., 1990; Kahneman & Miller, 1986; Landman, 1987).

Counterfactuals cut both ways: "upward counterfactuals" involve believing that things could have been so much better "if only I'd ...," while "downward counterfactuals" involve seeing how much worse things could have been "if ..." Differing conditions can make upward or downward counterfactuals more salient. Take, for example, research conducted into how Olympic medalists respond to winning a silver medal in comparison to those who win a bronze medal (Medvec, Madey, & Gilovich, 1995). Most would guess that silver medalists would be much happier than bronze medalists, but this proves not to be so. Questionnaires completed by Olympic medalists, along with ratings of their videotaped behavior when awarded their medals, makes clear the fact that bronze medalists appear to be much happier than silver medalists. It may be the counterfactuals that each of the medalists considers salient differs: The silver medalist compares his achievement against the counterfactual of having nearly won the gold (upward counterfactual) whereas the bronze mentalist considers his accomplishment in the context of the downward counterfactual of having not won any medal whatsoever (McMullen, Markman, & Gavanski, 1995; Roese, 1994). Medvec, Madey, and Gilovich (1995) note that silver medalists "... focus not on what they accomplished but on what they *almost* accomplished ... [whereas for bronze medalists] finishing second instead of third represents little change because in both cases the person won a medal but failed to capture the coveted gold. The contrast between third and fourth places, however, is more dramatic: third place earns a medal, whereas fourth place leaves one off the medal stand and among the pack" (p. 261).

A final factor that renders counterfactuals salient is the decision to act (versus to not act) after having weighed one's options, which creates conditions favorable to a consideration of upward counterfactuals and, with it, regret. Actions tend to be much more salient—more noteworthy and memorable—than instances when one could have acted but chose not to[6] (Gleicher et al., 1990; Kahneman & Miller, 1986;

Kahneman & Tversky, 1982b; Landman, 1987). If one elects to do nothing (to let things ride), one is much less susceptible to generating bothersome upward counterfactuals in the short run than if one chooses actively to intervene to make a change. If that decision turns out for the worse, one might use the imagined outcome of not acting (leaving things as they are) as the upward counterfactual against which to compare one's seeming folly for having ventured to try to actively alter the course of affairs—tempting fate rather than leaving well enough alone.

Conditions that forbid counterfactual thinking

Having considered the sorts of conditions that favor the generation and consideration of counterfactuals, we now turn to circumstances when one can ill afford to permit oneself to regret the present situation that had been of one's own making. Sometimes circumstances forbid consideration of counterfactuals and, with it, regret. In such cases, regret threatens to disrupt a tenuously balanced situation that cannot bear the weight of considering how things might otherwise be. Take, for example, the case of Jodi, a professional woman with three young children who had chosen to become the guardian of her brother's three children, all of whom are under the age of eight. The abuse and neglect that these children had suffered haunted Jodi for a long time, so when the authorities caught wind of what was happening at her brother's house and stepped in, taking the children into protective custody, Jodi stepped forward and offered to serve as their foster parent. Jodi, who worked full time, had not seriously thought the matter through—she had not given due consideration to what it would be like having six young children under her roof. And when the kids were taken into custody, she hadn't given a second thought as to whether she might come to regret her decision. Nor was she able to do so now—on the first anniversary of the date they were taken into custody, and her niece and two nephews moved in. In such instances, allowing herself to imagine how things might have been had she *not* decided as she had, threatened a precariously balanced situation that had her working 24/7 to handle a houseful of kids—three of whom were emotionally challenged having been damaged by the abuse they had suffered.

Regretting action vs. regretting inaction

One of the best known and most frequently replicated findings in the study of regret appeared in a seminal paper by Kahneman and Tversky

(1982b). Research subjects were asked which of two hypothetical characters (George or Paul) would be prone to feel more regret after deciding *to act* (George) or *to not act* (Paul). In each case, the two characters lost an identical sum of money by making different investment choices. Paul considers selling his stock in one company and purchasing stock in another, but decides against doing so, whereas George acts on his decision to make the switch. Even though each suffered a comparable financial loss as a result of their decision, a staggering 92 percent of research subjects predicted that George would feel a greater sense of regret, having decided to disrupt the status quo rather than stay the course as Paul had done. This experiment demonstrates that *inaction* proves to be less salient and tends *not* to be regarded as an actual decision, which, in fact, it very much is. Gilovich and Medvec (1995b) sum up the results noting,

> People find it easy to imagine how taking an action that one *need not have taken* would produce tortured thoughts about what could have or should have been. Individuals are thought to "own" their actions more than their inactions, and so an action that leads to negative consequences is considered more likely to induce a disquieting sense of "this did not have to be" or "I brought this on myself." (p. 264, italics added)

Hence, *action* is considered salient in comparison to *inaction* that generally flies under the radar.

There are inherent problems in the design of the experiment that compared George's and Paul's investment decisions. Life outside the lab rarely works in precisely the same manner—the ultimate outcome of our actions cannot always be known or computed in so exact a fashion—making such experiments more theoretical than naturalistic in nature. Oftentimes, an outcome only becomes apparent over the course of time and the ultimate outcome may remain in flux for extended periods—sometimes even remaining indeterminate. Accordingly, results of contrived experiments that make crystal clear the precise outcome of an action or of a failure to act, do not truly represent naturally occurring situations that often have no clear-cut or quantifiable outcome. Furthermore, the George and Paul experiment addresses situations that are acute in nature, the outcome of which is readily apparent—allowing for the comparison of action and inaction, in which case action proves decidedly salient relative to inaction.

Experiments demonstrating that action taken is more salient than actions not taken have been replicated many times over and have gone on to be regarded as irrefutable by those working in the field of counterfactual research (Gleicher et al., 1990; Kahneman & Miller, 1986; Landman, 1987). It is important to note that another set of studies (Gilovich & Medvec, 1994, 1995b) suggests the exact opposite: that individuals are often haunted by regrets about *not* having acted when opportunity arose and they subsequently imagine how much better life would have been if only they *had* acted back when. At first glance, it appears as if these sets of studies contradict one another until one realizes they were measuring two different sorts and sources of regret.

Asking individuals to look back over the course of their lives and consider what they regret having done or not having done skews regret in favor of *inaction* (opportunities not taken) for one simple reason: action produces a finite result (e.g., the decision to purchase a stock did or did not prove profitable). By comparison, imagined outcomes of a *failure to act* can imaginatively mushroom over time to include an entire array of distinct and compounding possibilities (Gilovich & Medvec 1995b). In fact, over time, individuals are much more inclined to regret the *road not taken*. They may come to believe it would have completely changed their lives had they only "seized the day" and acted decisively by taking advantage of what, in retrospect, they realize to have been "a golden opportunity" rather than shrinking from the challenge as they now deeply regret having done.

In one study (Kinnier & Metha, 1989), respondents reported feeling regret over not having acted more assertively in their life, not having taken more risks, not having spent more time with loved ones. Gilovich and Medvec (1994) conducted a similar study in which they asked subjects: "When you look back on your life to this point, what are your biggest regrets?", and found that individuals were twice as likely to regret things they might have done but, for whatever reason, had failed to do (missed educational opportunities, failure to "seize the moment," devoting insufficient time to personal relationships). These researchers also found the tendency to regret inaction increases with age—with older respondents reporting a three to one bias for regretting things they had failed to do. Furthermore, because acts of commission (doing) are often seen in retrospect as having a "silver lining" ("I learned so much from my mistakes so I am better prepared to make better decisions in the future"), it becomes easier to reconcile oneself to having made decisions that had not turned out well than it is to opportunities one had failed to have taken, which subsequently become more troublesome over time as one imagines how much better one's life could have been if only ...

What decision theory overlooks

According to classic decision theory, regret depends upon two factors: the *quality of the decision making* and the *nature of the outcome*. One of the many issues this model overlooks is the fact that regret also develops upon realizing that one had not given the "all" to realizing a chosen goal, independent of the quality of the decision or the outcome that developed as a result. Seeing a plan through to completion hinges on such factors as conscious, as well as unconscious, intent (whether one had been wholeheartedly committed to the plan), one's level of commitment (a matter of prioritization), and sheer effort (how hard one tries, how willing one is to sacrifice in the process of making a particular goal paramount above all others).

Another limitation of decision theory is its seeming insistence that an individual's decision to do X or to not do X should optimally be made strictly on a rational and conscious basis, carefully weighing options and taking care not to allow poor decision-making practices, irrational thinking, or neurotic processes to intervene. These theorists argue that if one goes about deciding in this manner then there is nothing whatsoever to regret, seeing that one had done everything in one's power to make the very best decision possible (Landman, 1993). Reasoning aside, every human knows on a gut level that he cannot summarily dismiss regret as an inappropriate and/or capricious emotion just because an individual believes he had gone about deciding in an optimal manner.

Decision making draws upon a number of psychological and emotional factors: needs, desires, wishes, beliefs, intentions, etc., not all of which are included in the thinking of strict cognitive theorists, which is a third issue that decision theory glosses over. Zeelenberg (1999a)—a leading researcher in the subject of regret—notes:

> Theories of rational choice view decision making as a cold cognitive process. Decision makers are supposed to rationally calculate for all possible courses of action the utility of each possible outcome, and weigh the utilities with probability that each outcome will occur.

> They then choose the course of action that provides them with the highest (expected) utility. Emotions typically are neglected in these theories. In reality, however, decision outcomes are known to be powerful antecedents of emotional experience and these emotions may well influence the choices we make. (pp. 325–326)

A failure to consider the extent to which emotions play a definitive role in decision making is yet another oversight of those working in the field of decision theory.

The decision theory model also disallows for unconscious decision making, when, in fact, the lion's share of decision making goes on at an implicit level beyond the individual's conscious awareness. In a review article published in *Science*, Custers and Aarts (2010) offer noteworthy examples of how nonconscious forces help shape our decisions and our behaviors, referencing a multitude of studies that demonstrate the extent to which our actions may be influenced by subliminal stimuli that "prime" us to act in particular ways with us none the wiser. Dijksterhuis and Aarts (2010) note that these findings strongly suggest it is reasonable to think in terms of *unconscious will and unconscious intention*, in opposition to the widespread tendency to see volition (choice, decision making) strictly as a function of conscious thought. Hence, "deliberate" behavior need not be *consciously* deliberate, nor need we consider the process of "deliberation," which leads to choice, something that necessarily requires a conscious weighing of alternatives. Failure to make room for unconscious processes is yet another of the oversights of decision theory.

Some acts—particularly those of omission (not doing)—may appear to lack evidence that a conscious decision-making process had been operating. Take, for example, a patient in his late forties who, in retrospect, regrets having not gotten a Mother's Day present for his young children to give his wife. The patient reports that it *had not even occurred to him* to do so and he only became painfully aware of the oversight when he had taken his wife and kids out for Mother's Day brunch but hadn't anything for his kids to give their mom. The patient explained that his own mother was out of the country so he hadn't thought to get her a gift, and seeing that he'd previously been triggered to think of getting his wife a gift when he'd gotten one for his mother, that task had fallen through the cracks.[7] Here is an instance when regret developed not because of a failure of conscious decision making but instead because an unconsciously determined "oversight."

Not only can unconscious/preconscious process give rise to regret, irrational thinking may do so as well, which flies in the face of decision theory that posits decisions be made on both a conscious and a rational basis. Consider the case of an individual who regrets not having remembered to conduct a superstitious ritual—say, wearing her "lucky socks" on the day of an exam—and as a result is fearing hearing how she'd performed on an exam she'd just taken. Not only are unconscious forces at play in this instance (why she'd forgotten to wear her "lucky socks" in this particular instance), irrational ones are at play as well (magical thinking), something the classic decision theory tends not to allow for. Regret can also develop irrationally when one's expectation of what one was capable of knowing at the time a decision had been made grossly overestimates what that individual could possibly have known. Unrealistic expectations can beget regret when an individual fails to perform in accordance with what he thought he was capable of knowing before the fact.

Clinical implications

Much like guilt, which serves a behavioral regulatory function insofar as it keeps us on the straight and narrow relative to both self-imposed and societally imposed expectations, regret provides comparable benefits by creating a "signal" pain in order to caution the individual against deciding or behaving in ways he will *yet again* regret just as he had the last time out. Regret is constructive and adaptive to the extent it heightens our resolve to anticipate regret in an effort to avoid it in the future. Anticipated regret provides genuine benefit just so long as it remains within bounds by functioning like a signal affect generating a productive, though limited, amount of psychic discomfort that alerts us to the possibility that we may be on the verge of making yet another regrettable decision.

At the same time, as with guilt, regret can become so intense and tenacious that it begins to look persecutory in nature, at which point regret becomes maladaptive and symptomatic. Rather than optimizing future decision making, regret becomes self-punitive in nature as evidenced by its: 1) being overly intense (the punishment is out of proportion to the crime), 2) resulting in the regretful individual's failure to take into consideration factors that had contributed to his deciding or acting as he had in the past (the punishment is unmerciful, self-empathy is precluded), 3) being predicated on one's lending the regretted action or decision an inflated sense of importance (the punishment is unjust) and, 4) capacity to serve as a vehicle for satisfying masochistic tendencies (the punishment is purposely, if unconsciously designed to be cruel) (Taylor, 1985). The detrimental effects of regret are many and varied. It can lower one's self-esteem,[8] cause one to doubt one's decision-making abilities, unleash a torrent of self-reproach, preoccupy the mind to a distracting degree, interfere with effective decision making, preclude one's capacity to be forgiving of oneself, and leave the individual feeling downright miserable.

The self-punitive nature of regret becomes readily apparent when one considers a common expression associated with regret: "I'm kicking myself ... [for deciding and/or acting as I had]." McMullen, Markman, and Gavanski (1995) note that if counterfactuals do not enhance a given individual's feelings of control (by educating the individual as to how best to proceed in the future—the "silver lining" effect) (Gilovich & Medvec, 1995b), "[These individuals will] experience the full brunt of the negative affect associated with considering how things could have been better" (p. 157).

The lament "I should have known *then* what I know *now*" tends to be an unfair charge since such retrospective thinking implies that one had, at the time, the knowledge needed to make a better decision—the sort of decision one would be inclined to make if one were deciding today. To the extent that an individual unfairly hinges his negative self-assessment on such thinking, this constitutes cause for clinical intervention. The same can be said of instances when an individual loses track of the emotional factors that had encumbered or impaired his decision making and goal pursuing behavior at the time, having lost sight of just how daunting the task had seemed at the time, which the passage of time has let fade from view (Gilovich, Kerr, & Medvec, 1993). As a result, "[W]e curse ourselves by asking 'Why didn't I at least try?' and torment ourselves with accusations that 'I'm just too timid' or 'I'm too indecisive'" (Gilovich & Medvec, 1995b, p. 277). The less one remembers about why one had struggled with deciding to act, the more one will fault oneself for not having acted, leading one to become plagued with regret about matters that had been harder to bring about than one can now imagine.

Efforts to anticipate and avoid future regret—in the wake of regretting one's past performance—can go into overdrive, threatening to bog down the decision-making process to the point it may even be brought to a grinding halt for no other reason than one's professed need to be absolutely sure—surer than may be possible—that one isn't yet again heading down a path that one will later regret. The would-be decider may avoid deciding altogether (Beattie, Baron, Hershey, & Spranca, 1994; Gilovich & Medvec, 1995a), engage in an endless investigation to determine which among the available options is best (Janis & Mann, 1977), drag his feet (Sirois, 2004), become paralyzed with indecision, beg others to tell him what to do, or engage in the typically futile practice of endlessly weighing the pros and cons of his varied options in the misguided belief that doing so will ultimately render the "right" decision apparent. Excessive efforts to avert regret may cause an individual to "play it safe" by never taking a risk (Zeelenberg, Beattie, van der Pligt, & de Vries, 1996); alternately, it may eventuate in his taking an impulsive leap of faith in a desperate effort to push past paralysis, which—in the process—paradoxically heightens the chance he will end up feeling the very emotion he'd been trying so hard to avoid from the start.

The following vignette illustrates how much weight certain individuals place on making the "right" decision—one they will not regret—as they decide between alternate paths that could result in very different outcomes, very different lives. Deciding prospectively how each of the choices will pan out sometimes assumes an unrealistic capacity to predict the future, which is not to deny instances when the positive benefits offered by one among the many varied options are readily determinable. Setting these exceptions aside, let's consider the following material.

Clinical vignette

Mahnaz is a twenty-three-year-old graduate student I'd been treating for over a year for recurrent panic attacks, generalized anxiety, and unresolved interpersonal difficulties she was having with her folks. Mahnaz had been accepted to two medical schools in two different states—one a bit more academically impressive than the other—and she was struggling with the question of which to attend. While the school with the better academic reputation was offering her a larger scholarship, she imagined she would be more comfortable attending the other school, which was located in the state in which she had grown up where family and friends still resided. Her home-state school was geographically adjacent to the one in which she was now living, which was "home" to many of her newest friends upon whom she had grown to depend for emotional support.

Unsure of which school was better suited to her needs, and scared to make a decision she might regret years later, Mahnaz resorted to the time-honored tradition of polling friends. Some insisted that it was a "no brainer—go to the 'better' school! Everybody knows that!" These friends considered it an "awful" idea for the patient to limit herself to her comfort zone, suggesting that she would come to regret having done so by the time graduation rolled around. But those who knew her well had a different opinion insofar as they understood how much of a role anxiety played in Mahnaz's life. These friends were more sympathetic to the idea of her attending a school that was not only situated in a more "friendly" locale but one that wasn't quite so academically challenging as to intensify her anxiety given her driving ambition that caused her to need to be the best.

The patient wanted my help determining which of the two options was least likely to be the one she would later come to regret, since the task of avoiding regret weighed heavy on her mind. The degree of certainty the patient was seeking struck me as one that could not possibly be achieved, though I understood how pressured she felt by that task. I offered my opinion that we were not in a position to know as much as she wished to be able to know, so we could not say for certain that she would not make a decision she might later regret. It seemed conceivable that she could end up regretting attending each school but for different reasons, so simplifying the matter by posing it in a black-and-white fashion made little sense. Besides, comparing between alternatives—as Kahneman (1995) notes—relies on the imaginative and fallible process of "mental simulation," which cannot deliver absolute answers about how the future will play out to the degree some wish it might.[9]

The psychoanalytic view

Psychoanalysts have not attended much to the subject of regret, with a few notable exceptions (Cooper, 2004; Kavaler-Adler, 1989, 1992, 2004; Shabad, 1987). Patients do not tend to present with the complaint of being plagued by regret, though it may turn out in the course of treatment that this is, in fact, very much the case. Every clinician can easily recognize the clinical manifestations of regret spelled out in this chapter: the way in which fear of regret can disrupt the decision-making process

and the extent to which individuals suffer from overly intense or prolonged periods of harsh self-reproach, from tendencies to become so
preoccupied with past failures as to preclude one's ability to attend sufficiently to the matters at hand, from unfair assessments of their prevailing psychic state at the time a decision had been faced that made
deciding more difficult than one can now imagine, etc.

The clinical task of working with patients suffering from maladaptive
levels of regret involves helping them work through their feelings of
regret. First and foremost, this involves helping the patient realize that
she is struggling with regret and its associated feelings (loss, disappointment, sadness, self-reproach, a lowering of self-esteem, heightened self-doubt, etc.), so that she can fully experience the feeling on the
way to exploring the root causes of those feelings. If a patient shows
signs of being plagued with regret, he must first be helped to recognize
as much before any progress can be made. In this regard, "[R]egret is a
signpost of hope if it can be consciously felt and processed" (Kavaler-
Adler, 2004, p. 40).

Accepting responsibility for having authored situations that one
regrets is another important step toward working through regret—to
accept what Shakespeare (*Julius Caesar*) noted when he wrote: "The fault
dear Brutus, is not in our stars but in ourselves" (Scene 2, p. 6). Patients
must first address their tendencies to blame others (e.g., parents, even
unfavorable fate) before they can move on to the central task of mourning
lost possibilities that can never be, no matter how badly one longs for
a second chance to undo past actions and recapture lost opportunities.
One may have to reconcile oneself to a lesser gain by making sure one
does not repeat a regrettable decision next time around, and that may
prove enough for some, though others may either continue to long to
regain lost opportunities or continue to make the same mistakes having
failed to learn a redeeming lesson from past regrets.

Cooper (2004) writes of patients who try to:

> ... resurrect or perpetuate a fantasy that things that in fact weren't
> possible would somehow magically now be possible ... [which]
> allows us to deny the reality of time and to deny death by asserting
> magical, childlike thinking about how, if we wish things to be so,
> they will be. The universality of the notion "I could have been a
> contender" lies in the part of our character that always wishes that
> we could be someone or something else. (p. 569)

Shabad (1987) notes how regret can sometimes arise in the course of treatment as patients come to take stock of the extent to which they'd missed out on what life has to offer. Realizing that this had been the case, and further realizing it had been the result of neurotic tendencies to repeat the past rather than accepting novel situations as novel—as filled with possibilities, about which one begins to become aware as treatment progresses—sets the stage for the beginnings of the working through of regret. Such working through cannot begin to take place, however, until the patient suffers with the painful realization of the precious time he had lost and the valuable opportunities he'd let pass. Shabad notes this process—"the reawaking to life's preciousness" (p. 198)—may be set in motion "with the first glimmerings of a heretofore denied mortality and the uneasy sense of time slipping away" (p. 197). Shabad suggests that "The continued retention of symptoms can be viewed as a form of self-punishment for not having taken advantage of earlier opportunities when the 'iron was hot'" (p. 199).

The centrality of mourning lost opportunities is emphasized in the writings of Kavaler-Adler (1989, 1992, 2004) who sees the capacity to face regret as "pivotal in psychic change and self-integration" (2004, p. 39), believing that failure to work through regret is an important source of resistance in certain patients. Kavaler-Adler (1992) notes that "Facing regret is an entryway into the developmental enhancement of interiority and observing ego reflection" (p. 40).

Grunbaum (1974) addresses the savageness with which certain individuals punish themselves for acting in ways they now regret. Without specifically referring to the consequences of a harsh superego, he offers a plea for compassion that has implications when treating individuals struggling with tendencies to maliciously punish themselves. Grunbaum believes that one only becomes able to work through things one's come to regret after one ceases to punish oneself in such an uncompassionate fashion. To this end, he calls for the humane treatment of those who have erred when he refers to "the moral requirement that *gratuitous* suffering [for regrettable actions] be avoided as a principle of justice" (p. 20), arguing that "*reformative or educative punishment* [should strictly serve as a] *deterrent* against the repetition of past behavior" (p. 19).

A final thought or two

There is an aspect of counterfactual thinking that must be kept in mind if one hopes to understand its role in facilitating regret. Concluding that an alternate decision would have resulted in a more desirable outcome requires a bit of imaginative thinking that involves entertaining hypothetical possibilities that are often unknowable. Kahneman (1995) describes how counterfactual thinking hinges on:

> ... mental simulation [which is] a form of elaborative thinking in which one imagines the unfolding of a sequence of events, from an initial counterfactual starting point to some outcome. The outcome that is "observed" in the simulation is considered true, or at least likely to be true ... *it is experienced as an act of observation, not as an act of construction*. Indeed, the high confidence that is sometimes attached to the outcomes of mental simulations derives precisely from the sense that the outcome is observed, not contrived at will ... [but] there is no magic in mental simulations and no guarantee that it correctly represents the causal relationships of the real world. (pp. 378–380, italics added)

The notion that proper decision making makes clear which choice among the varied options is most ideal, and that one is free to engage in such ideal decision-making procedures, are dubious propositions given that they disallow for a consideration of unconscious psychological forces that often have a hand in one's decision-making process and in one's efforts to wholeheartedly pursue a chosen goal to completion. An idealized view of the matter insists that one can always transcend impeding psychological and/or emotional factors, and protestations to the contrary are nothing more than a cop-out. There will always be those who paint psychoanalytic psychotherapists as making apologies for patients that essentially excuse them from having to accept ultimate responsibility for the error of their ways rather than holding themselves accountable. The anticipatory function of regret, as it's been spelled out in this chapter, attests to the extent that this is *not at all* the case. But when regret persists beyond its signal function of preventing one from making the same regrettable mistake time and time again, and goes on to become symptomatic, it is essential that that individual examine the unconscious factors that were operating behind the scenes that helped determine why he'd decided or acted as he had. Anticipated regret without accompanying understanding of these background dynamics may oftentimes not be sufficient to help one change one's ways.

If one operates under the illusion that one is completely free to choose, one will be predisposed to regret decisions that *had not* been in one's control to the degree one might like to believe. Given such conditions, regret helps reinforce the illusion that one is in a position to both know which among the alternatives will prove to be the best path to pursue and to be fully equipped to actualize that goal. Such beliefs function like a compromise formation: Rather than confront the awesome limits of human ability the individual instead pays the price of feeling regret that issues from believing that it *had been* within his power to know the best path and to successfully see it to fruition, even if things hadn't played out in that fashion.

While many limit regret to outcomes that had been of one's own making, there are times when regret issues from circumstances that were, in fact, beyond one's control. Regret that follows on the heels of coming painfully close to achieving a highly desired goal (e.g., for Olympic silver medalists), hinges on a sense that the outcome *had* decidedly been under one's control ("if only I had tried a tad harder, remained a bit more vigilant, been better prepared ..."), which may or may not be so. While a desired goal is sometimes within our reach, at other times believing as much is predicated on an illusion that we possess superhuman knowledge, power, and ability. Such illusions help us avoid confronting reality (the limits of our power and ability)—a task that some find extraordinarily challenging. This touches on the idea that "People may blame themselves excessively for negative outcomes if they had control over some of the event antecedents, even if those events were in no way causal to the outcome" (Sherman and McConnell, 1995, p. 205).

Consider the example of Peter T, a recently divorced professional man in his mid-fifties who was lamenting his failure to have been the sort of father he wished to have been. By all accounts, it sounded as if he had done a decent enough job fathering his three grown children. None had voiced any complaints about the sort of father he had been, but this did not stop Mr. T from looking back with regret, believing he could have been a more active and emotionally present father in his children's lives. As the patient and I explored the issue, it became readily apparent that he was laboring under the influence of a wish to be a very different father than his father had been—a man of immense presence who the patient experienced as overwhelmingly imposing. Feeling that his father had cast him in the darkness of his father's shadow left Mr. T dedicated to the task of being a very different sort of father with his own kids. To that end, he tended to veer in the opposite direction to such a degree that he ended up feeling as if he absented himself, which he now very much regretted. I suggested to the patient that his regret was predicated on a belief he was completely free to be the father he now, in retrospect, wishes to have been. But even if he had realized at the time that this had been his goal, he was still under the sway of unconscious factors that he would need to work through before he could be freed to be that type of dad he wished he could be above and beyond the negative model his father had provided.

The notion that one's life would have been remarkably different if only one had done this or that can be seen as the makings of fairy tales. This doesn't suggest that change isn't possible, that making the right decisions doesn't matter. People's lives do change—sometimes quite dramatically—as a result of pivotal decisions they'd made, but believing such opportunities are within everyone's reach can leave individuals deeply regretting their past decisions, actions, and/or inactions. The idea that change is within one's reach if only one had the foresight to make good decisions and the wherewithal to see them through to completion is a bit of an idealized pipedream. Certainly, there are times when opportunity comes knocking and no one answers the door, when a significant change in one's life circumstances was within reach, and yet one failed to grasp it for reasons that, in retrospect, may strike one as frivolous. Under such conditions, one is left regretting a failure to act. Forgetting how hard it had been at the time to do just that intensifies regret and leaves one disappointed and dismayed with one's less than noble behavior—an attitude that often reflects an inability to appreciate how things had seemed at the time one was facing the lion head on. What I am saying is not meant to discourage dreamers from imagining better lives, nor is it meant to make excuses that let those who failed to act off the hook. It is only meant to remind us all that gazing into crystal balls about what the future holds, or what it might have held if only we had …, is nothing short of pure speculation much of the time. We may become so impressed with visions of what could have been that we lose sight of the hypothetical nature of such dreaming. It's essential we remember that, in the final analysis, the counterfactuals against which we compare our present lives and our past decisions oftentimes can't be known to truly represent how things would have played out if only we'd made better decisions or had worked harder to see the chosen plan through to completion. In this regard, compassion often fails when regret begins to flare.

Notes

1. Potentially leaving the patient to feel that he should have known *then* what he clearly knows *now*—regardless of whether there is ample justification for believing as much, which isn't to deny instances when an individual had, in fact, been in a position to prospectively anticipate regret had he given the matter more thought.
2. Notable exceptions are Cooper, 2004; Kavaler-Adler, 1989, 1992, 2004; and Shabad, 1987.
3. It is noteworthy that these theorists tend to overlook failures to perform (e.g., actions that are required to successfully actualize a decision) as another important source of regret which gets lost in the shuffle of emphasizing the centrality of decision making in the genesis of regret.
4. Guilt, shame, and remorse being notable exceptions.
5. Here, we are speaking strictly from the standpoint of classic decision theory. As we shall see further along, there are other conditions under which regret can develop.
6. Which is only true in the short run in comparison to instances when one looks back on the entirety of one's life, as will be discussed shortly.
7. This explanation is merely the patient's articulated account of why he had acted as he had. Naturally, the reasons he had failed to remember to buy his wife a present are undoubtedly more complex, necessarily involving unconscious process about which the patient was unaware when he was reporting this event in session.
8. Or, more to the point, further lower one's self-esteem given that low self-esteem is hypothesized to contribute to one's propensity to feel regret in the first place (Josephs et al., 1992).
9. The patient elected to attend her home-state school and felt resolved in her decision.

REFERENCES

Abraham, C., & Sheeran, P. (2003). Acting on intention: the role of anticipated regret. *British Journal of Social Psychology*, 42: 495–511.

Abraham, K. (1924). The influence of oral eroticism on character formation.
In: *Selected Papers of Karl Abraham, M. D.* (pp. 393–406). New York:
Brunner/Mazel, 1955.

Akhtar, S. (1996). "Someday ..." and "if only ..." fantasies: pathological
optimism and inordinate nostalgia as related forms of idealization.
Journal of American Psychoanalytic Association, 44: 723–753.

Akhtar, S. (1999). *Inner Torment: Living Between Conflict and Fragmentation.*
Northvale, NJ: Jason Aronson.

Akhtar, S. (2002). Forgiveness: origins, dynamics, psychopathology, and
technical relevance. *Psychoanalytic Quarterly*, 71: 175–212.

Akhtar, S. (2009). *Comprehensive Dictionary of Psychoanalysis.* London: Karnac.

Akhtar, S. (2015). Patience. *Psychoanalytic Review*, 102: 93–122.

Alvarez, A. (2012). *The Thinking Heart: Three Levels of Psychoanalytic Therapy
with Disturbed Children.* London: Routledge.

Anka, P. (1968). *My Way.* (Recorded by F. Sinatra, 1969.) Los Angeles, CA:
Reprise Records.

Balter, L. (2006). Nested ideation and the problem of reality: dreams and
works of art in works of art. *Psychoanalytic Quarterly*, 75: 405–445.

Bar, S. (2015). Professor Dan Ariely talking about FoMO. www.youtube. com. Accessed March 25, 2015.

Barnes, J. (2013). *The Sense of an Ending*. London: Vintage.

Beattie, J., Baron, J., Hershey, J., & Spranca, M. (1994). Psychological determinates of decision attitude. *Journal of Behavioral Decision Making, 7*: 129–144.

Beckett, S. (1953). *Watt*. London: Faber, 2009.

Begley, L. (1993). *The Man Who Was Late*. New York: Alfred Knopf.

Bell, D. (1982). Regret in decision-making under uncertainty. *Operations Research, 30*: 961–981.

Bion, W. R. (1959). *Experiences in Groups*. New York: Basic Books.

Bion, W. R. (1961). *Experiences in Groups and Other Papers*. London: Tavistock.

Bion, W. R. (1962a). Learning from experience. In: *Seven Servants: Four Works*. New York: Jason Aronson, 1977.

Bion, W. R. (1962b). The psycho-analytic study of thinking. *International Journal of Psychoanalysis, 43*: 306–310.

Bion, W. R. (1963). Elements of psycho-analysis. In: *Seven Servants: Four Works*. New York: Jason Aronson, 1977.

Bion, W. R. (1967). *Second Thoughts: Selected Papers on Psychoanalysis*. New York: Jason Aronson.

Bion, W. R. (1970). *Attention and Interpretation*. London: Tavistock.

Bishop, E. (1983). *The Complete Poems*. New York: Farrar, Straus and Giroux.

Bjälkebring, P., Svenson, O., & Slovic, P. (2016). Regulation of experienced and anticipated regret in daily decision-making. *Emotion, 16*: 381–386.

Blos, P. (1967). The second individuation process of adolescence. *Psychoanalytic Study of the Child, 22*: 162–186.

Bollas, C. (1987). The transformational object. In: *The Shadow of the Object: Psychoanalysis of the Unthought Known* (pp. 13–29). New York: Columbia University Press.

Boninger, D., Gleicher, F., & Strathman, A. (1994). Counterfactual thinking: from what might have been to what may be. *Journal of Personality and Social Psychology, 67*: 297–307.

Brandchaft, B. (2007). Systems of pathological accommodation and change in analysis. *Psychoanalytic Psychology, 24*: 667–687.

Braudy, L. (2005). *BFI Film Classics: On the Waterfront*. London: British Film Institute.

Bromberg, P. M. (1983). The mirror and the mask—on narcissism and psychoanalytic growth. *Contemporary Psychoanalysis, 19*: 379–381.

Brontë, C. (1846). Regret. In: *Poems of Currer, Ellis, and Acton Bell* (pp. 325–326). London: Smith, Elder, 1888.

Brontë, E. (1847). *Wuthering Heights*. Oxford: Oxford University Press, 1995.

Burns, P., Riggs, K., & Beck, S. (2012). Executive control and the experience of regret. *Journal of Experimental Child Psychology, 111*: 501–515.

Caruth, C. (1996). *Unclaimed Experience: Trauma, Narrative, and History.* Baltimore, MD: Johns Hopkins University Press.

Cather, W. (1911). The joy of Nelly Deane. In: *Coming Aphrodite! and Other Stories.* New York: Penguin, 1999.

Chamberlain, H. S. (1912). *The Foundations of the Nineteenth Century.* London: John Lane, The Bodley Head.

Chin, C. (1993). The relationship between regret and rumination. Honors thesis in psychology, University of Michigan, Ann Arbor, MI.

Chown, J. (2003). Visual coding and social class in "On the Waterfront". In: J. E. Rapf (Ed.), *On the Waterfront* (pp. 106–123). Cambridge: Cambridge University Press.

Civitarese, G., & Ferro, A. (2013). The meaning and use of metaphor in analytic field theory. *Psychoanalytic Inquiry, 33*: 190–209.

Coetzee, J. M. (1998). *Boyhood.* London: Vintage.

Coetzee, J. M. (1999). *Disgrace.* London: Vintage.

Coetzee, J. M., & Kurtz, A. (2015). *The Good Story: Exchanges on Truth, Fiction and Psychoanalytic Psychotherapy.* London: Harvell Secker.

Coleridge, S. T. (1798). *The Rime of the Ancient Mariner and Other Poems.* New York: Dover, 1992.

Collins German Dictionary (2016). Entry on "regret". www.collinsdictionary.com. Accessed July 12, 2016.

Conrad, J. (1900). *Lord Jim.* New York: Penguin, 1989.

Cooper, S. (2004). Psychoanalysis preparatory to psychotherapy: the ambiguity of reflection when patients return to psychoanalysis. *Contemporary Psychoanalysis, 40*: 557–576.

Coulda Woulda Shoulda. (2003). From the album, "One Heart". Columbia Entertainment CD.

Custers, R., & Aarts, H. (2010). The unconscious will: how the pursuit of goals operates outside of conscious awareness. *Science, 239*: 47–50.

Dickens, C. (1860). *Great Expectations.* New York: Penguin Classics, 1994.

Dickinson, E. (1960). *The Complete Poems of Emily Dickinson.* T. H. Johnson (Ed.). Boston, MA: Little Brown.

Dictionary.com (2016). Entry on "regret". Accessed July 6, 2016.

Didion, J. (2005). *The Year of Magical Thinking.* New York: Alfred Knopf.

Dijksterhuis, A., & Aarts, H. (2010). Goals, attention, and (un)consciousness. *Annual Review of Psychology, 61*: 467–490.

Dutton, D. J. (2007). "Proponents and critics of appeasement", published in the *Oxford Dictionary of National Biography* online. www.oxforddnb.com. Accessed July 23, 2016.

Eidelberg, L. (Ed.) (1968). *Encyclopedia of Psychoanalysis*. New York: Free Press.

Eliot, G. (1871). *Middlemarch*. New York: Penguin, 1994.

Emerson, R. W. (1957). *Selections from Ralph Waldo Emerson*. S. Whicher (Ed.). Boston: Houghton Mifflin.

Epstein, L. (1979). Countertransference with borderline patients. In: L. Epstein & A. H. Feiner (Eds.), *Countertransference* (pp. 375–406). New York: Jason Aronson.

Erikson, E. H. (1950). *Childhood and Society*. New York: W. W. Norton, 1963.

Euripides (405 BC). *The Bacchae of Euripides*. D. Sutherland (Trans.). Lincoln, NE: University of Nebraska Press, 1968.

Faimberg, H. (2014). The paternal function in Winnicott: the psychoanalytical frame. *International Journal of Psychoanalysis, 95*: 629–640.

Fairbairn, W. R. D. (1952). Schizoid factors in the personality. In: *An Object Relations Theory of the Personality* (pp. 3–27). New York: Basic Books.

Fallon, T. (2014). *Disordered Thought and Development: Chaos to Organization in the Moment*. New York: Jason Aronson.

Fenichel, O. (1945). *The Psychoanalytic Theory of Neurosis*. New York: W. W. Norton, 1972.

Ferenczi, S. (1916). *First Contributions to Psycho-Analysis*. London: Hogarth, 1952.

Fodor, N. (1950). Varieties of nostalgia. *Psychoanalytic Review, 37*: 25–38.

Fonagy, P., & Target, M. (1996). Playing with reality: I. Theory of mind and the normal development of psychic reality. *International Journal of Psychoanalysis, 77*: 217–233.

Freud, S. (1895d). The psychotherapy of hysteria. In: *Studies on Hysteria*. *S. E., 2*: 253–305. London: Hogarth.

Freud, S. (1899a). Screen memories. *S. E., 3*: 301–323. London: Hogarth.

Freud, S. (1900a). *The Interpretation of Dreams*. *S. E., 4–5*. London: Hogarth.

Freud, S. (1912e). Recommendations to physicians practising psycho-analysis. *S. E., 12*: 109–120. London: Hogarth.

Freud, S. (1912–13). *Totem and Taboo*. *S. E., 13*: 1–161. London: Hogarth.

Freud, S. (1914g). Remembering, repeating, and working-through (further recommendations on the technique of psycho-analysis). *S. E., 12*: 147–156. London: Hogarth.

Freud, S. (1915e). The unconscious. *S. E., 14*: 159–216. London: Hogarth.

Freud, S. (1916a). On transience. *S. E., 14*: 303–307. London: Hogarth.

Freud, S. (1916–17). *Introductory Lectures on Psycho-Analysis*. *S. E., 15–16*: 243–463. London: Hogarth.

Freud, S. (1917e). Mourning and melancholia. *S. E., 14*: 117–140. London: Hogarth.

Freud, S. (1919h). The uncanny. *S. E., 17*: 217–252. London: Hogarth.

Freud, S. (1920g). *Beyond the Pleasure Principle*. *S. E., 18*: 7–64. London: Hogarth.

Freud, S. (1930a). *Civilization and Its Discontents. S. E., 21:* 64–145. London: Hogarth.

Gavanski, I., & Wells, G. (1989). Counterfactual processing of normal and exceptional events. *Journal of Experimental Social Psychology, 45:* 268–273.

Gay, P. (1988). *Freud: A Life for Our Time.* New York: W. W. Norton.

Geerken, I. (2004). Mortal regret in "Wuthering Heights". *Journal of Narrative Theory, 34*(3): 373–406.

Gilbert, D., Morewedge, C., Risen, J., & Wilson, T. (2004). Looking forward to looking backward: the misprediction of regret. *Psychological Science, 15:* 346–350.

Gilovich, T., & Medvec, H. (1994). The temporal pattern to the experience of regret. *Journal of Personality and Social Psychology, 67:* 357–365.

Gilovich, T., & Medvec, V. (1995a). The experience of regret: what, when, and why. *Psychological Review, 102:* 379–395.

Gilovich, T., & Medvec, V. (1995b). Some counterfactual determinants of satisfaction and regret. In: N. J. Roese & J. M. Olson (Eds.), *What Might Have Been: The Social Psychology of Counterfactual Thinking* (pp. 259–282). Hillsdale, NJ: Lawrence Erlbaum.

Gilovich, T., Kerr, M., & Medvec, V. (1993). Effect of temporal perspective on subjective confidence. *Journal of Personality and Social Psychology, 64:* 552–560.

Gleicher, F., Kost, K., Baker, S., Strathman, A., Richman, S., & Sherman, S. (1990). The role of counterfactual thinking in judgment of affect. *Personality and Social Psychology Bulletin, 36:* 284–295.

Graham, A. D. (2011). The Motto. From the album, *The Motto,* produced by Republic Records, Los Angeles, CA.

Gray, P. (1987). On the technique of analysis of the superego—an introduction. *Psychoanalytic Quarterly, 56:* 130–154.

Greenberg, M. G. (2012). The psychology of regret. http://www.psychologytoday.com. Retrieved October 31, 2016.

Greenson, R. R. (1958). On screen defenses, screen hunger and screen identity. *Journal of the American Psychoanalytic Association, 6:* 242–262.

Greenspan, S. I. (2007). Infant-caregiver interactions and the Developmental, Individual-difference, Relationship-based (DIR) model: Implications for psychopathology and the psychotherapeutic process. *Journal of Child and Adolescent Psychotherapy, 6:* 211–244.

Grosskurth, P. (1986). *Melanie Klein: Her World and Her Work.* New York: Alfred Knopf.

Grotstein, J. (1981). *Splitting and Projective Identification.* New York: Jason Aronson.

Groundhog Day (1993). Directed by H. Ramis, produced by Columbia Pictures.

Grunbaum, A. (1974). Free will and laws of human behavior. *Psychoanalysis and Contemporary Science, 3:* 3–39.

Hardy, T. (1898). *The Complete Poems*. J. Gibson (Ed.). New York: Macmillan, 1994.

Harte, F. B. (1867). Mrs. Judge Jenkins. In: *The Complete Works of Bret Harte*. Amazon Kindle Edition, 2014.

Heller, J. (1966). *Something Happened*. New York: Charles Scribner's Sons, 1974.

Hemingway, E. (1936). The Snows of Kilimanjaro. In: *The Complete Short Stories of Ernest Hemingway: The Finca Vigia Edition* (pp. 56–87). New York: Charles Scribner's Sons.

Horowitz, M. (1975). Sliding meanings: a defense against threat in narcissistic personalities. *International Journal of Psychoanalytic Psychotherapy*, 4: 167–180.

Hoyt, M. F. (1983). Concerning remorse with special attention to its defensive function. *Journal of the American Academy of Psychoanalysis*, 11: 435–444.

Ishiguro, K. (1989). *The Remains of the Day*. New York: Vintage International.

James, H. (1881). *The Portrait of a Lady*. New York: Oxford University Press, 1947.

Janis, I., & Mann, L. (1977). *Decision-Making: a Psychological Analysis of Conflict, Choice, and Commitment*. New York: Free Press.

Jaques, E. (1965). Death and the midlife crisis. *International Journal of Psychoanalysis*, 46: 502–514.

Johnson, A. M., & Szurek, S. A. (1952). The genesis of antisocial acting out in children and adults. *Psychoanalytic Quarterly*, 21: 323–343.

Josephs, R., Larrick, R., Steele, C., & Misbett, R. (1992). Protecting the self from the negative consequences of risky decisions. *Journal of Personality and Social Psychology*, 62: 26–37.

Juni, S. (1991). Remorse as a derivative of psychoanalysis. *American Journal of Psychoanalysis*, 51: 71–81.

Kahneman, D. (1995). Varieties of counterfactual thinking. In: N. J. Roese & J. M. Olson (Eds.), *What Might Have Been: The Social Psychology of Counterfactual Thinking* (pp. 375–396). Hillsdale, NJ: Lawrence Erlbaum.

Kahneman, D., & Miller, D. (1986). Norm theory: comparing reality to its alternatives. *Psychological Review*, 93: 136–153.

Kahneman, D., & Tversky, A. (1982a). The simulation heuristic. In: D. Kahneman, P. Slovic, & A. Tversky (Eds.), *Judgment under Uncertainty: Heuristics and Biases* (pp. 201–208). New York: Cambridge University Press.

Kahneman, D., & Tversky, A. (1982b). The psychology of preferences. *Scientific American*, 246: 160–173.

Kasimatis, M., & Wells, G. L. (1995). Individual differences in counterfactual thinking. In: N. J. Roese & J. M. Olson (Eds.), *What Might Have Been: The Social Psychology of Counterfactual Thinking* (pp. 81–101). Hillsdale, NJ: Lawrence Erlbaum.

Katan, A. (1951). The role of "displacement" in agoraphobia. *International Journal of Psychoanalysis*, 32: 41–50.

Kavaler-Adler, S. (1989). Discussion of "Perspectives on Transference". *Psychoanalysis and Psychotherapy, 7*: 80–84.

Kavaler-Adler, S. (1992). Mourning and erotic transference. *International Journal of Psychoanalysis, 73*: 527–539.

Kavaler-Adler, S. (2004). Anatomy of regret: the critical turn towards love and creativity in the transforming schizoid personality. *American Journal of Psychoanalysis, 64*: 39–76.

Kavaler-Adler, S. (2006a). From neurotic guilt to existential guilt as grief: the road to interiority, agency, and compassion through mourning, Part I. *American Journal of Psychoanalysis, 66*: 239–260.

Kavaler-Adler, S. (2006b). From neurotic guilt to existential guilt as grief: the road to interiority, agency, and compassion through mourning, Part II. *American Journal of Psychoanalysis, 66*: 333–350.

Kavaler-Adler, S. (2013). *Regret: From Death Instinct to Reparation and Symbolization through Vivid Case Studies*. London: Karnac.

Kernberg, O. F. (1975). *Borderline Conditions and Pathological Narcissism*. New York: Jason Aronson.

Kernberg, O. F. (1980). *Internal World and External Reality: Object Relations Theory Applied*. New York: Jason Aronson.

Kernberg, O. F. (1992). *Aggression in Personality Disorders and Perversions*. New Haven, CT: Yale University Press.

Kierkegaard, S. (1843). *Fear and Trembling*. London: Penguin Classics, 1985.

Kinnier, R., & Metha, A. (1989). Regrets and priorities at three stages of life. *Counseling and Values, 33*: 182–193.

Klein, M. (1929). Personification in the play of children. *International Journal of Psychoanalysis, 19*: 193–214.

Klein, M. (1935). A contribution to the psychogenesis of manic-depressive states. *International Journal of Psychoanalysis, 16*: 145–174.

Klein, M. (1937). Love, guilt, and reparation. In: *Love, Guilt and Reparation and Other Works – 1921–1945* (pp. 306–343). New York: Free Press, 1975.

Klein, M. (1940). Mourning and its relation to manic depressive states. In: *Love, Guilt and Reparation and Other Works – 1921–1945* (pp. 344–369). New York: Free Press, 1975.

Klein, M. (1957). *Envy and Gratitude*. New York: Basic Books.

Klein, M. (1960). On mental health. In: *Envy and Gratitude and Other Works 1946–1963*. London: Hogarth, 1975.

Kleiner, J. (1970). On nostalgia. *Bulletin of the Philadelphia Association for Psychoanalysis, 20*: 11–30.

Kramer, S., & Akhtar, S. (1988). The developmental context of internalized preoedipal object relations: clinical applications of Mahler's theory of symbiosis and separation-individuation. *Psychoanalytic Quarterly, 57*: 547–576.

Kris, E. (1956). On some vicissitudes of insight in psychoanalysis. *International Journal of Psychoanalysis, 37*: 445–455.

Lachkar, J. (1998a). *The Many Faces of Abuse: Treating the Emotional Abuse of High-Functioning Women.* Northvale, NJ: Jason Aronson.

Lachkar, J. (1998b). Narcissistic/borderline couples: a psychodynamic approach to conjoint treatment. In: L. Sperry & J. Carlson (Eds.), *The Disordered Couple* (pp. 159–284). New York: Brunner/Mazel.

Lachkar, J. (2003). *The Narcissistic/Borderline Couple: New Approaches to Marital Therapy.* New York: Taylor & Francis.

Lachkar, J. (2008a). *The V-spot: Healing the "Vulnerable" Spot from Emotional Abuse.* New York: Jason Aronson.

Lachkar, J. (2008b). *How to Talk to a Narcissist.* New York: Taylor & Francis.

Lachkar, J. (2012). *The Disappearing Male.* New York: Jason Aronson.

Lachkar, J. (2014). *Common Complaints in Couple Therapy: New Approaches to Treating Marital Conflict.* New York: Routledge.

Lachkar, J. (in press). *Courts – Beware of the Borderline Personality: Implications for Mediation.*

Landman, J. (1987). Regret: a theoretical and conceptual analysis. *Journal for the Theory of Social Behavior, 17*: 135–160.

Landman, J. (1993). *Regret: The Persistence of the Possible.* New York: Oxford University Press.

Laplanche, J., & Pontalis, J.-B. (1967). *The Language of Psychoanalysis.* New York: W. W. Norton.

Lee, L. (2003). "On the Waterfront": script analysis conventional and unconventional. In: J. E. Rapf (Ed.), *On the Waterfront* (pp. 61–84). Cambridge: Cambridge University Press.

Lévi-Strauss, C. (1978). *Myth and Meaning.* New York: Schocken.

Linehan, M. M. (1993). *Cognitive Behavioral Treatment of Borderline Personality Disorder.* New York: Guilford Press.

Little, M. (2008). The role of regret in informed consent. *Journal of Bioethical Inquiry, 6*: 49–59.

Long, R. E. (1997). *The Films of Merchant Ivory: Newly Updated Edition.* New York: Harry N. Adams.

Loomes, G., & Sugden, R. (1982). Regret theory: an alternative theory of rational choice under uncertainty. *Economic Journal, 92*: 805–824.

Lunchbox, The (2013). Directed by R. Batra, produced by Sikhya Entertainment.

Machina, M. (1987). Decision making in the presence of risk. *Science, 236*: 537–542.

Mason, A. (2016). Personal communication, November 5.

McEwan, I. (2001). *Atonement: A Novel.* New York: Doubleday.

McMullen, M., Markman, K., & Gavanski, I. (1995). Living in neither the best nor worst of all possible worlds: antecedents and consequences of upward and downward counterfactual thinking. In: N. J. Roese & J. M. Olson (Eds.), *What Might Have Been: The Social Psychology of Counterfactual Thinking* (pp. 133–168). Hillsdale, NJ: Lawrence Erlbaum.

Medvec, V., Madey, S., & Gilovich, T. (1995). When less is more: counterfactual thinking and satisfaction among Olympic medalists. *Journal of Personality and Social Psychology, 69*: 603–610.

Meltzer, D. (1976). Temperature and distance as technical dimension of interpretation. In: A. Hahn (Ed.), *Sincerity: Collected Papers* (pp. 374–386). London: Karnac, 1995.

Melville, H. (1924). *Billy Budd and Other Stories.* New York: Penguin, 1986.

Merriam-Webster's Collegiate Dictionary (8th Edition) (1993). Regret (p. 985). F. C. Mish (Ed.) Springfield, MA: Merriam-Webster Press.

Merriam-Webster Dictionary. http://www.merriam-webster.com/dictionary.

Metzl, M. N. (2014). The continuum of mourning: anatomy of regret: "From Death Instinct to Reparation and Symbolization through Vivid Clinical Cases" by Susan Kavaler-Adler. *DIVISION/Review, 11*: 4–5.

Miller, W. I. (2003). *Faking It.* New York: Cambridge University Press.

Moore, B., & Fine, B. (Eds.) (1968). *A Glossary of Psychoanalytic Terms and Concepts.* New York: American Psychoanalytic Association.

Moore, B., & Fine, B. (Eds.) (1990). *Psychoanalytic Terms and Concepts.* New Haven, CT: Yale University Press.

Munro, A. (2001). What is remembered. In: *Hateship Friendship Courtship Loveship Marriage* (pp. 219–242). New York: Vintage.

Munro, A. (2011). Gravel. In: *Dear Life* (pp. 99–109). London: Vintage, 2013.

de M'Uzan, M. (1969). The same and the identical. In: G. Saragnano (Ed.), *Death and Identity: Being and the Psycho-Sexual Drama* (pp. 3–15). London: Karnac, 2013.

de M'Uzan, M. (1976a). Countertransference and the paradoxical system. In: G. Saragnano (Ed.), *Death and Identity: Being and the Psycho-Sexual Drama* (pp. 17–32). London: Karnac, 2013.

de M'Uzan, M. (1976b). The work of dying. In: G. Saragnano (Ed.), *Death and Identity: Being and the Psycho-Sexual Drama* (pp. 33–48). London: Karnac, 2013.

de M'Uzan, M. (1983). The person of myself. In: G. Saragnano (Ed.), *Death and Identity: Being and the Psycho-Sexual Drama* (pp. 55–71). London: Karnac, 2013.

de M'Uzan, M. (2013). *Death and Identity: Being and the Psycho-Sexual Drama.* G. Saragnano (Ed.). London: Karnac.

Niazi, M. (1986). Humesha der kar deta hoon main. In: *Tez Hava Aur Tanha Phool* (p. 32). Islamabad, Pakistan: Dost Publications, 2008.

Niederland, W. (1968). Clinical observations on the "survivor syndrome". *International Journal of Psychoanalysis, 49*: 313–315.

Novick, K. K., & Novick, J. (2005). *Working with Parents Makes Therapy Work.* Lanham, MD: Jason Aronson.

O'Brien, T. (1978). *Going After Cacciato.* New York: Delacorte Press.

Ogden, T. (1994). The analytic third: working with intersubjective clinical facts. *International Journal of Psychoanalysis, 75:* 3–19.

Ogden, T. (2005). On holding and containing, being and dreaming. In: *This Art of Psychoanalysis* (pp. 93–108). New York: Routledge.

On the Waterfront (1954). Directed by E. Kazan, produced by Columbia Pictures.

Oxford Advanced Learner Dictionary. http://www.oxforddictionaries.com/

Oxford English Reference Dictionary (1995). Oxford: Oxford University Press.

Parker-Pope, T. (2011). What's your biggest regret? *The New York Times.* Retrieved March 23, 2011.

Phillips, A. (2010). *On Balance.* London: Penguin, 2011.

Phillips, A. (2012). *Missing Out: In Praise of the Unlived Life.* New York: Farrar, Straus and Giroux.

Pine, F. (1997). *Diversity and Direction in Psychoanalytic Technique.* New Haven, CT: Yale University Press.

Plath, S. (1960). *The Collected Poems of Sylvia Plath.* New York: Harper Perennial, 1981.

Ponsot, M. (2016). *Collected Poems.* New York: Alfred Knopf.

Proust, M. (1913). *Remembrance of Things Past.* Ware, UK: Wordsworth Editions, 2006.

Proust, M. (1913–1927). *In Search of Lost Time.* New York: Penguin Classics, 2004.

Rapf, J. E. (2003). Introduction: "The Mysterious Way of Art": making a difference in *On the Waterfront.* In: J. E. Rapf (Ed.), *On the Waterfront* (pp. 1–18). Cambridge: Cambridge University Press.

Reider, N. (1953). Reconstruction and screen function. *Journal of the American Psychoanalytic Association, 1:* 389–405.

Remains of the Day, The (1993). Directed by J. Ivory, produced by Merchant Ivory Productions.

Richard, R., van der Pligt, J., & de Vries, N. (1996). Anticipated regret and time perspective: changing sexual risk-taking behavior. *Journal of Behavioral Decision Making, 9:* 185–199.

Roese, N. (1994). The functional basis of counterfactual thinking. *Journal of Personality and Social Psychology, 66:* 805–818.

Roese, N. J. (1997). Counterfactual thinking. *Psychological Bulletin, 121:* 133–148.

Roese, N. J., & Olson, J. M. (1995). *What Might Have Been: The Social Psychology of Counterfactual Thinking.* Hillsdale, NJ: Lawrence Erlbaum.

Rorty, A. (1980). Agent-regret. In: A. Rorty (Ed.), *Explaining Emotions* (pp. 489–506). Berkeley, CA: University of California Press.

Rosen, I. (2009). Atonement. In: S. Akhtar (Ed.), *Good Feelings: Psychoanalytic Perspectives on Positive Attitudes and Emotions* (pp. 371–401). London: Karnac.

Rosenfeld, H. (1964). On the psychopathology of narcissism: a clinical approach. *International Journal of Psychoanalysis, 45*: 332–337.

Rossetti, C. (1647). *The Complete Poems.* New York: Penguin, 2001.

Rowlings, J. K. (1999). *Harry Potter and the Prisoner of Azkaban.* London: Bloomsbury.

Run Lola Run (1998). Directed by T. Twyker, produced by X-Filme Creative Pool.

Rycroft, C. (1968). *A Critical Dictionary of Psychoanalysis.* London: Penguin, 1972.

Safire, W. (1994). On Language: Shoulda-Coulda-Woulda. *The New York Times.* www.nytimes.com/1994/05/15/magazine. Accessed July 10, 2015.

Sandberg, T., & Conner, M. (2008). Anticipated regret as an additional predictor in the theory of planned behaviour: a meta-analysis. *British Journal of Social Psychology, 47*: 589–606.

Sandler, A. M. (1982). Psychoanalysis and psychoanalytic psychotherapy of the older patient. A developmental crisis in an aging patient: comments on development and adaptation. *Journal of Geriatric Psychiatry, 15*: 11–32

Savage, L. (1951). The theory of statistical decision. *Journal of the American Statistical Association, 46*: 55–67.

Scarfone, D. (2013). Preface. In: G. Saragnano (Ed.), *Death and Identity: Being and the Psycho-Sexual Drama* (pp. vii–ix). London: Karnac.

Schafer, R. (1980). Action language and the psychology of the self. *Annals of Psychoanalysis, 8*: 83–92.

Schafer, R. (2005). Cordelia, Lear, and forgiveness. *Journal of the American Psychoanalytic Association, 53*: 389–409.

Schulberg, B. (1955). *Waterfront.* New York: Primus.

Schulberg, B., & Silverman, S. (2001). *On the Waterfront: The Play.* Chicago, IL: Ivan R. Dee.

Schwartz, B. (2004). *The Paradox of Choice: Why More is Less.* New York: HarperCollins.

Seelau, E., Seelau, S., Wells, G., & Windschitl, P. (1995). Counterfactual constraints. In: N. J. Roese & J. M. Olson (Eds.), *What Might Have Been: The Social Psychology of Counterfactual Thinking* (pp. 57–80). Hillsdale, NJ: Lawrence Erlbaum.

Segal, H. (1957). Notes on symbol formation. *International Journal of Psychoanalysis, 38*: 391–397.

Segal, H. (1964). *Introduction to the Work of Melanie Klein*. New York: Basic Books.

Segal, H. (1981). *The Work of Hanna Segal: A Kleinian Approach to Clinical Practice*. New York: Jason Aronson.

Settlage, C. F. (1989). The interplay of therapeutic and developmental process in the treatment of children: an application of contemporary Object Relations theory. *Psychoanalytic Inquiry, 9*: 375–396.

Shabad, P. (1987). Fixation and the road not taken. *Psychoanalytic Psychology, 4*: 187–205.

Shah, A. (2015). Nayak: a therapeutic journey. In: A. Bingham (Ed.), *Directory of World Cinema: India* (pp. 20–21). Bristol, UK: Intellect.

Shakespeare, W. (1599). *The Tragedy of Julius Caesar*. In: W. A. Neilson & C. J. Hill (Eds.), *The Complete Plays and Poems of William Shakespeare A New Text*. Boston, MA: Houghton Mifflin Company, 1970.

Shakespeare, W. (1606). *King Lear*. San Francisco, CA: Ignatius Press, 2008.

Shakespeare, W. (1623). *The Tragedy of Macbeth*. In: W. A. Neilson & C. J. Hill (Eds.), *The Complete Plays and Poems of William Shakespeare A New Text*. Boston, MA: Houghton Mifflin Company, 1970.

Shelley, M. (1818). *Frankenstein*. New York: Penguin, 1992.

Sherkow, S. P. (2001). Reflections on the play state, play interruptions, and the capacity to play alone. *Journal of Clinical Psychoanalysis, 10*: 531–542.

Sherman, S., & McConnell, A. (1995). Dysfunctional implications of counterfactual thinking: when alternatives to reality fail us. In: N. J. Roese & J. M. Olson (Eds.), *What Might Have Been: The Social Psychology of Counterfactual Thinking* (pp. 199–232). Hillsdale, NJ: Lawrence Erlbaum.

Shimanoff, S. (1984). Commonly named emotions in everyday conversation. *Perceptual and Motor Skills, 58*: 512–514.

Siassi, S. (2013). *Forgiveness in Intimate Relationships: A Psychoanalytic Perspective*. London: Karnac.

Simonson, I. (1992). The influence of anticipating regret and responsibility on purchase decisions. *Journal of Consumer Research, 19*: 105–118.

Singletary, W. M. (2015). An integrative model of autism spectrum disorder: ASD as a neurobiological disorder of experienced environmental deprivation, early life stress and allostatic overload. *Neuropsychoanalysis, 17*: 81–119.

Sirois, F. (2004). Procrastination and counterfactual thinking: avoiding what might have been. *British Journal of Social Psychology, 43*: 269–286.

Sirois, F., Monforton, J., & Simpson, M. (2010). If only I had done better: perfectionism and counterfactual thinking. *Personality and Social Psychology Bulletin, 36*: 1675–1692.

Solnit, A. J. (1987). A psychoanalytic view of play. *Psychoanalytic Study of the Child, 42*: 205–219.

Solomon, J. (2007). *The Book of Regrets: Thoughts, Memories and Revelations from a Celebrated Cast*. London: JR Books.

Sonnenberg, S. M. (1972). A special form of survivor syndrome. *Psychoanalytic Quarterly, 41*: 58–62.

Sophie's Choice (1982). Directed by J. Pakula, produced by Incorporated Television Co.

Spence, D. P. (1980). *Narrative Truth and Historical Truth: Meaning and Interpretation in Psychoanalysis*. New York: W. W. Norton.

Steele, C. (1988). The psychology of self-affirmation: sustaining the integrity of the self. *Advances in Experimental Social Psychology, 21*: 261–302.

Stein, H. H. (2003). *Double Feature: Discovering our Hidden Fantasies in Film*. New York: Open Road.

Steiner, J. (1985). Turning a blind eye: the cover up for Oedipus. *International Review of Psycho-Analysis, 12*: 161–172.

Steiner, J. (1993). *Psychic Retreats: Pathological Organizations in Psychotic, Neurotic and Borderline Patients*. London: Routledge.

Sterba, E. (1940). Homesickness and the mother's breast. *Psychiatric Quarterly, 14*: 701–707.

Stevenson, C. L. (1944). *Ethics and Language*. New Haven, CT: Yale University Press.

Styron, W. (1979). *Sophie's Choice*. New York: Vintage.

Sugden, E. (1985). Regret, recrimination, and rationality. *Theory and Decision, 19*: 77–99.

Taylor, G. (1985). *Pride, Shame, and Guilt: Emotions of Self-Assessment*. New York: Clarendon Press.

Thalberg, I. (1963). Remorse. *Mind, 73*: 545–555.

Thefreedictionary.com (2016). Entry on "regret". Accessed July 12, 2016.

Turner, M. (1996). *The Literary Mind: The Origins of Thought and Language*. New York: Oxford University Press.

Tversky, A., & Kahneman, D. (1981). The framing of decisions and the psychology of choice. *Science, 211*: 453–458.

Waelder, R. (1936). The principle of multiple function: observations on multiple determination. *Psychoanalytic Quarterly, 41*: 283–290.

Webster's New World Dictionary (1987). New York: World Publishing.

Werman, D. (1977). Normal and pathological nostalgia. *Journal of the American Psychoanalytic Association, 25*: 387–398.

Whittier, J. G. (1856). Maud Muller. In: T. R. Lounsbury (Ed.), *Yale Book of American Verse* (pp. 148–152). New York: Forgotten Books, 2011.

Wiktionary (2016). https://www.google.com/etymology_of_the_word_regret. Accessed February 16, 2016.

Williams, B. (1981). *Moral Luck*. New York: Cambridge University Press.

Winnicott, D. W. (1945). Primitive emotional development. *International Journal of Psychoanalysis, 26*: 137–143.

Winnicott, D. W. (1953). Transitional objects and transitional phenomena. *International Journal of Psychoanalysis, 34*: 89–97.

Winnicott, D. W. (1956). On transference. *International Journal of Psychoanalysis, 37*: 386–388.

Winnicott, D. W. (1958). The capacity to be alone. *International Journal of Psychoanalysis, 39*: 416–420.

Winnicott, D. W. (1960). Ego distortion in terms of true and false self. In: *Maturational Processes and the Facilitating Environment* (pp. 140–152). New York: International Universities Press, 1965.

Winnicott, D. W. (1965). *The Maturational Processes and the Facilitating Environment: Studies in the Theory of Emotional Development*. London: Hogarth and the Institute of Psycho-Analysis.

Winnicott, D. W. (1969). The use of an object. *International Journal of Psychoanalysis, 51*: 711–716.

Winnicott, D. W. (1971). *Playing and Reality*. London: Tavistock.

Winnicott, D. W. (1974). Fear of breakdown. *International Review of Psycho-Analysis, 1*: 103–107.

Wurmser, L. (1981). *The Mask of Shame*. Baltimore, MD: Johns Hopkins University Press.

Yeats, W. B. (1936). *Selected Poetry*. A. N. Jeffares (Ed.). London: Macmillan, 1968.

Zeelenberg, M. (1999a). The use of crying over spilled milk: a note on the rationality and functionality of regret. *Philosophical Psychology, 12*: 325–340.

Zeelenberg, M. (1999b). Anticipated regret, expected feedback and behavioral decision-making. *Journal of Behavioral Decision Making, 12*: 93–106.

Zeelenberg, M., Beattie, J., van der Pligt, J., & de Vries, N. (1996). Consequences of regret aversion: effects of expected feedback on risky decision-making. *Organizational Behavior and Human Decision Processes, 65*: 148–158.

Zeelenberg, M., van Dijk, W. W., & Manstead, A. S. R. (1998). Reconsidering the relation between regret and responsibility. *Organizational Behavior and Human Decision Processes, 74*: 254–272.

Zeelenberg, M., van Dijk, W. W., & Manstead, A. S. R. (2000). Regret and responsibility resolved? Evaluating Ordóñez and Connolly's (2000) conclusions. *Organizational Behavior and Human Decision Processes, 81*: 143–154.

Zeelenberg, M., van Dijk, W. W., Manstead, A. S. R., & van der Pligt, J. (1998). The experience of regret and disappointment. *Cognition and Emotion, 12*: 221–230.

Zeelenberg, M., van Dijk, W. W., Manstead, A. S. R., & van der Pligt, J. (2000). On bad decisions and discomfirmed expectancies. *Cognition and Emotion, 14*: 521–541.

Zeul, M. (2001). "The Remains of the Day". In: G. O. Gabbard (Ed.), *Psychoanalysis and Film*, 109–130, London: Karnac Books.

INDEX